AMERICAN LABOR

FROM CONSPIRACY TO COLLECTIVE BARGAINING

ADVISORY EDITORS

Leon Stein   *Philip Taft*

THE STORY OF THE CIO

Benjamin Stolberg

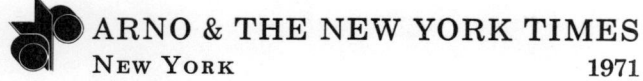
ARNO & THE NEW YORK TIMES
NEW YORK   1971

LIBRARY
FLORIDA STATE UNIVERSITY
TALLAHASSEE, FLORIDA

Reprint Edition 1971 by Arno Press Inc.

Reprinted from a copy in the U.S. Department of Labor Library
LC# 77-156426
ISBN 0-405-02944-6

American Labor: From Conspiracy to Collective Bargaining—Series II
ISBN for complete set: 0-405-02910-1
See last pages for titles.

Manufactured in the United States of America

THE STORY OF THE CIO

THE STORY OF THE

BENJAMIN STOLBERG

THE VIKING PRESS · NEW YORK
1938

PUBLISHED IN OCTOBER 1938

COPYRIGHT 1938 BY THE VIKING PRESS, INC.
PRINTED IN U. S. A. DISTRIBUTED IN CANADA BY
THE MACMILLAN COMPANY OF CANADA, LTD.

PREFACE

THIS BOOK IS partly history and theory, and it is partly journalism.

A reconstruction movement in American labor like the CIO cannot be understood outside of its historic setting, and it has no meaning except in terms of its fundamental intellectual drives. They are as much a part of *The Story of the CIO* as is its unfolding drama. But that part is already history. Another convention, a great strike, an industrial victory, or a factional defeat cannot change this background.

The rest of the book is journalism. It is the biography of the CIO from its birth until today. It reports its struggles on the industrial front and behind the lines. It deals with living men and issues, with shifting factors and emerging facts. And like all journalism, this part of the story has to end with the printer's deadline.

I want to thank the many friends in the CIO, among both the leaders and the rank and file, who have helped me. Their experience and knowledge is the living material of my research. Many of them have read this book not only in manuscript but as it was being written. But of course they are not responsible for my opinions and conclusions.

BENJAMIN STOLBERG

August 25, 1938
New York City

The author is indebted to the editors of the Scripps-Howard Newspapers and to the editors of the *Nation* for permission to incorporate material which has appeared in their publications.

CONTENTS

Preface		v
I:	Why the CIO?	3
II:	Founders of the CIO	27
III:	Big Steel and Little Steel	66
IV:	The New Vigilantism	92
V:	Factionalism	123
VI:	The Automobile Workers	156
VII:	The Maritime Workers	187
VIII:	New Unions in New Fields	206
IX:	White Collar and Professional Workers	245
X:	What's Ahead?	268
Index		285

THE STORY OF THE CIO

CHAPTER I

WHY THE CIO?

THE CIVIL WAR made us a nation; in spite of our regional differences, one people. The Spanish-American War marked our entry in a minor role on the imperialist stage. It was during this period of economic Reconstruction, which lasted much longer than the political Reconstruction, that we had our industrial adolescence. It was then that the foundations of American big industry were laid, and that we changed from a mercantile society with a simple industrial economy to modern industrial capitalism.

This change was not brought about by statistical bureaucrats through a series of Five Year plans. The men who plotted this transformation did not do it with charts and curves. They plotted with personal greed and social ruthlessness. They knifed each other, they cheated the public, they fought and bribed and browbeat. They were daring, able, wasteful, and unscrupulous. Now and then some of them realized dimly that these jungle methods were also clearing a new industrial frontier. And into this new frontier they carried over many of the characteristics of the original frontiersman. But his virtues they turned to vices. While he was rugged, they were hard. While he was driven by a passion for independence, not unmixed with speculative greed, their energy was galvanized wholly by the obsession for profit and for power. But for all that, at the turn of the century our industrial frontier was cleared, almost at the very moment our physical frontier had closed. And some twenty years later, when our tyro imperialism of saving the Cubans by taking the Philippines had graduated into the financial imperialism of saving the world for democracy, we had the greatest and most effective industrial plant under the sun. In the process we had also acquired the technological experience to run this plant—and to be run by it. Today we are at once the ablest masters and the most helpless victims of a purely industrial civilization, which is characterized by an enormous practical acumen at the service of social innocence.

Now what sort of labor movement has grown up in opposition to the industrial freebooters who have made America the society it is?

Unlike the builders of trusts our labor movement, from the Civil War to the mid-eighties, was dreamy, almost mystical, crackpot-idealist, thoroughly ineffectual, now and then breaking out in moody and resentful fits of violence, provoked by industrial barbarism. And when its radicalism was not romantic and unreal, it was angry and benighted. Labor vacillated between various types of Utopian socialism and the Know Nothing syndicalism of the Noble and Holy Order of the Knights of Labor. The Utopian socialisms were of either the Robert Owen or the Fourier variety, which by that time had deteriorated into dismal and futile colonies; or they consisted of sectarian denominations whose creeds had been blown across the Atlantic by the winds of doctrinal struggles. The Knights of Labor, on the other hand, was a crazy mixture of labor populism and lower-middle-class bigotry. Obviously this odd assortment of run-down Utopian communes, of imported socialist sects, and of native labor Know Nothingism, was no match for the Robber Barons who, for all their robberies, represented a historical advance. They were industrializing a continent. They were modernizing a petty and diffused economy into powerful trusts and monopolies with a terrific power to destroy and build, to exploit and punish. It was not until Samuel Gompers founded "pure and simple" trade unionism that American labor began to speak a language to which big business and industry had to listen.

The American Federation of Labor began as an alliance of skilled craft tribes, out to conquer for themselves a place on this new frontier of large-scale industry. Its tactics were essentially guerrilla tactics. And Gompers was ideally suited for such warfare. Strong, crafty, bigoted, absolutely selfless, and one with his task, he threw overboard all the ideological ballast of European socialism and of all other revolutionary doctrines of the time. He determined that American labor should travel philosophically light, thus fixating in the mind of organized labor an anti-intellectual obsession which lasted for almost half a century and gradually stupefied the leadership of the A. F. of L. But until America became a world empire, when ignorance was no longer a source of undivided strength but of complex confusion, "pure and simple" trade unionism was the most effective way of entrenching skilled labor at the expense of the unskilled masses. For the philosophy of the A. F. of L., which consists in having no philosophy at all, appealed to every middle-class instinct of the American mind, especially during the era of industrialization. And American labor was of that mind, too. For while this process of industrialization was going on, the physical frontier was still expanding, and its unlimited opportunities delayed and hid our class stratification. Hence the A. F. of L. did not fight the employer on the basis of a class consciousness, which it repudiated. It fought him in defense of our traditional conception of the Common Man, to which everyone subscribed. It avoided all sectarian abstractions, all Utopian fantasies, all government "interference," including all labor legislation. In the beginning the A. F. of L. fought even the various workmen's compensation acts on the same grounds that big business fought government regulation. Both organized labor and big business were imbued with the same simple idea: let us rely on our economic strength; let us fight it out!

Pure and simple trade unionism had a Decalogue simplicity about it, seemingly free of all economic idolatries. It was based on the belief that labor had only one right, the right to organize for collective bargaining within the logic of capitalist production and within its ethics of fair play. And from this right flowed ten simple commandments: organize by separate crafts; demand more wages; fight for fewer hours; get better conditions in the shop; break no contracts; obey the oligarchy of the chiefs; commit no adultery with socialists or communists or

WHY THE CIO?

other such "theorists"; covet not the function of capital or the protection of government; abstain from all partisan politics; and strike when necessary. These are the stone tablets which Gompers handed down to the children of the A. F. of L. from the Mount Sinai of Pittsburgh in 1881.

In short, Gompers realized that the frontier of American big industry required guerrilla tactics of fighting, and that it could not include the unskilled masses, whose labor market was constantly flooded by new waves of immigration. In his earliest days Gompers went into organizational campaigns with a gun on his hip, and he and his fellow-organizers traveled not on luxurious expense accounts but on the bumpers. By the end of the century, the A. F. of L. was entrenched as our dominant labor movement. But it had also built up an aristocracy of labor with a completely middle-class outlook both on life and work, an outlook which was bound to defeat it in the long run. For in accepting the logic of capitalist production, the A. F. of L. also accepted its theory of labor as a commodity. Thus pure and simple trade unionism gradually became *business* unionism. Its business was to corner craft skill through craft monopoly, to control the market of the isolated craft through union recognition, and to sell its labor on the best possible terms through collective bargaining. Work, in this view, is a thing for sale; the employer is a customer; the union official is a business agent; and labor is a commodity subject to price-fixing.

This view of labor, not as a creative function, but as

a commodity, is of course the main characteristic of the property-mindedness of our industrial system. And in accepting this view in principle, the A. F. of L. thereby accepted both the outlook and the way of life of the middle classes, of which it quickly became an integral part. Like the petty bourgeois, the skilled craftsman developed a contempt for the unskilled immigrants and native proletarians who manned our basic industries. He drew the color line in his union, thus forcing the Negro into a long and tragic history of strike-breaking. Jealous of their craft monopolies, the various trades in each industry spent a great deal of their energy in "jurisdictional disputes" with one another, which arise whenever two of them claim the same set of workers. But these same crafts combined quickly to fight the least tendency toward industrial unionism, the amalgamation into one union of all workers in one industry. The labor oligarchy feared industrial unionism because it would eliminate many a sinecure. And the skilled worker feared that his strategic place in industry might be swamped by the industrial organization of labor, not realizing that technological improvement was constantly displacing his skill.

For a long time the skilled worker was able to increase his wages through his monopolistic craft control and by the tendency of the employers to give him preferential treatment, so as to divide him from the masses. And as he gradually raised his standard of living, he could live like the petty bourgeois he was—politically, socially, and culturally. He bitterly opposed every hint of class consciousness in labor. Indiscriminate Red-baiting became his favorite sport. He fought the rise of a labor party, and voted the Republican or Democratic ticket. And in many communities the central labor bodies, especially the building trades, became the allies of the corrupt political machines. During the World War he shared the chauvinism of the middle classes and fought in defense of all those forces which finally clinched the power of finance capital over American life.

It was during the World War that the middle-classification of the A. F. of L. was completed. The evolution of the original guerrilla fighter into a petty trade union Babbitt was consummated. Through the New Era, from Harding to Hoover, labor leaders were addressing not union locals but Chambers of Commerce and Rotary lunches. Organized labor went into banking, life insurance, realty speculation, necessarily as satellites of big finance. Labor's conception of its own place in industrial society became ever more ambiguous, contradictory, and feeble. For as the A. F. of L. was rising in false middle-class consciousness, it naturally weakened as organized labor. And its craft structure expressed functionally this split between its middle-class delusions and its working-class needs. The Federation became ever more archaic in a society of expanding technology and contracting finance control. By refusing to reconstruct itself, as industry had done long before, from independent small units into trusts and monopolies, that is, from craft guilds into industrial unions, it lost its grip even on its "pure and simple" functions of protecting these crafts. Thus, during the nineteen-twenties, the business unionism of the A. F. of L. became increasingly *small* business unionism. The Hutchesons and Whartons, the Freys and Tracys, who run the A. F. of L., hate industrial unionism for exactly the same reasons that the corner grocer hates the A. & P. Industrial unionism would drive them out of business. The craft union is out of date. It is a specialty shop of skilled labor in a world in which big industry requires ever fewer specialists of labor. And yet the A. F. of L. insists that the man who has become a living screw-driver is a skilled mechanic. The only thing that the A. F. of L. cannot decide is whether he is a machinist, a carpenter, an electrician, or the master of some other skill he does not practice.

But to organize the unorganized masses, who lack skills, is precisely what the A. F. of L. neither can do nor can afford to do. Its entire history has been a continuous training in avoiding this very task. This does not mean that the A. F. of L. oligarchy does not yearn to conquer the unorganized fields. But it is afraid. On several occasions an A. F. of L. union has refused to admit workers who were organized in a strike by outside "agitators," especially if their admission would have enlarged the union considerably. For at the next convention of the union the new delegates, fresh from their militant experience, would have smashed the entrenched machine. This is precisely what happened after the great textile strike in Passaic in 1927. The officers of the United Textile Workers did not dare to triple their membership. William Green undoubtedly wanted to organize the automobile workers during the NRA and after. But he felt about the automobile industry as an old and impotent man feels about a young and desirable woman. He wants her, yet he is afraid. The jurisdictional disputes in the A. F. of L. about as yet unorganized workers are partly the rationalizations of such impotence. They are just as much an expression of emotional anxiety as they are of economic self-protection by the hierarchy.

Green indeed expresses perfectly this dread of industrial unionism, far more so than the arch-reactionaries on his Executive Council, some of whom at least have the bigotry of their backwardness. Like all miners, Green believes in industrial unionism. But he can't stand up against the Hutchesons and Whartons, for his complete lack of backbone keeps his beliefs from ever rising to convictions. A mildly honest man, he would like to have principles, but he is too soft to hold them. A timorously kindly man, when frightened he displays the hysterical unscrupulousness of the weak when cornered. Sensing his own limitations but not knowing their boundaries, because everything about him is so vague and so ill-defined, he is forever dazed by the fact that he is a National Figure. This refulgent daze of public life, which keeps him in a state of constant pleasurable excitation, he will defend to the last gasp. To this defense he brings a profusion of meaningless gifts. Master of an empty vocabulary, of bellicose platitudes, of half-baked ideas, he bases his facts on false premises and his premises on wrong facts, skipping from irrelevance to non-sequitur to nonsense to arrive triumphantly at the final fallacy. Such is a speech by William Green, who lives only to make speeches. It is like an oration by Ed Wynn in *Hooray for What!*—but the satire is unintentional. Westbrook Pegler felicitously called him the "all-American mushmouth." Green shouts himself momentarily into a sense of artificial conviction, as a little boy whistles to keep up his courage. And between speeches he administers the confusions and evasions of his own making. Nothing describes the atmosphere of the A. F. of L. better than this militant myopia, righteous mediocrity, and pompous pother of the lay Baptist preacher from Coshocton, Ohio, who is its president.

Since the CIO was formed in 1935 the A. F. of L. has also grown by some 800,000 members—partly due to the stimulation of the CIO and partly due to scabbing on the CIO. "Traitor!" roars John Lewis at Bill Green. Lewis is wrong. Green is merely the prisoner of his own weaknesses.

From 1923 until the great depression Green was traveling all over the country selling the conservatism of the A. F. of L. to the big industrialists. But they did not weaken in their sales resistance. Periods of prosperity are a narcotic for labor organization, and big industry used the boom to build up an enforced company union membership of almost 2,000,000, approximating the size of the Federation. At the same time, the A. F. of L. bureaucracy was fighting every sign of discontent or criticism within labor. Partly it wished to curry favor with big industry; and partly, Red-baiting by the labor oligarchy is also a characteristic of a boom era, when strikes are few and the help of the militants need not be even surreptitiously enlisted as it is in crises. In short, during the New Era the A. F. of L. was in a state of peaceful degeneration.

There were only two exceptions to this sorry picture, the miners and the needle trades workers. The United Mine Workers, from the very beginning a strictly industrial union, have a long and militant history. The two great tailoring unions, the International Ladies' Garment Workers Union and the Amalgamated Clothing Workers, have always been semi-industrial unions, and their long though stale socialist background had endowed them with sufficient skepticism of the New Era. But during the second half of the twenties, these unions too suffered from prosperity. And, precisely because of their radical traditions, they were far more defenseless against the growing influence of Stalinism, whose program at that time called for "boring from within" the labor movement, and whose nature I shall discuss later in detail. Unlike the vast majority of the A. F. of L. unions, the miners, and especially the needle trades, were allergic to the dust the Stalinists were raising. For by that time Stalin was already in the saddle, and his American stooges in the Workers Party were not a radicalizing but a disruptive force in the labor movement. In the United Mine Workers the Stalinists were handled rather roughly. John Lewis simply heaved them out, along with his other critics, whenever they showed their heads above ground. But the needle trades were almost wrecked by the struggle. In 1925 the Stalinists who had worked their way into the Amalgamated Clothing Workers began to sabotage union activities, especially during strikes, in order to discredit the leadership. In 1926 the Stalinists captured the new Joint Board of the International Ladies' Garment Workers and conducted what was probably the most incompetent, irresponsible, and wasteful strike in the history of the union. They dissipated $3,500,000 of the union treasury, of which only $1,500,000 went for strike benefits. The rest was never accounted for. After terrific internal upheavals the Stalinists were finally defeated in the needle trades, except in the Fur Workers Union.

But by the time these industrial and semi-industrial unions had checked the Stalinist penetration, prosperity had crashed into the inevitable depression and our domestic trade collapsed. Even in normal times the mining and the tailoring industries function in a highly competitive, over-expanded, and erratic market. The depression exacerbated all these problems. Even so, the progressive traditions of these unions and their industrial form of organization helped them to survive not only the boom but also the collapse. But the bulk of the A. F. of L. unions were completely demoralized. Prosperity had weakened their fiber, and the depression laid them completely low. Then came Roosevelt and the New Deal.

The New Deal needed organized labor to save big

business. Three months after Roosevelt came to power, the NIRA was passed, and the NRA, its administrative apparatus, was set up. The NRA was essentially a price-fixing mechanism to enable big industry to regain the control of scarcity which it had lost in the excitement of the boom. But this price-fixing mechanism was useless unless it could be effectively enforced, unless the chiseling and the cheating among the industrialists could be kept down to a minimum, and unless wages could be kept up to support the buying power of the masses. That's where organized labor was to come in. It was to police, through collective bargaining, the "social planning" of stabilizing prices in an economic system which is partly irresponsibly competitive and partly dictatorially monopolistic. And to enable organized labor to perform this miracle, Sections 7A and 7C legalized its right to organize and guaranteed its minimal functions. With one stroke of the pen the NIRA turned our "pure and simple" labor movement, which would have nothing to do with government "interference," into a semi-public unionism whose organization was part of a government program; at least in theory. Section 7A insisted that "employees shall have the right to organize and bargain collectively through representatives of their own choosing . . . [and] that no employee . . . shall be required to join any company union." And Section 7C empowered the President to fix "such maximum hours of labor, minimum rates of pay, and other conditions of employment as he finds to be necessary to effectuate" the codes in recalcitrant industries. But of course the NIRA left to labor the actual job of organizing the unorganized workers and of obtaining optimum conditions.

There is one thing the New Deal did not venture even to suggest. It did not tell organized labor that it must reform itself into industrial unionism, which obviously is the only form under which it might conceivably have fulfilled its function of policing industry. For one thing, the New Deal was afraid of antagonizing by such a suggestion the A. F. of L. hierarchy. And for another thing, a successful drive for industrial unionism would render labor far too powerful for Mr. Roosevelt's program of reviving capitalism. Industrial unionism is a truly radicalizing force; the NRA was a truly compromising dream.

On the Labor Advisory Board of the NRA the President appointed John L. Lewis, Sidney Hillman of the Amalgamated, George L. Berry of the Printing Pressmen, and of course William Green. But as soon as the NRA began to function, it ran into difficulties with Mr. Green and the Executive Council of the A. F. of L. Mr. Green's chronic fear of organizing the unorganized masses quickly brought on his collapse. Lewis and Hillman had to spend a good deal of their time holding him up. With Green the rest of the A. F. of L. collapsed as well, except in those highly skilled trades, such as the printing and building trades, which for years had been entrenched as trade union aristocracies and did not need the NRA. Green babbled about organizing "10,000,000 as the next step" and "25,000,000 ultimately," but from

June to October 1933, the A. F. of L. managed to organize less than half a million workers outside the coal and clothing industries. And most of these half-million workers were organized into "federal labor unions," which is a method of granting A. F. of L. charters directly to individual plants with the understanding that later the workers in these plants will be apportioned to the various crafts to which they "belong." What really happened during the summer and fall of 1933 was that Mr. Green was doing all he could to stem the industrial union drive which had developed spontaneously in the basic industries. He actually told Mr. Gerard Swope of the General Electric Company, who was on the Industrial Advisory Board of the NRA, that the A. F. of L. could not undertake to organize the workers in the General Electric unless it could divide them into fifteen separate crafts. Mr. Green even "settled" strikes by permitting established unions to scab on newly formed unions. With his approval, the United Brotherhood of Carpenters filled the places of striking studio stage hands, and the International Brotherhood of Electrical Workers filled the places of some 4000 strikers in the motion picture studios.

John Lewis and Sidney Hillman, on the other hand, exploited to the utmost the opportunities under Section 7A. Throughout the summer of 1933 the United Mine Workers carried on an intensive organization drive. Lewis even organized, by a series of brilliantly executed "spontaneous" strikes, the unorganized fields of Alabama, Kentucky, and West Virginia. And when the coal code was finally adopted, the miners were almost completely organized, and were able to exercise their power in the codification. Hillman, who rose above the usual tension between the Amalgamated Clothing Workers and the International Ladies' Garment Workers, considered himself the spokesman of all the needle trades and did an excellent job in helping them to organize their industries. These first six months of the NRA determined the rate of growth of the different unions as long as the NRA lasted. And the difference between the miners and the needle trades on one hand and the rest of the A. F. of L. on the other is best gauged by the following figures: Between 1933 and 1935 the industrial and semi-industrial unions grew by 132 per cent, while the craft unions grew by only 13 per cent. But after the first six months of the initial enthusiasm engendered by Section 7A, the organization drive of labor spent itself rapidly. The employers revived the company unions with the aid and comfort of General Hugh Johnson and Mr. Donald Richberg, who "interpreted" such unions as complying with Section 7A. And when finally the Supreme Court in May 1935 declared the NRA unconstitutional, the Executive Council of the A. F. of L. heaved a sigh of relief; though, to be sure, by that time the NRA was as much a hindrance as it was a help to labor.

Still, the NRA had dramatized the issue of organized labor. And as the NRA was dying, the rank and file of labor took up the issue. The whole of American labor, both organized and organizable, was in turmoil. The workers in the basic industries were clamoring for organization, *and they wanted industrial organization.* Unrest against the oligarchy spread in the rank and file. Powerful leaders, such as Lewis and Hillman and Dubinsky, began to lead the opposition movement. But the louder the industrial unionists knocked at the doors of the Executive Council, the more they frightened the old men of the crafts.

Finally, at the 1934 convention of the A. F. of L. in San Francisco, the issue burst into the open. Resolutions for industrial unionism were introduced from all over the floor. They were introduced by the Pennsylvania State Federation of Labor, by the American Federation of Teachers, by the Mine, Mill and Smelter Workers, by the United Hatters, Cap and Millinery Workers, by the cleaners and dyers, by numerous federal local unions of automobile workers, of radio and television workers, of electrical workers, rubber workers. The movement became a stampede. But all that John P. Frey, head of the Metal Trades Department of the A. F. of L. and secretary of the Committee on Resolutions, could think of doing to counter this storm was to call for more rigid enforcement of the jurisdictional rights of the crafts and for the organization of more federal locals in the basic industries as against national industrial unions.

The avalanche of resolutions was referred to the Committee on Resolutions, which for over half a century had functioned as a lethal chamber for all opposition. But this time a sharp struggle took place within the Committee itself between John L. Lewis and John P. Frey. The Old Guard had to compromise. And what the resolutions committee reported out indicated the depth of the cleavage that had taken place inside. For the compromise did not represent an adjustment but a mere postponement of the conflict. With spurious diplomacy it admitted the merits of both sides, and let it go at that. And here is the gist of this compromise resolution:

During recent years there have developed new methods. This has brought about a change in the nature of the work performed by millions of workers in industries which it has been most difficult or impossible to organize into craft unions. The systems of mass production are comparatively new and are under the control of the great corporations and aggregations of capital which have resisted all efforts at organization.

The American Federation of Labor is desirous of meeting this demand. We consider it our duty to formulate policies which will fully protect the jurisdictional rights of all trade unions organized upon craft lines and afford every opportunity for development and accession of those workers engaged upon work over which these organizations exercise jurisdiction.

However, it is also realized that in many of the industries in which thousands of workers are employed a new condition exists requiring organization upon a different basis to be most effective.

To meet this new condition the Executive Council is directed to issue charters for National or International unions in the automotive, cement, aluminum, and such other mass production and miscellaneous industries as in the judgment of the Executive Council may be necessary to meet the situation.

That the Executive Council shall at the earliest practical

date inaugurate, manage, promote, and conduct a campaign of organization in the iron and steel industry.

That in order to protect and safeguard the members of such National and International unions as are chartered, the American Federation of Labor shall for a provisional period direct the policies, administer the business, and designate the administrative and financial officers of such newly organized unions.

The leader of the drive for industrial unionism in the convention and in the resolutions committee from the very start was John L. Lewis. He was supported by Charles P. Howard of the printers, David Dubinsky of the ladies' tailors, Sidney Hillman of the men's tailors, Max Zaritsky of the milliners, and of course by the leaders of the new unions on the floor. Lewis accepted the compromise resolution, for that was all the industrial unionists could get from the Old Guard. But in his interpretation of it he spoke over the heads of the Old Guard to the whole of organized labor, with an eye to the next year's convention. "What does it mean?" he asked. "It means the outlining of a definite policy on the part of the A. F. of L. for the organization and the bringing into the fold of trade unionism in America of the teeming millions of workers here in America's base industries and its miscellaneous trades." His interpretation was, in a way, a threat. He put it up to the Executive Council. If it should fail, opposition to it at the next convention would be far more formidable.

The craft separatists were worried. Arthur O. Wharton of the machinists rose several times to make sure that the granting of an industrial charter to the "automotive" industry would not cut into his bailiwick in auto rebuilding and repair work and in garages. William L. Hutcheson of the carpenters, John Coefield of the plumbers, J. A. Franklin of the boilermakers, other Old Guard leaders, suspicious and alarmed, asked similar questions. Finally John P. Frey assured them that after all the Executive Council was to interpret this resolution. That satisfied them. Most of them were on it. But the atmosphere was tense. The issue was obviously crucial, though no one as yet dared to render it irreconcilable. The convention cheered the "unanimous" adoption of the resolution. But it finally disbanded with the uneasy sense that the future of the A. F. of L., and of American labor as a whole, was alarmingly uncertain.

Next year at Atlantic City the Executive Council reported. It reported that during the summer it had granted an industrial charter to the auto workers, except those engaged in the manufacture of auto parts and in skilled jobs; in short, it reported that it had not granted a real industrial charter to the workers in this industry. And Green failed to mention that he had forced upon the new union as president Francis J. Dillon, an old hack A. F. of L. organizer, to protect the "jurisdictional" claims of the crafts. The Executive Council further reported a number of new federal local unions in auto parts, in gasoline stations, in rubber, aluminum, radio, cement, gas and by-product coke, in lumber, in other industries. But it also added that a survey "of the strength of organizations established in cement, aluminum, gas, **coke and by-products, and radio,** convinced the Executive Council that the time had not yet arrived when international unions could be established in the named industries." It also reported its intention to grant "a charter to rubber workers . . . upon proper application to cover all those in that industry while engaged in the mass production of rubber products, same not to cover or include such workers who construct buildings, manufacturing or installing of machinery, or engage in maintenance work or in work outside of the plants or factories"; which again meant that it had no intention of granting to the rubber workers a real industrial charter. Finally, it reported that "owing to the internal difficulties within the Amalgamated Association of Iron, Steel and Tin Workers, we did not deem it advisable to launch an organizing campaign for the steel industry until that breach was healed."

To sum up, the Executive Council reported that it had done nothing in a complicated way, and that it meant to do less if possible. It had thrown down the masses in the basic industries. It reported its own bankruptcy.

The report was met by twenty-one resolutions from the floor calling for unrestricted industrial unionism in the basic industries. And this time the Committee on Resolutions was no longer unanimous. There was no compromise. There were a majority and a minority report. Colonel John P. Frey presented the majority report signed by eight members of the committee, urging the convention to back up the Executive Council. Charles P. Howard presented the minority report signed by six members of the committee, among them Lewis, Howard, and Dubinsky. The minority report came out for unqualified industrial unionism. "We refuse to accept," read Howard, "existing conditions as evidence that the organization policies of the A. F. of L. have been successful. The fact that after fifty-five years of activity and effort we have enrolled under the banner of the A. F. of L. approximately 3,500,000 of members of the 39,000,000 of organizable workers is a condition that speaks for itself. . . . Industrial organization is the only solution."

And finally the minority report insisted: "The Executive Council of the A. F. of L. is expressly directed and instructed to issue unrestricted charters to organizations formed with the policy herein enunciated. The Executive Council is also instructed to enter upon an aggressive organization campaign in those industries in which the great mass of workers are not now organized, issue unrestricted charters to workers organized into independent unions, company-dominated unions, and those organizations now affiliated with associations not now recognized by the A. F. of L. as bona fide labor organizations."

Lewis rose to defend the minority report. He was angry. He indicted the record of the A. F. of L. as "twenty-five years of constant, unbroken failure." He showed how the pitiful gains of the Federation during the NRA had melted away since. He blamed himself for trusting the Old Guard the year before in San Francisco. "I was beguiled into believing that an enlarged Executive Council would honestly interpret and administer the policy—the policy we talked about for six days in committee, the policy of issuing charters for industrial unions in the mass production industries. . . . At San Francisco they seduced me with fair words. Now, of course, having learned that I was seduced, I am enraged and I am ready to rend my seducers limb from limb."

He went on: "If we fail to have this convention adopt this policy [industrial unionism], then of course the responsibility falls upon the A. F. of L. And the world and the workers will believe now and for the future that the A. F. of L. cannot and will not make a contribution toward the obvious need of our present economic conditions. . . ." And, always the miner aware of the menace of unorganized steel, he concluded: "I will accept your judgment, if you make it, as an evidence of the fact that your minds are closed on this question and that my people whom I represent can expect no help or no assistance from the A. F. of L. in the organization of the steel industry, and we will be compelled to carry on as best we can in the mining industry, knowing that our terrible adversary, the steel industry in this country, having tasted blood, may at any time open up and attempt to destroy the union which I have the honor to represent."

From that moment on, the struggle between craft as against industrial unionism became irreconcilable. The Mine, Mill and Smelter Workers complained that the International Association of Machinists was scabbing on them. The federal local unions of the radio workers asked for a national industrial charter, and complained of their difficulties with the International Brotherhood of Electrical Workers. The automobile workers entered an appeal against the decision of the Executive Council in refusing them an unrestricted industrial charter. The cement workers, the rubber workers, the aluminum workers, all newly organized workers, objected to the majority report. The convention turned into bedlam.

But the Old Guard won. The majority report was adopted by a vote of 1,802,400 as against 1,093,300. Even so, this was a miracle. Ever since the eighties, the progressives had fought for industrial unionism. They never could muster more than a few scattered votes. Now more than one-third of the A. F. of L. was for it.

After the vote was taken, the rubber workers introduced a formal resolution asking again for an unrestricted industrial union charter. Hutcheson would not let this resolution be introduced on the ground that the majority report had already been adopted. Lewis objected to such quibbling. A few acrimonious remarks were exchanged by the two men, who stood near each other. Hutcheson called Lewis a "bastard."

Lewis closed in on Hutcheson and hit him on the jaw. Hutcheson crashed against a table. That blow resounded across the American labor movement, and split it in two. Lewis was through with the A. F. of L.

Three weeks later the CIO was founded. And five weeks later, on November 23, Lewis wrote Green a brief letter: "Dear Sir and Brother: Effective this date, I resign as vice-president of the American Federation of Labor."

CHAPTER II

FOUNDERS OF THE CIO

On November 9, 1935, the CIO opened shop in Washington with seven unions and almost 1,000,000 members.[1] Lewis became chairman and Howard secretary. John Brophy, an old leader of the opposition to Lewis in the United Mine Workers, was appointed as director. The three most powerful charter unions were the United Mine Workers, 500,000 strong; the Amalgamated Clothing Workers, 150,000; and the International Ladies' Garment Workers Union, 200,000. Of the United Hatters, Cap and Millinery Workers, only the men's headgear workers joined, with a membership of about 7000; and since then they have left the CIO. The United Textile Workers, with a membership of 65,000, were taken over in March 1937 by the Textile Workers Organizing Committee, whose fortunes I shall discuss in a later chapter. The remaining charter members were the Oil Field, Gas Well and Refinery Workers, with about 40,000 members; and the International Union of Mine, Mill and Smelter Workers, with 15,000.

In this chapter I shall trace the story of the five founding unions which are still in the CIO; and especially, of course, of the miners and the men's and women's clothing workers, which have been the backbone of the move-

---

[1] The CIO is often credited with eight charter unions, but the late Charles P. Howard of the printers joined only as an individual.

ment. They furnished the top leadership, the rank and file of organizers, the cash, and the enthusiasm. When the A. F. of L. suspended the CIO in August 1936, it kicked out not only one-third of its membership, but most of its brains and all of its militancy.

Clearly the promise of the CIO was great. But its performance during the next two years was almost miraculous. At its Atlantic City conference in November 1937, it boasted 32 organizations with a membership of almost 3,750,000, a figure which was only some 12 per cent overoptimistic.[1] But the CIO could also boast, and that quite demonstrably, that in the industries it had organized, especially in the mass production industries, it had raised wages by $1,000,000,000 a year, cut hours by some 2,000,000 a week, and improved working conditions everywhere. It had organized 75 per cent of the steel industry, 70 per cent of the automobile industry, 65 per cent of the rubber industry, and about one-third of the maritime and textile industries. The CIO is constantly adding organizations in new fields—in the public utilities, in

---

[1] At the Atlantic City conference the CIO reported the International Typographical Union (75,000) and the United Hatters, Cap and Millinery Workers (25,000) as member unions, while in fact these two unions were not in the CIO. Then the Textile Workers Organizing Committee claimed a membership of 400,000 by the simple device of counting the turnover membership during its organization drive; in fact, the TWOC never had more than 200,000 members at any time, and the business recession brought even this figure down considerably. Finally, the publicity director of the CIO, Mr. Len De Caux, accepted none too critically the figures of several Stalinist-controlled unions. Thus the United Cannery, Packing and Allied Workers, largely a paper organization, credited itself with 100,000 members, which was about five times the number it actually had.

FOUNDERS OF THE CIO 29

the meat packing, toy, and furniture industries.[1] And all along it has made good use of its political weight, both directly and indirectly. Moreover, the CIO is not only a great institutional success. It is of paramount importance to American industry and life. It is revamping American labor from an archaic horse-and-buggy craft separatism into modern industrial unionism.

On August 4, 1936, the Executive Council of the A. F. of L. voted fourteen to one to break up organized labor into two major camps rather than run the risk of endangering their control of it. They voted to suspend the CIO unless it disbanded within one month.[2] Suspension under such circumstances could lead only to final expulsion. John Lewis immediately announced, as a matter of course, that the CIO was to go on. The split involved many more organizations than were immediately implicated. Toward the end of 1936 the whole of organized labor was split wide open—in every state federation of labor, in every local labor council, in every A. F. of L. union down to its smallest unit. And as time went on, the struggle grew in bitterness.

The Executive Council had voted illegally. It acted against the plain constitutional provision of the A. F. of L., which permits only its annual conventions to suspend without a time limit or to expel constituent unions, and then only by a two-thirds vote. And the possibility

---

[1] In this book I am not discussing the organizations which the CIO set up after its Atlantic City conference, which marked its second birthday.
[2] Since then all the founding unions of the CIO, with the exception of the International Ladies' Garment Workers, have been expelled.

of such a vote at the next convention was excluded because the suspended unions were not to be admitted. Since the CIO unions would not be party to such crassly illegal proceedings, they refused to defend themselves before the Executive Council. Accordingly the Executive Council was put into the absurd predicament of having to act as judge in a case which had no defendant. One of its henchmen, Colonel John P. Frey, acted as plaintiff. Frey is known as the "scholar" among the labor bureaucrats. He is as much of a scholar as a Kentucky colonel is a military expert. Incapable of the least theoretical conception, pseudo-learned, pompous, verbose, reactionary, he was for many years the highbrow front for the late Samuel Gompers. Gompers, himself an ignoramus, inordinately admired Frey's gift of handing out platitudes with an air of academic authority which bowled over Congressional committees or the jerkwater members of learned societies.

The suspension proceedings before the Executive Council gave Frey a wonderful opportunity to display his gifts. With much misquotation from the classics and garbled allusions to history, the colonel traced his own cockeyed misinterpretation of American trade unionism, and wound up with an indictment of the CIO for "rebellion" and "dual unionism." Industrial unionism, he insisted, was not the issue. Green has frantically echoed this absurdity all along: "Not industrial but dual unionism is at stake!" That of course just isn't so. To be sure, industrial unionism is bound increasingly to displace craft separatism. But this "dual" nature was forced upon the CIO by the blindness of the A. F. of L. oligarchy. The only issue was and still is industrial unionism. And the only "insurrection" the A. F. of L. bureaucracy faced, and will continue to face, is the rebellious mood of American labor, especially in the mass production industries. The unorganized workers, led by the progressive forces within the Federation, object to the scarcity program in labor organization which guarantees to the Old Guard the continuance of their sinecures. It is Green and Company who are engaging in dual unionism by sabotaging everywhere the efforts of American labor to organize along industrial lines. And this sabotage does not shrink from outright strike-breaking. Since the CIO came into existence, the A. F. of L. has grown by some 800,000 members. Part of the increase was a secondary effect of the CIO drive. But a good number of these the A. F. of L. has been able to recruit by "recognizing" company unions and by enlisting ordinary scabs in CIO strike campaigns.

John Lewis and the Miners

Ever since the foundation of the A. F. of L., radicals of every hue, both inside and out, have tried to amalgamate the crafts in each industry into industrial unions. The Socialists fought for it way back in the nineties. And in 1894 they defeated Gompers for the presidency of the A. F. of L., for the first and last time, by throwing their votes to John McBride of the United Mine Workers, who was an industrial unionist, though the issue was primarily the effort of the Socialists to put through their political program. In this century there were the Industrial Workers of the World, who were especially active before the war, and various amalgamation movements in the nineteen-twenties. The main program of all these dissenters has always centered in industrial unionism.

But this time the issue was not taken up by the Wobblies or other idealists who had dwelt in the radical wilderness outside the dominant labor movement, or were mere sports within it. Forced by the technological strides of industry, by the depth of the depression, by mass unrest, and by the ever more obvious idiocy of craft division, the fight was taken up by some of the ablest and most powerful leaders of the A. F. of L. itself. And the strongest of them all is John L. Lewis. Only Lewis had the following and prestige to start the CIO by taking with him one-third of the Federation.

Lewis has the patient strength to weather dark and disheartening periods. In the later nineteen-twenties, the United Mine Workers had dwindled to a membership of some 150,000. The industry itself was a chaos of wildcat over-expansion. The unorganized fields in West Virginia, Alabama, Kentucky, throughout the South, seemed unassailable fortresses, defended by armies of corrupt sheriffs and their deputized gangsters. And these unorganized fields, with their low wages and preferential freight rates, were capturing the market from the union territory. Opposition to Lewis, based on increasing unrest in the rank and file, was bitter beyond belief. Through it all, Lewis was imperturbable, driving his critics to distraction. In his opinion, objective factors were responsible for the mess in the industry and for the depression in the union. But Lewis is by nature an effective personality, and he has a withering contempt for failure brought about by what seems to him sheer ineptitude, cowardice, and job-holding. When he finally became convinced that the "pure and simple" trade unionism of the A. F. of L. in the mazes of modern industrial society just made no sense, he went to work to change it—and if necessary to wreck it. And for the sort of leadership that means breaking with the past without regrets, Lewis has just the right personal equipment.

Lewis is a natural public figure, dramatic by instinct, not by mere publicity. He talks with the picturesque, ponderous, but effective gravity of an almost Biblical style, of whose abusiveness he is past master. And his orotundity, flamboyant in cold print, goes over big on the platform. He can make his flamboyance seem like a pillar of fire. Every time he raises his hand, it turns into a finger-post. His great strength as a leader lies in the sense of security he gives to the led. Mentally direct, emotionally as shaggy as he looks, Lewis is absolutely fearless with the insensitive courage of those who don't know when they're licked, and therefore seldom are. He is shrewd, and would be more so if he were less contemptuous of opposition. He is intelligent, but he thinks directly on the surface. Impatient of subtlety, where indirection is a virtue he is apt to lose. He can step quickly into the breach, discarding and innovating as the situation dictates. But he has no collateral insights, his imagination is purely practical, and his tactics are conditioned by the fight, never developed into general principles. He is tough in the good sense: he never gives way on what he thinks are essentials, but will compromise on everything else. Unfortunately, the fact that his practical sagacity is so much greater than his theoretical imagination often leads him astray as to what is and is not essential. Thus, he has not been "worried," at least not until lately, about the infiltration of the Stalinists into the CIO. During the nineteen-twenties, he used to throw them out of the union, and he is firmly convinced that he can do so again when necessary. He is wrong. At that time they were unwelcome guests. Now Stalinism is a movement of stealthy and devious penetration. That is why the factionalism which they are fostering in the CIO is so disruptive. But Lewis goes on relying entirely on what experience has taught him, without gauging imaginatively the underlying social forces.

In short, Lewis is a competent and courageous opportunist, who is felt primarily in action. And like most men of action, he tends to be dictatorial. Often he decides on major policies without consulting even the most important leaders beyond the circle of his intimates. One of the reasons David Dubinsky and Homer Martin differ with him on the issue of peace with the A. F. of L. is his failure to consult them. On the other hand, he will give some subordinate free rein on a highly crucial matter. In some ways, Lewis is completely unpredictable.

But, for all his faults, Lewis has the outstanding virtue, in an exaggerated and dramatic form, of representing the pragmatic nature of the progressive forces in American labor. And there is probably no better way of tracing this progressive evolution from trade unionism to industrial unionism in the American working class than in the empirical education of John L. Lewis. Lewis began his career as an organizer for Sam Gompers, he was one of the king-pins in the A. F. of L. machine, and for years he was considered by all left-wingers the leading reactionary in the oligarchy. He arrived at his present outlook not through opposition to the oligarchy, but through the sheer force of his experience. In this he represents a fundamental shift in the attitude of American labor itself. Moreover, the mining industry has suffered more than any other from the contradictions of modern industrialism. And Lewis came to know its mechanisms better than any other trade union leader of importance.

His knowledge of the coal industry, and through it of industrial organization in general, is enormous and detailed. Besides, though the radicals throughout the nineteen-twenties considered him an arch-reactionary, he thought of himself always as a progressive, partly because he began in local union politics as a rebel, and partly because of the traditional radicalism of his union. Didn't he always invite Rena Mooney to address the miners' conventions for the Mooney-Billings defense committee, and didn't he see to it that she never left empty-handed? Didn't the Resolutions Committee in every convention of his union, which was always under his thumb, endorse such radical measures as the thirty-hour week, or the nationalization of the coal industry, or the Plumb Plan? Didn't he always speak his mind about the "masters" of finance capital? It was partly because he believed in his own progressivism that he fought the radicals in his own union, not only ruthlessly, but with a sort of moral passion. He got rid of Frank Farrington, the Illinois "progressive," by proving that Farrington was in the pay of the coal operators. He got rid of Alex Howat, the Kansas radical, an honest but almost illiterate roughneck, by railroading him out of the union for insubordination. His sergeants-at-arms used to throw his left-wing opponents out of the conventions of the United Mine Workers by the scruff of their necks. Finally, he got rid of John Brophy, whom he considered an impractical idealist—as indeed he is—by accusing him in 1928 of fomenting "dual unionism."

But in fact Lewis was not a progressive until the very end of the nineteen-twenties, and it was not until the NRA was in full swing that his progressivism became conscious. It was then that he came out unequivocally for industrial unionism for the whole of labor, so that it might organize the basic industries and present a monolithic front to modern industrial monopoly.

John Lewis's people have been miners as far back as any record shows, and the record goes back for many generations. His father, Thomas Lewis, came from Wales and settled in Lucas, Iowa, where John was born on February 12, 1880. The father got a job in the mines and joined the Knights of Labor. In 1890 Tom Lewis was active as a rank-and-filer in the foundation of the United Mine Workers, and almost immediately got himself permanently blacklisted in the entire coal industry. The Lewis boys had to go into the mines and support the family. In his youth, John Lewis drifted into all sorts of mining, all over the country—gold, copper, soft and hard coal. A start in life under such hard conditions may drive some gifted temperaments either into ineffectual bitterness or into ineffectual idealism. On Lewis it had the effect of toughening him realistically. He became a leader in his union local, often, to be sure, through means which a Debs would have eschewed. Lewis never moved without building and tightening his machine. He never hesitated to win first and to be fair afterwards. And he also had the ability to inspire deep loyalty in the crowd around him. His fights with his enemies were often so extraordinarily bitter that for years one heard about John Lewis as having "sold out." There never was a word of truth in it. Unlike other leaders of the miners, who became operators, Lewis was never moved by such petty ambitions. John Lewis is interested in gathering and building power, not in selling it.

This does not mean that in his early days Lewis rose to power by being drafted for his high-mindedness. But he got there just the same. In 1917 he became first vice-president of the United Mine Workers, after a few years as organizer in the A. F. of L. under Sam Gompers. Frank Hayes, then president of the union, was seldom on the job, and Lewis really ran the union. In 1919 he became acting president and in 1920 president. And whoever is president of the U.M.W. usually stays, for the miners do not elect their national officers at conventions but by mail. Lewis's machine out in the field saw to it that he got the right mail. It is the common belief in the union that in 1926 John Brophy was really elected president. But if he was, he never served.

During the nineteen-twenties Lewis won more victories than any other labor leader. The miners won every national strike. He settled most of these strikes with victorious agreements. And when that was impossible, he at least held on to his slogan, No Backward Step! He never agreed to a reduction in wages on a national scale, to a worsening of conditions, to a formal weakening of the union. And that at a time when the rest of American labor was giving way to the company union everywhere.

Yet every victory left the union more exhausted, more disorganized, numerically dwindling. And while the union refused to take "a backward step" nationally, the separate districts had to take one backward step after another, because the industry was getting sicker. The coal operators everywhere were chiseling on the contracts. Standards were disintegrating. Mines lay idle. The coal market was shrinking erratically. Electricity and oil were cutting in. Periods of wildcat over-expansion were followed by monopolistic compression, and in one monopolistic squeeze after another some 200,000 miners lost their jobs within a decade. The anthracite miners, who were in the more stabilized sector of the industry, more or less held their own. But the soft coal field was gradually crumbling into coal dust. Toward the end of the great prosperity, the union had only 150,000 dues-paying members. To be sure, it continued to pay the A. F. of L. a tax for 400,000 members, in order to retain its powerful vote in the A. F. of L. conventions. But in 1928 the union had to have its per capita tax to the A. F. of L. remitted. There just weren't enough dues-paying members to meet the bill. And all along, radical opposition within the union against Lewis was fermenting, partly because every effort to organize West Virginia, Alabama, and Kentucky was drowned in blood. The truth was that John Lewis's great victories for the union were all Pyrrhic victories. They were won on the dotted lines of contracts, not in the coal fields.

Now, John Lewis is by temperament not satisfied with formal victories which actually are defeats. Accordingly, with every new "victory," he became more puzzled. Why did the union succeed on the map in his office, and fail in the industrial field? Lewis began to study the industrial process. And though he did not become a revolutionary, he finally did become convinced that some sort of *planning* was essential in the coal industry.

When Lewis became boss of the union in 1919, the coal industry was crazily over-expanded. But the suicidal contradictions of this over-expansion, the chaos it was creating in the industry, were hidden by the immediate post-war boom. Lewis was prepared neither by training nor experience to see through the economics of this over-expansion. He saw his duty primarily in strengthening the union, so that it might keep pace with the illusory growth of the industry. He did not realize that such anarchic growth was bound to wreck both the industry and the union.

His first great victory—and it was a true victory in its educational effect on himself—came from the national coal strike of 1919. On November 8, eight days after the strike was called, Judge Anderson of the United States District Court in Indiana issued an injunction which forbade the miners even to "think" about the strike. Lewis called off the strike officially, but somehow not a single miner went back to work. With this grapevine strategy he forced President Wilson to appoint a Bituminous Coal Commission. That was the first time Lewis disregarded the A. F. of L. dread of government "interference" in industry. The Commission recommended a wage increase of 27 per cent for miners, and corresponding increases for common labor, for trappers, and for boys. No change was made in basic hours. The operators had to accept. Of course, the coal industry being what it is, the agreement bristled with the usual exceptions, technical differentials, and other loopholes for chiseling by the operators. Under this agreement the average miner, getting as much work as the industry could offer, earned no more than $900 to $1000 a year, a good deal less than the totally inadequate $1600 which the Department of Labor then computed as essential to a standard of minimum health and decency for the American family. Still, the men returned feeling that they had gained something. But the almost immediate and wholesale knifing of the agreement by the operators created an infinite amount of trouble. Local, mostly wildcat, strikes were chronic, and the unorganized fields, particularly in West Virginia and Alabama, were constant sores. Obviously, the Bituminous Coal Commission lacked teeth.

Nation-wide coal strikes occur only when the coal operators refuse to enter negotiations at the expiration of a contract. The next national strike was in 1922. And it ended with a tri-State agreement, which involved Ohio, Indiana, and Illinois as the basis for a national settlement. The union officially fought for a thirty-hour week, by which it really meant a minimum of thirty hours, for most men were working only from one to three days a week. Once more the union won largely a paper victory, for though it got an eight-hour day, the chaos in the industry kept most of the mines closed. Lewis did, however, gain a 10 per cent wage increase.

After this tri-State agreement, the destructiveness of wildcat over-expansion began to tell in earnest. Lewis realized that there were "twice too many mines and twice too many miners." It was then that he woke up to the fact that what the industry needed above all was real stabilization, a conception which he later extended to include the whole of our economy. And he began to advocate real government regulation of the coal industry, a tremendous forward step for an A. F. of L. leader. "Some national authority over the coal industry is necessary, call it what you may," Lewis testified before the Bland Committee of the House of Representatives. He came out for "an industrial bill of rights," and suggested a permanent coal commission representing capital, labor, and the ever-mythical "public."

The tri-State agreement was to last till April 1, 1924. On February 19, 1924, the Jacksonville agreement was signed to last until 1927. It was signed by the operators and the miners of Illinois, Indiana, Ohio, and western Pennsylvania, again as the basis for a national settlement. The old conditions were renewed. This was considered a tremendous victory because at that time the rest of labor was losing all along the line to the company unions. But no sooner was the Jacksonville agreement signed than the coal operators began to sabotage it with all sorts of new and fancy subterfuges. They started "group" leasing and other such "co-operative" undertakings, which threw the men out of work wholesale. The unionized fields became completely disorganized. Toward the end of 1924, 40 per cent of the coal mines in the country were non-union. One year later, 60 per cent were non-union. For the Coolidge administration, under pressure from Mr. Hoover, who was then Secretary of Commerce, allowed the scab operators in the Southern unorganized coal fields preferential freight rates so as to kill union production. It was during this period of the Jacksonville agreement that Lewis had most of his trouble with the left wing, which expressed the disgust of the rank and file. The opposition wanted him to organize the unorganized fields. Lewis showed that the non-union fields were owned by the same Wall Street interests that owned the union fields and manipulated both, and he claimed that the Southern territory, especially in West Virginia, could not be organized short of a civil war. The slightest attempt at organization in those fields was accompanied by murder, evictions, and general terror. The coal operators' association of West Virginia, under the leadership of their president, Tom Lewis, a former president of the United Mine Workers, spent millions in plant-fortification, on guns and cartridges and tear gas.

Lewis's answer was to intensify his agitation for government regulation of the industry. When the Jacksonville agreement broke down in 1927, he fought for the Watson coal stabilization bill, which was finally introduced in 1930. The stress of the depression kept it from consideration, but in January 1932 it was revised and introduced by James Davis in the Senate and Clyde Kelley in the House. During these years, from 1927 on, the miners of course carried on negotiations and signed agreements, more or less renewals, with the operators. But by this time, Lewis's main interest was directed toward the sort of industrial planning which was eventually enacted in the NIRA, and which indeed was foreshadowed by the Davis-Kelley bill. The Davis-Kelley bill was designed to stabilize coal production. It guaranteed to labor the right to organize in authentic as against company unions. And it made it mandatory on the government to license and to impose minimum conditions on interstate coal corporations. Needless to say, the Hoover administration got the bill shelved.

It was during the last year of the disastrous Hoover

regime that Lewis concluded that what was wrong with coal was what was wrong with all industry. And on February 17, 1933, he appeared before the Senate Committee on Finance advocating a program of industrial stabilization for our entire productive mechanism. He came out for the suspension of the Sherman Anti-Trust Act, though of course also for iron-clad guarantees to labor. In essence, these proposals, together with the ideas which grew out of the discussion of the Davis-Kelley bill, resulted in the formulation of the NIRA. The whole conception of the NIRA was originally worked out in detail by John L. Lewis with the able technical assistance of W. Jett Lauck, who for years has been his economic adviser. And the NIRA, as finally adopted, embodied in essence Lewis's recommendations. The licensing feature which he had advocated in the Davis-Kelley bill became the model under the NIRA of the codes of fair competition. And the labor guarantees of the Davis-Kelley bill became the famous Section 7A.

When the NIRA became law in June 1933, Lewis immediately stepped into the opening, and began a drive to organize the unorganized workers. In his own industry he did wonders. Between June and November 1933, he almost doubled his membership. By November he had over 400,000 dues-paying members. He pushed and fought and called a series of brilliantly executed strikes through which he forced the operators to sign the coal code. And finally he had even Kentucky, West Virginia, and Alabama in the bag. Even the coal-diggers in the so-called captive mines, which supply the steel industry directly and are owned by the United States Steel Corporation, joined the union. And when the NRA was declared unconstitutional in May 1935, Lewis had organized over 95 per cent of the industry. Today the United Mine Workers are 600,000 strong. In the meantime, in April 1934, a new agreement was signed between the operators and the union. The workers were guaranteed a seven-hour day, a five-day week, a basic wage scale of $5.00 a day in the North and $4.60 in the South.

The old-line craft unions, on the other hand, broke down the moment the NRA began. Jurisdictional disputes among the crafts broke out like a rash all over the country. Green quickly accepted General Johnson's special interpretation of Section 7A for the automobile industry, an interpretation which practically recognized the company union. Green sabotaged all organizing efforts, warning his organizers to slow down. Under such circumstances it was obviously impossible for labor, even though it had the law on its side, to oppose the great industrialists who insisted that Section 7A permit the organization of company unions under some other name. It was then that Lewis appreciated that the stabilization of industry without the complete organization of labor was a mockery, and that the effort to organize labor in the mass production industries along craft lines was criminal folly. The reason the United Mine Workers had been able to organize up to the hilt during the first six months of the NRA was precisely that they were an industrial union, that Hutcheson of the carpenters could not "claim" the carpenters in the mines. And Lewis determined that craft unionism must no longer be allowed to stand in the way of organizing American labor.

When Lewis decided to strike out along industrial lines, he relied primarily on the United Mine Workers of America. The U.M.W. has so far contributed to the CIO over $2,700,000, and is still assessing itself $30,000 a month toward its support. The steel industry was organized directly by officials of the miners. Most regional directors of the CIO today are United Mine Workers. The CIO borrowed the full-time services of Lewis's closest friends and collaborators in the miners' union—Phil Murray, Van A. Bittner, Pat Fagan, Bill Mitch, board members, district presidents, organizers galore. And the rank and file of the U.M.W. enthusiastically endorsed this policy. Of course the very drive of the CIO has also helped the mine workers. In spite of the fact that the original Guffey-Snyder coal bill was declared unconstitutional by the Supreme Court, and that the new Coal Act lacked teeth, and in spite of the business recession, the union was able to keep the operators to their contracts. Indeed, in the Appalachian fields, where the vast majority of soft coal miners are employed, the union was able to improve both pay and conditions.

Next to Lewis in authority in the CIO is Phil Murray, first vice-president of the U.M.W. and director of the steel drive. He has been Lewis's friend and collaborator for a quarter of a century. With his gentle Scotch burr, Murray is the born diplomat, the natural pourer of oil on troubled waters, a gift which does not weaken in the least his skill in a fight. Like Lewis, he understands thoroughly the processes of modern industry, and his intelligence is more practical than imaginative. His realism is at once curiously idealistic at bottom and totally unsentimental on top. Murray had a lot to do with advising Lewis on how to handle Messrs. Thomas Lamont and Myron Taylor in coming to an agreement in Big Steel. After that was done, he proceeded to charm some 470 little steel masters into following the big boys. And though he was in charge of the lost strike in Little Steel in the summer of 1937, the campaign in steel is none the less one of the greatest feats in American labor history, sharing honors only with the automobile drive.

The other close associates whom Lewis commandeered from the U.M.W. for the CIO are typical lieutenants, though by no means his stooges. Lewis undoubtedly has dictatorial tendencies, but once he trusts a man, that man is his own boss within the ambit of his loyalty to Lewis. I know of no union in which the top leaders work more closely in policy and yet more independently in administration than in the U.M.W. In fact, Lewis's habit of trusting those whom he has once accepted has been one of the major reasons for the factionalism in the CIO. Today he is surrounded by many new men whom he does not really know and whom he over-trusts. It is one thing for him to trust Phil Murray or Van Bittner, who want what he wants, and quite another thing to trust such strangers as Len De Caux, the editor of the CIO *News* and publicity director of the CIO, or Harry Bridges, director of the West Coast CIO.

As time has shown, probably the worst major appointment Lewis made was that of John Brophy as director of the CIO. When Lewis unequivocally came out for industrial unionism, Brophy, who for years had been his bitterest opponent in the U.M.W., came to see him. "I want to help," said Brophy. And Lewis, who for all his toughness of fiber has a deep sentimental streak, said: "All right, you be the director." Of course, at that time no one guessed that the CIO would go like wildfire. It was still supposedly only a committee to fight for industrial unionism within the A. F. of L. But even so, the choice was too impulsive. Brophy was born to be a visionary in opposition to those in power. Responsibility confuses him. And his idealism is rendered ineffectual by his utter guilelessness, which makes him the tool of all sorts of adventurers who exploit his "revolutionary" emotions. This does not mean that Brophy is simple. In fact, he is often profound in his glimpses into the labor movement and its history. Like the character in Dostoievsky's *Idiot*, he is surprisingly wise and brilliant in flashes, but utterly child-like and naïve in social politics. On his wall in his home he has a portrait of Lenin and a picture of Christ, which indicates the depth of his confusion. A devout Catholic, whose son is studying for the priesthood, a devout radical, a poor and absent-minded administrator, Brophy understands probably better than any other labor leader why the CIO came into being, and knows almost less than anyone else just what's going on around him. By 1937 he came completely under the influence of the Stalinists in his office. It was he who maneuvered the appointment of Harry Bridges, the leader

of the West Coast longshoremen, to the directorship of
the West Coast CIO. This move has since disrupted the
CIO on the Pacific, as I shall show. It is Brophy who,
influenced by the Stalinists, lends the authority of the
CIO to their maneuvers in those unions in which they
play a part. And as in the case of all confused idealists and somnambulistic saints, responsibility has finally
changed John Brophy's standards. Today his influence
in the CIO is pernicious.

Brophy is significant as a symptom of Lewis's weakness as a leader. On the other hand, the tremendous drive
of the CIO, its organizational success, Lewis's capacity
to rouse his great union to a magnificent outpouring of
energy and sacrifice, reveal his strength as a leader.

The Amalgamated

After the miners, the two great tailoring unions in
the men's and women's clothing industries supplied most
of the energy to the drive in the CIO. And just as the
United Mine Workers were more or less responsible for
the campaign in steel, a cognate industry, so the Amalgamated Clothing Workers and the International Ladies'
Garment Workers, but especially the Amalgamated, were
in charge of the drive in the closely related textile industry.

The history of the Amalgamated began with a dra-
matic strike in the shops of Hart, Schaffner & Marx in
Chicago late in 1910, which soon spread all over the city.
It was led by a fiery young cutter, Sidney Hillman.
Hart, Schaffner & Marx settled the strike in 1911, with

an arbitration scheme which finally developed into a bipartisan trade board headed by an impartial chairman. The strike magnetized to the side of labor a great many liberals, middle-class intellectuals, and social workers, of whom the late Jane Addams was the outstanding personality. These good people made a lasting impression on young Hillman. In the course of years he gradually gave up his early radicalism, not of course in favor of the narrow bigotry of an A. F. of L. bureaucrat, but in favor of the kind of "industrial statesmanship" which relies primarily on delicate union-management co-operation. The Hart, Schaffner & Marx arbitration scheme became the model for the elaborate arbitration machinery set up wherever the Amalgamated was victorious. And it is this emphasis on diplomacy in industry, rather than on militant protection of the union, which gives the Amalgamated its distinctive character and a reputation for social vision in liberal and highbrow circles.

The personality of Sidney Hillman plays an extremely important part in the history of the Amalgamated, because to an unusual extent it is a one-man show. In most unions control is vested in a board whose members usually have behind them the power of their personal following in the union. The board may be an entrenched oligarchy with a common interest, but it is a machine of intermeshing personalities. Hillman, however, has succeeded in surrounding himself with subordinate administrators, none of whom possesses real political power in his own right, and all of whom are his admirers, with the exception of Joseph Schlossberg, who holds the office but not the power of secretary-treasurer. It's Hillman and his Circle. Some of these administrators and organizers are extremely competent lieutenants, and some of them are mere glorified office boys and bookkeepers. But altogether they form a chorus forever hymning the achievements of the Amalgamated, so that in reading their statements and reports it is hard to distinguish between their social vision, by this time almost professional, and the objective truth.

In the course of years this attitude could not help but develop Hillman's self-esteem into self-overestimation. And his great flair for publicity, combined with his energy and ambition, has almost persuaded the public to accept him at his own valuation. To be sure, of late the newspaper fraternity, especially in Washington, is becoming somewhat skeptical of his Statesmanship, and the rank and file of the men's clothing workers, who gauge success by wage scales, have been pretty tired of it for some time. I do not say all this in a spirit of carping criticism. But I have come to the conclusion that few things more effectively sap a labor union than the sort of indiscriminate adulation that Mr. Hillman seems to need. For many reasons, for some of which one cannot blame him, and which I will analyze in detail later, the Textile Workers Organizing Committee, under his chairmanship, has made a poor job of it. Yet Hillman insisted during the rocket-like beginning of the drive that it was one of the greatest successes in the history of American labor.

Hillman's preoccupation with the arbitral technique

in the men's clothing industry was bound to lead him in time to be as concerned for the organization of the employers as for the organization of the workers. He always prides himself on looking at "the industry as a whole." On several occasions the Amalgamated banks in New York and in Chicago saved employers from impending bankruptcy. In each specific instance the rescue was justified; it saved the workers their jobs. But in the long run the price the Amalgamated has had to pay for such a broad attitude is reflected in its wage scales, which are by no means what they might have been if, like the International Ladies' Garment Union, it had been less open-minded in seeing the employers' side. And we must not forget that the Amalgamated, unlike the International, has the advantage of dealing mainly with large shops.

The historic function of a trade union is not to put most of its energy into perfecting a sensitive *modus vivendi* with industrialists in order to smooth the edges of the rasping contradictions of capitalist production. Its historic function is to move, no matter how gradually, toward a new society in which these contradictions are resolved. It's all a case of emphasis: a union which forever and on principle looks out for the "entire industry" is bound to become enervated in time, no matter how intelligent its tactics may seem at the moment. This quality of Social Vision on the part of Hillman has also taken his union into all sorts of ventures—banking, housing enterprises, into the Russian-American Industrial Corporation in 1922, even into men's clothing production—

all of which again have tended to "widen the horizon" of the union at the inevitable expense of its protective function.

And now let us go back for a moment into Amalgamated history. The union became nationally established in 1914, as local after local split away from the antediluvian United Garment Workers, led since 1903 by the reactionary Tom Rickert, and joined the Amalgamated. The A. F. of L., of course, declared the Amalgamated a dual union, but finally in 1932 admitted it into the fold. The jurisdictional disputes between the Amalgamated and the United were adjusted on the basis of the status quo: the Amalgamated retained the entire men's clothing field and the United retained the overalls. Four years later, the Executive Council of the A. F. of L. suspended the Amalgamated for its charter membership in the CIO. And in 1938 the Council expelled it.

When the NRA was organized, Hillman became a member of its Labor Advisory Board. And with his usual energy he exploited Section 7A in behalf of all the needle trades. The ladies' tailors, the millinery workers, all needle workers, considered him their friend and spokesman in the Administration, and he more than lived up to their expectations. During the NRA, from 1933 to 1935, the Amalgamated rose from a membership of about 125,000 to 150,000, and to 160,000 in 1936, according to its own figures; though the Handbook of American Trade Unions of the Department of Labor gives it only 125,000 members as of March 1, 1936. Today the Amalgamated claims 225,000 members and may well have them, for since the CIO it has branched out to include various allied trades. Although exact figures are unavailable, the Amalgamated claims to have taken in during the last three years 3000 neckwear workers, 7000 journeymen tailors, 6000 workers in cleaning and dyeing establishments, and 25,000 laundry workers in the linen supply industry, as well as 25,000 shirtmakers. It has also conducted a drive in the rest of the men's cotton garment industry, from pants to pajamas. In short, the NRA and the CIO drives together have netted the Amalgamated almost 100,000 members in these last five years.

On September 11, 1933, the NRA code reduced hours in the men's clothing industry to 36 a week, and granted a minimum wage of 40 cents an hour in the North and 37 cents in the South. Excepting in the more highly skilled crafts, such as that of the cutters, this minimum wage rapidly became the maximum wage throughout the country, though not in the centers where the big shops are. But even there the average was not more than about $18 a week.

By 1936, wages in the industry had gone up to a country-wide average of $18.43 a week. This wage scale created enormous unrest among the workers, and something had to be done. Accordingly, early in 1937 Hillman insisted on a substantial increase, and this time on a *national* scale. The new agreement, signed on February 14, announced the startling victory of a 12 per cent increase. The increase was to go into effect on May 15, covering 85 per cent of the industry. "This agreement," the *Monthly Labor Review* of the Department of Labor stated, "was in the form of a joint press release, and represents the first bargaining of national scope in the men's clothing industry." Unfortunately, this wage increase was practically confined to the press release, for various factors kept it from being reflected in the pay envelopes. Since the agreement was not to go into effect for another three months, the manufacturers crowded in all the overtime possible in order to accumulate enormous stocks at lower wages. And after that the depression set in, and kept the industry working at about 70 per cent of normal. Hence, in spite of the great "victory" of 12 per cent, the average wage for 1937 did not exceed $18.84 throughout the country. And in the big clothing centers—New York, Rochester, Baltimore, Chicago, and Philadelphia—few workers made more than $22 to $25 a week, which of course is included in the national average.

The NRA gave Hillman the proper scope for his energies as an organizer. But it also gave scope to his brain trust proclivities, a tendency which Mr. Roosevelt cannily exploited, making him feel that he is the Felix Frankfurter of labor. Since 1933 Hillman has become a sort of unofficial spokesman of the Roosevelt administration in the labor movement; at least he has managed to convey this impression to the public. John Lewis, who quite rightly thinks that labor should represent labor, and hence should play with the administration rather than fall for it, is at times slightly annoyed by the loftier vision of Mr. Hillman, who is trying to make Labor's Nonpartisan League a left tail to the Democratic Party kite. But Lewis appreciates the energy of the man, who from the very start has given the CIO his enthusiastic support. Hillman and other officers of his union have given a great deal of their time to it, especially in the organization of the textile workers, toward which the Amalgamated has contributed $500,000. The Amalgamated has also contributed $100,000 to the steel drive, and another $100,000, up to 1938, to the national CIO.

When the Supreme Court declared the NIRA unconstitutional in May 1935, the Amalgamated immediately went to work to hold the lines already gained and to push further organization. It is between then and now that it has added to itself thousands of workers in the merchant tailoring, neckwear, cleaning and dyeing, linen supply, and cotton goods industries. The NRA code of the thirty-six-hour and five-day week is still general in the industry, and union standards have been upheld—at least on paper.

The International

The International Ladies' Garment Workers Union was founded in 1900 by seven small unions in four cities. It rose from several semi-skilled sweatshop trades which had survived the Knights of Labor. It is our only great American trade union with a long and consistent radical tradition, which reaches back into the eighties and nineties. The early leaders of the women's tailors, mostly in New York and Philadelphia, were the sweatshop philosophers of the Jewish and German immigration in the last two decades of the last century. Many of them were socialists, members of Daniel De Leon's Socialist Labor Party, some were anarchists, some syndicalists, some anarcho-syndicalists. All of them had brought their social philosophies with them from the other side, philosophies which they forever discussed in the cellars of the industry over their sewing machines. In fact, the boss was often one of them, and would violently defend Marx against Bakunin, or vice versa.

These various revolutionary philosophies gave the International a certain worldly-wise and continental proletarian outlook in its early years. The *Jewish Daily Forward* played an immense political role in the union for a long time, in fact until the accession to power of David Dubinsky. Dubinsky's socialism is purely nostalgic, like a Wall Street broker's memories of his Iowa childhood. And as far as the rank and file is concerned, their socialism went the way of the international socialist movement, becoming ever more conservative and "safe and sane." Moreover, in recent years the influx of second-generation American girls, mostly of Italian, Negro, and old American stock, has tended to contribute toward the highly practical day-to-day progressive business unionism of the International. Still, its socialist background does come out in the various causes it supports, and in the generosity of its gifts to socialist, labor, and liberal enterprises. And this background is evident also in its genuine progressivism, in its educational program for its members, and in its eagerness for political action.

The great strikes which really established the union—the Uprising of the Twenty Thousand in 1909 (the strike of 20,000 shirtwaist makers in New York City) and the melodramatic cloak and suit strike in 1910 known as the Great Revolt—serve as historic landmarks in the consciousness of the International. They established an arbitral relation with the manufacturers which has continued since. Today, the relation between capital and labor in the women's clothing industry is far more stable than the market of the industry. Indeed, the highly competitive, over-expanded, and dizzily seasonal character of the industry makes an understanding between the union and the manufacturers' association essential. This union-management relation is based not so much on class collaboration, as in the men's clothing industry, as on constant realistic bargaining. Now and then this process of bargaining is punctuated by brief strikes and lockouts, which result in signing on the dotted line—dotted by a long tradition of mutual self-preservation.

During the NRA the International took every advantage of Section 7A, and organized the industry nearly 70 per cent. It rose from a membership of about 50,000 to 150,000 by October 1933, and to almost 200,000 by May 1935, when the NRA was declared unconstitutional. Today the International has 260,000 members out of a possible 300,000. In the cotton garment trades the NRA reduced hours from 40 or more to 36 a week, though since then hours in the industry have often gone back to 40. In the coat and suit and in the dress sections of the industry, the NRA reduced hours from 40 to 35 a week, where they technically remain. But since then the new depression has reduced them considerably.

In its wage scales, the International has done better than the Amalgamated under the NRA and especially since; and in comparable work it has done a great deal better. For one thing, the national minimum wage of $14 a week under the NRA did not tend, as in the case of the Amalgamated, to become a maximum for the needle workers, because it was limited to "non-manufacturing" workers such as shipping clerks. In the women's coat and suit section, which comprises 19 per cent of the industry, the average wage in 1933 was $29.13; and in the dress manufacturing section, which covers 41 per cent of the industry, it was $19.51. The average wage for the entire women's clothing industry in 1933 was about $16.50 a week. Obviously 40 per cent of the workers—in the cotton garment, children's wear, and undergarment sections—received miserable wages. In fact, they had no minimum scale, and in 1933 they worked so few hours that their wages were around $13 a week. But since then the International has been able to raise wages steadily in these less skilled sections of the industry. By 1936, the International managed to raise its weekly average throughout the country to $18.80, and by 1937 to $19.30. Unfortunately, the business depression has hit the women's clothing industry pretty hard. And since the fall of 1937 it has been operating at only about 75 per cent of normal.

The CIO drive has contributed relatively little to the International, either in membership or in better agreements. The union has done as well as it could these last few years. It could not very well do better because of the highly seasonal nature of the industry; because of its subdivision into inside manufacturers, jobbers, and contractors; and because of the large number of unskilled workers in the manufacture of low-priced goods.

Though a Socialist in his youth, David Dubinsky is really the first president of the International who rose entirely on his record as a trade unionist. His predecessors had all been political personalities in the socialist or syndicalist movements. Dubinsky is by nature, if not by philosophy, one of the more conservative leaders in the CIO. He is a shrewd politician, a hard bargainer, resilient, and full of fun. He is very proud of being a "lowbrow," partly as a reaction to Mr. Hillman's highbrowism, though he knows trade union organization, both in theory and practice, from the ground up. Few men know as well as he just what goes on inside the labor movement, especially in New York City. Besides his union, to which he gives some fifteen hours a day of his great administrative ability, he is interested in labor's political action, particularly in the American Labor Party in New York.

In the CIO itself Dubinsky has not been very active

FOUNDERS OF THE CIO 61

since early 1937 because of the tension between himself and John L. Lewis. This tension is due to the fact that Dubinsky has been the leading advocate in the CIO of peace with the A. F. of L. For this end he has been maneuvering in both camps, which, in view of the bitterness between them, has not helped him in either, especially in the CIO. In 1938, however, peace between the two organizations became so remote that Dubinsky postponed his efforts in its behalf. Another reason for the coolness between Lewis and Dubinsky is Sidney Hillman, whom Lewis finds a great deal more amenable, and who in turn is jealous of Dubinsky's emergence as the most powerful leader in the needle trades.

The Metal Miners

The Western Federation of Miners had a long and glorious and melodramatic history before it became respectable and called itself the International Mine, Mill and Smelter Workers Union. It was founded in 1893, a year after the bloody lockout of Coeur d'Alene, as an industrial union in the metalliferous mining fields of the West. And for the next twelve years it was engaged in some of the most desperate struggles in American labor history. The murder of ex-Governor Steunenberg in 1905, for which Charles Moyer and Bill Haywood of the Western Federation were tried and acquitted, a *cause célèbre* which made the reputations of both Senator Borah and Clarence Darrow, epitomized the industrial relations in this industry. In 1905 the Western Federation was instrumental in founding the I.W.W., of which

Bill Haywood became the most picturesque leader. In 1911 this union joined the A. F. of L., and in 1916 it became the International Mine, Mill and Smelter Workers Union, thus officially renouncing its wild revolutionary youth. Soon after this renunciation the union collapsed, and continued in a state of complete stagnation until the NRA. But during the NRA it revived, increasing its membership from 1500 in 1933 to over 16,000 in 1936.

In May 1935, the union called a strike at the Eagle-Picher Company, a large lead and zinc mine near Joplin, Missouri. The company replied with a lockout, broke the strike, and set up a company union known as the Blue Card Union, from the color of its membership card. Early in 1937 the A. F. of L. granted a charter to this company union and called it the Tri-State Metal, Mine and Smelter Union. Ever since, the A. F. of L. has used this "independent" union as a scab agency against the CIO. And when the Mine, Mill and Smelter Workers conducted a new organization campaign against the same company, the Blue Card thugs led a murderous attack against the CIO organizers at their union hall on April 12, 1937.

The Mine, Mill and Smelter Workers joined the CIO at the very start. Since then the union has raised its membership to over 50,000. In August 1937, however, it lost a strike at the largest silver mine in the world, the Sunshine Silver Mine at Wallace, Idaho. But it won a sit-down strike in July 1937 at the American Smelting and Refining Company of Perth Amboy, New Jersey, where it gained union recognition and a slight raise in wages. These two strikes are characteristic of the union: it does poorly in the mining end, and much better in the smelting and refining end of the industry. The reason is that smelting is done all over the country, while metal mining is confined to a few Western States, and owned by enormous trusts which also own the local governments. But in the smelting and refining plants the union has been able to sign contracts all the way from Perth Amboy, New Jersey, to Juneau, Alaska. It signed collective bargaining agreements in Utah, in British Columbia, in Ontario, and even in the Coeur d'Alene region in Idaho. It won practically all the elections under the National Labor Relations Board. Today it has over a hundred collective bargaining agreements, and it is getting itself ready for intensive drives among the workers of the Anaconda Copper, Phelps-Dodge, and the American Smelting and Refining Company. Under the unexciting but steady leadership of Reid Robinson and John M. Sherwood, it is making sure progress with the help of the CIO, which is supplying it with organizers and with money.

The Oil Workers

After many failures, the A. F. of L. finally managed in 1918 to organize a small nucleus of oil workers into the Oil Field, Gas Well and Refinery Workers Union. During the war this union grew slightly, but in the depression of 1920 it broke down entirely. In 1933, at the beginning of the NRA, it had a membership of some 300. The NRA acted as an elixir on the union. By 1936 it had 42,000 members, and in February 1937 it boasted 75,000 members.

Remembering its history under the A. F. of L., the union gladly joined the CIO as a charter member. And to give it a push—for the industry in its production and distribution ends together has approximately 1,000,000 workers—Lewis appointed in March 1937 a Petroleum Workers Organizing Committee. The Committee consisted of Philip Murray, Charles P. Howard, and Harvey Fremming, the president of the union. Fremming is a simple and pedestrian person, rather unskillful in collective bargaining. The committee has considerably stimulated the growth of the union, which early in 1938 claimed 100,000 members. Of course, it could not crack on a national scale the giant corporations in the industry —the Standard Oil-Rockefeller interests, the Gulf Oil-Mellon interests, and the Shell Oil-Deterding interests. But it has managed to achieve a somewhat shaky but none the less nation-wide contract with the Consolidated Oil Company of the Sinclair group. By 1937 it also had agreements which cover six Cities Service plants, two Standard Oil subsidiaries, seven Texaco plants, three Pure Oil plants, and a number of independents. These agreements are all signed locally, but in general follow the lines of the national so-called Sinclair Agreement, which provides for an elaborate system of seniority, for wage rates based on detailed job classification with extra pay under special circumstances, for time-and-a-half for overtime, and for a forty-hour week. There is no preference in employment for union members. And though a general check-off is not provided for, the worker can ask the company to deduct his dues and turn them over to the union. During the life of the agreement, strikes and lockouts are prohibited, and an arbitral machinery for grievances is provided. One of the great hopes of the union lies in the fact that the oil industry is "depression-proof." The production of crude oil is rising every year. And the CIO has every intention of tackling the oil industry in a big way these next few years.

CHAPTER III

BIG STEEL AND LITTLE STEEL

THE AMALGAMATED ASSOCIATION of Iron, Steel and Tin Workers was founded in 1876. Though nominally an industrial union, it never got a foothold among the unskilled workers. Even before the disastrous Homestead strike in 1892, it consisted mainly of skilled puddlers, heaters, and nailers. The Homestead strike, which was drowned in blood by the Carnegie Company with the use of Pinkertons, company police, sheriffs, and hoodlums, broke the union. And from that time on, especially after the foundation of the United States Steel Corporation in 1901, the Amalgamated merely vegetated in the steel areas. It gave up every pretense of functioning, and in the words of its president, Mike Tighe, confined itself to "giving way to every request made by the steel men when they insisted upon it." Old Man Tighe, a simple and kindly soul, and known far and wide as an excellent family man, maintained his Lilliputian machine in a small office in Pittsburgh. This machine had two simple functions: to pay the reasonable salaries of its officers, and to sabotage every effort of the "Reds" to have the union call a convention.

In 1918 and 1919, the government wanted to stimulate production in the basic industries, especially in steel. It even toyed with the idea of acknowledging labor's right to organize. The workers in the steel industry were restless, and the opportunity for organizing steel seemed excellent. But since nobody expected the Amalgamated to do anything, the A. F. of L. in 1919 set up a National Committee for the Organizing of Iron and Steel Workers under the leadership of William Z. Foster, today the puppet-chairman of the Communist Party but at that time an excellent organizer. The committee took over Mike Tighe's skeleton union, and put the skeleton into the closet, exactly as was done seventeen years later by the CIO.

In 1919 conditions in the industry were comparable to those in England at the beginning of the Industrial Revolution. Under the benevolent piety of the late Judge Gary, who never saw a blast furnace until after his death, the steel industry still enjoyed the twelve-hour day, the seven-day week, and the twenty-four-hour shift every two weeks. Foster, of course, wanted to introduce industrial unionism, but he decided "to achieve the results of industrial unionism without sacrificing the craft unionism of the A. F. of L." He had to give way to the jurisdictional obsession of the Federation. And during the strike the workers were being allocated to twenty-four craft organizations, whose main "organizing" campaign consisted in dividing them up on paper before they were organized in fact. Since even by that time the automatic steel-mill rolling process had displaced over 95 per cent of the skilled workers, this jurisdictional fantasy introduced a note of tragic farce. These squabbles finally defeated the strike, though the drive had managed to organize some 365,000 workers. The steel trust, of course, exploited the bickerings in the A. F. of L., the post-war political reaction, and especially the racial divisions among the workers, playing upon the "Americanism" of the few skilled craftsmen. Gangsters, spies, coal and iron police slugged and murdered. The strike collapsed. The Amalgamated Association went back to sleep. And the steel companies began to build their company unions.

Unlike Rip van Winkle, Mike Tighe never woke up. Even the NRA could not rouse him from his sleeping-sickness. The steel companies were able to write their own codes as they pleased, palming off their company unions as meeting the requirements of Section 7A. By October 1933, 85 per cent of the steel industry was organized in company unions under various deceptive names.

But trouble was brewing. Coal is a cousin of steel. And John L. Lewis, who knows a great deal about the steel industry, because it owns the so-called "captive mines," insisted that steel must be organized. For years he had begged William Green to attempt the task. At the San Francisco convention of the A. F. of L. in 1934, he once more raised the question. And he forced the decision by the convention that the A. F. of L. should "at the earliest practical date inaugurate, manage, promote, and conduct a campaign of organization in the iron and steel industry." The burden of the drive was placed upon the Executive Council. But, as we have seen, at the 1935 convention of the A. F. of L. in Atlantic City, the Council reported back that it "did not deem it advisable to launch an organizing campaign for the steel industry," until "the internal difficulties within the Amalgamated Association of Iron, Steel and Tin Workers were healed."

These "difficulties" had been raised by a militant rank-and-file movement which for some time had been developing in the steel centers. Local leaders sprang up here and there and everywhere, took charge of this new mass unrest, and demanded "an aggressive campaign for union recognition, to be backed up if necessary by a general strike in the industry"; to which Mike Tighe replied: "We ain't a strike organization." But he could not down the gathering storm which had developed at the convention of the Amalgamated in 1934. At this April convention the younger delegates had succeeded in putting through a motion to present the union demands to the steel industry on May 20, and to follow with a strike if these demands were not met by June 15. They demanded the recognition of the union, one dollar an hour, a six-hour day, and a five-day week. The convention elected a committee of ten rank-and-file leaders to execute this motion. But this rank-and-file committee got nowhere, either with the steel trust or with the Amalgamated, which even refused them desk space in the union headquarters.

In the meantime, the steel companies were laying in a heavy supply of ammunition, tear gas, and other such paraphernalia for a regular little civil war. And Mike Tighe was busy denouncing the committee as "Communist," in spite of the fact that the Communist Party was vilifying it for its refusal to be captured by the Stalinists. The committee was given the run-around both by the union and by the Roosevelt administration. President Roosevelt, General Johnson, and Donald Richberg had persuaded the steel barons to allow the organization of a Steel Labor Board similar to the one in the automobile industry, which sold out the automobile workers. The problem was to get the workers to accept the board instead of calling a strike. For this purpose William Green and Mike Tighe called a special convention, supposedly to decide on the strike, but actually to knife it. They took full parliamentary advantage of the inexperience of the committee of ten. They dragged out the sessions with all kinds of technicalities, and finally managed to get the convention to accept the Steel Labor Board. After the convention, the rank-and-filers tried to reorganize themselves, but they had lost their strategic moment, and managed only to get themselves expelled, not only individually, but by whole lodges. The expelled lodges formed themselves into a new union, which was reunited with the Amalgamated in the summer of 1935. But by that time the situation was quite hopeless. The Amalgamated had run down to 8600 members.

Thus things stood when the CIO was formed in November 1935. Late in February 1936, John Lewis offered to the A. F. of L., in the name of the CIO, $500,000 toward a fund of $1,500,000 to organize steel along industrial lines. Green turned down the offer. Thereupon the CIO offered $500,000 to the Amalgamated, on the same condition, having in the meantime worked up a great deal of rank-and-file sentiment. And at the convention of the Amalgamated in April 1936, Mike Tighe and Louis Leonard, secretary of the Amalgamated, were finally forced to accept the offer. An agreement was signed between the Amalgamated and the CIO, which set up the Steel Workers Organizing Committee. The committee immediately displaced the Amalgamated, pensioned off Mike Tighe and Louis Leonard, and went to work. The American Iron and Steel Institute, which includes 95 per cent of the industry, representing a $5,000,000,000 investment, realized that the CIO meant business. And one of the first things it did was to publish a full-page ad in 375 newspapers at a cost of over $400,000, declaring that it never would recognize the independent organization of the steel workers.

Under the energetic and astute chairmanship of Philip Murray, the S.W.O.C. was extraordinarily effective from the moment it was organized on June 3, 1936. It began a tremendous campaign throughout the steel areas of the country, with widespread publicity, radio talks, and mass meetings. It began training a vast corps of organizers. It got Governor Earle and Senator Guffey of Pennsylvania to promise protection to the organizers and the workers, and relief in the event of strikes. Within four months, its three regional offices—in Pittsburgh, Chicago, and Birmingham—had organized 35 sub-regional offices, and were employing 158 full-time organizers. But Phil Murray's greatest triumph was his getting one company union after another to go over to the S.W.O.C. The steel industry replied by discharging innumerable union members, by hiring spies and gangsters, by running full-page ads in the local press. But the company unions continued to go over to the S.W.O.C. And a great many of the "undercover" men from the steel trust were loyal union members, put there by the S.W.O.C. The company executives found all their "information" scrambled. Small companies began to sign up. The activities of the CIO in behalf of Roosevelt's re-election resulted in Democratic victories throughout Pennsylvania, even in Pittsburgh, and for the first time the tie between the steel trust and the corrupt Republican machines of Pennsylvania was broken. By December 1936, the S.W.O.C. had over 150 lodges and 125,000 members. Workers were flocking into the organization as fast as cards could be issued and one dollar for the first month's dues collected.

Suddenly, out of a clear sky, on March 1, 1937, the United States Steel Corporation recognized the S.W.O.C. It appeared that Myron C. Taylor, the strong, silent, far-visioned chairman of the corporation, had successfully conspired with John L. Lewis to usher in a new age of industrial peace and understanding. Little Steel, on the other hand, continued to corrupt the authorities, was busily subsidizing vigilantism, was turning its plants into arsenals, and was hiring the organized underworld in its fight against organized labor. Obviously, the public decided, the House of Morgan, which is Big Steel, is enlightened, and obviously the Graces, the Girdlers, the

Purnells, and the Weirs, who are Little Steel, are barbarians.

Such was, and still is, the picture in the public mind. And indeed, half of the picture is quite true. The Graces and the Girdlers *are* barbarians. During the strike in Little Steel, eighteen unarmed workers lost their lives, ten of them shot in the back. Hundreds were wounded, many seriously. The steel citadels in the Mohawk and Mahoning Valleys, in East and in South Chicago, were more like concentration camps than industrial centers. The Little Steel towns were under a reign of terror. But the other half of the picture in the public mind is not quite true. Big Steel was not exactly motivated by the Golden Rule. For much the same financial interests interpenetrate behind the scenes in the domination both of the United States Steel Corporation and of the large independent steel manufacturers. The powers which control steel form a club whose members more or less act together or split apart according to the dictates of a larger strategy.

United States Steel is controlled by the Morgans. But the Mellons and Kuhn, Loeb and Company are also large stockholders. The Mellons have also enormous stakes in Bethlehem; and through its relations with the Guaranty Trust Company, and otherwise, Bethlehem Steel is also tied up with the Morgans. The Pickands, Mather interests of Cleveland, whose dealings with the Morgans are close and manifold, are heavily interested in the Republic Steel Corporation, on whose board sits

J. F. Schoellkopf, Jr., of the Niagara Hudson Power Corporation, one of the largest utilities, with which the Morgans maintain intimate relations. And the Pickands, Mather group completely controls the Youngstown Sheet and Tube Company. Obviously, the enlightened gentlemen who dominate Big Steel are at least on speaking terms with themselves in Little Steel.

All this, of course, does not mean that there are no authentic and bitter rivalries for the market between the two groups. Nor does it mean that the Graces and the Girdlers and the Weirs are not outraged at the "treachery" of the interests which predominate in Big Steel. I had a long talk with Mr. Weir, and I can testify that his hatred of Myron Taylor goes all the way down to his shoes. Big Finance is never clearly conspiratorial, and is often at odds with itself, because its immediate interests and its long-range interests are as contradictory as is capitalism itself. But it is also true that Big Finance in steel, and elsewhere, has been consciously operating on two fronts against the mass organization of labor. One front is diplomatic, and the other is vigilante. And each front is watchfully awaiting the outcome on the other.

Big Steel

The independent steel barons, of course, hate the "irresponsible" John Lewis and the S.W.O.C. with murderous bitterness. Still, they hate Lewis as a Capone might hate a hard-hitting district attorney. It is impossible to hate John Lewis in the steel drive without respecting him.

Their really rabid and foaming rage is reserved for Myron Taylor. He "betrayed" them. He is the Judas in the garden of Bessemer, the Benedict Arnold of the Iron and Steel Institute. But the simple truth commands us to come to the defense of Mr. Taylor. He is merely one of the most expensive stuffed dress-shirts in the country, and he really was nothing but a figurehead in recognizing the S.W.O.C. To be sure, he signed the contract, but it was practically automatic writing. And here is the story of how the United States Steel Corporation came to recognize organized labor.

Mr. Myron Taylor was on the eve of his retirement from his long and successful career on the financial escalator. He is an impressive and handsome man in the clean-cut, strong-weak sense. He is platitudinous-profound, vain, and as bright as his best secretary. But his perfect linen is not stuffed with sawdust. It is stuffed with plaster of Paris, which gives him both the sense and the appearance of unbending strength. Mr. Taylor can't be told. He must be patiently flattered into thinking that it is he who does the telling.

The steel business was on the up-and-up all through 1936. It promised to be even better in 1937. The American market was excellent, and the foreign armament business was growing. Mr. Walter Runciman, president of the British Board of Trade, paid us a holiday visit in the spring of 1937, calling for a week-end at the White House, and spending much of his time with our international bankers and big industrialists. Mr. Runciman felt reasonably certain that the British rearmament program would bring a good deal of trade to the American steel-makers, especially in armor-plate. But, of course, the British wanted to be sure of continuous production.

The most enlightened man in the House of Morgan, professionally enlightened, is Thomas W. Lamont. By that I do not mean that Mr. Lamont could hold down, on his intellectual merits, an ordinary instructorship in economics at one of our leading universities. Next to Owen Young, he has written more piffle on economic matters than any other of our elder statesmen-behind-the-scenes. I mean to say that Mr. Lamont is shrewd not in the petty but in the worldly sense. Above all, he knows what is good for the House of Morgan. He appreciated that the United States Steel Corporation could not very well take on a slice of the British armament business and at the same time insist on refusing to bid for our own naval construction because it found the labor provisions of the Walsh-Healy Act objectionable. He also knew that the S.W.O.C. had by that time a majority of the workers in United States Steel, especially in the Pittsburgh district. He probably also knew that the S.W.O.C. had few members, and would have a lot of trouble, in Little Steel. He wanted good business, and hence continuous production in United States Steel, and he was much impressed with the fact that General Motors had lost a whole season's business through the great sitdown strike. He knew that the La Follette hearings were not doing big industry much good; and he realized that if the hearings should ever get around to an exposé of the United States Steel Corporation, the revelation of the number of gangsters, spies, and personnel fakers employed by his corporation would give him the shock of his life.

Moreover, he knew that the steel industry, in fighting the organization of the workers, was messing up its entire productive process. Carnegie Steel, the largest subsidiary of United States Steel, had 11,000 ratings in pay and status for 100,000 workers, merely to confuse all issues. He knew that the intransigent reaction of the Liberty League in the 1936 campaign had enormously strengthened the New Deal, which the House of Morgan, for all its courtesy toward it, detests. And finally he knew that John Lewis and Phil Murray had not changed overnight from conservative labor leaders to flaming revolutionaries, and that their record in the United Mine Workers—and Morgan dominates a lot of coal—has been not only highly responsible but the most rationalizing influence in this most irrational of industries. Mr. Lamont probably also suspected that the large independent steel companies, over which the House of Morgan has no immediate control, would keep the S.W.O.C. worrying. All these factors decided Mr. Lamont and the House of Morgan to become far-visioned industrial statesmen. This attitude was shared by Edward R. Stettinius, Jr., then the Morgan chairman of the finance committee of the United States Steel, and now the chairman of the corporation. Mr. Lamont's main problem was to make Myron Taylor believe that he had given birth to the big idea. The thing to do was to play on Myron's vanity.

Mr. Taylor held out for a long, long time—in fact, to the very last. But finally he became convinced that his recent trip to Europe had been for him a journey of deep meditation on the nature of modern industry, and that under the gaze of the Italian Primitives in his Florentine villa he had discovered what emerged as the famous Taylor Formula, with a capital F. The Taylor Formula is what the average high school boy calls union recognition. Secret meetings with John Lewis were arranged. And Lewis valiantly helped to build up the myth of Mr. Taylor's genius in industrial relations; it was a cheap price to pay. The House of Morgan kept out of the picture. And there was even a suggestion, made on whose authority no one knows, that the Ambassadorship to the Court of St. James might come Mr. Taylor's way on his retirement.

Accordingly, on March 1, 1937, Messrs. Taylor and Lewis were able to announce to a startled world that United States Steel had recognized the Association of Iron, Steel and Tin Workers of North America—which must have dumfounded Mr. and Mrs. Mike Tighe when they opened their morning paper. Benjamin F. Fairless, president of United States Steel, was no less surprised, though he learned about it the day before, which was a Sunday. On Monday morning, the company began cleaning out all the stooges, spies, and gangsters from its various plants, put away the tear gas and machine guns, and, as behooves enlightened industrial statesmen, began negotiations with Phil Murray and the other leaders of the S.W.O.C. On the next day, March 2, the agreement was signed without any fuss. The corporation recognized the union as the sole bargaining agency for its workers. It raised wages 10 per cent, as of March 16, with certain differentials. It established an eight-hour day, a forty-hour week, and time-and-a-half for overtime, and laid the foundations for the machinery of bargaining.

Within two months, some 260 lesser steel companies followed in the wake of Big Steel, including the large independent firm of Jones and Laughlin, though it took a short strike to persuade the latter. By early 1938 the S.W.O.C. had almost 450 firms signed up. Today some 450,000 workers are in the union. And many of the Big Steel executives are really co-operating with the S.W.O.C. in rationalizing the industry.

"You must talk to Edgar Lewis, president of Jones and Laughlin," my old friend Clint Golden, who is in charge of the S.W.O.C. in the Eastern States, insisted when I visited Pittsburgh in July 1937. Mr. Edgar Lewis is one of those paragon steel executives who actually want to produce steel in a state of industrial peace. Unfortunately, Mr. Lewis was out of town, and so I talked with Mr. Mossman, for many years the publicity director of Jones and Laughlin, and an uncle of Alf Mossman Landon. Mr. Mossman's attitude toward the Graces and the Girdlers makes him sound exactly like a union official. Jones and Laughlin is especially angry at Tom Girdler, for in 1936 the Republic Steel Corporation tried to swallow up Jones and Laughlin. Girdler had been superintendent and president of Jones and Laughlin for sixteen years, and when he left the company to head Republic Steel he knew all about Jones and Laughlin. Jones and Laughlin had developed an enormous business in making caps and stoppers for beer and soft drink bottles. These caps are made, by a formula developed by Jones and Laughlin, for the Crown Cork and Seal Company. Republic Steel has taken over a good deal of this business. "And this is the Tom Girdler," shouted Mr. Mossman, "who thinks that John Lewis is too 'irresponsible' to deal with."

Little Steel

On May 26, 1937, the S.W.O.C. called a strike against three of the large independents in steel: the Republic Steel Corporation, the Youngstown Sheet and Tube Company, and the Inland Steel Company. On June 11, it struck the Cambria plant of the Bethlehem Steel Corporation in Johnstown, Pennsylvania. The demand was union recognition. The S.W.O.C. did not as yet dare to tackle Weir's National Steel Corporation. Weirton, an industrial fief, was patrolled day and night by the notorious Hatchet Gang, an underworld organization hired by the company.

On May 26, 76,500 workers were called out. They struck on a steel front which starts at Chicago, swings along the lake front to Indiana Harbor, Cleveland, and Buffalo, and down through the Mahoning Valley from Warren to Youngstown, Ohio. On June 11, about 13,500 additional workers left the Cambria plant of the Bethlehem Steel Corporation in Johnstown. The Johnstown steel workers left in a sympathetic strike with some 350 trainmen on the Conemaugh and Blacklick Railroad, which is the transportation unit of the Cambria. Early in July, the S.W.O.C. called off the strike at the East Chicago plant of the Youngstown Sheet and Tube, and at the Inland Steel Company at Indiana Harbor. In fact, at about the same time the strike in Little Steel as a whole was unofficially abandoned. It had petered out. Why? The truth is that the strike was premature. The S.W.O.C. was over-enthusiastic. First, the easy victory in Big Steel had somewhat turned its head; second, the brilliant campaigns in the automobile and rubber industries had made it over-sanguine; and third, the organizers in the field completely misjudged the situation in the steel towns. In their optimism they exaggerated the number and the militancy of the unionized workers, and they under-estimated the vigilante spirit of the steel towns.

From the very first, Little Steel acted more intransigently than Big Steel. Indeed, at that time the executives of Little Steel controlled the Iron and Steel Institute, which had run the nation-wide ads against the S.W.O.C. Also, there can be little doubt that Little Steel was permitted by the large financial interests who dominate American big industry to test the strength of the CIO. In the beginning, both the Youngstown Sheet and Tube and the Inland Steel were tempted to follow Big Steel in recognizing the union. But they were brought into line by Grace and Girdler. Eugene Grace of Bethlehem Steel and Tom Girdler of Republic Steel were picked as the ideal men for the task of breaking the S.W.O.C. Each combines the big industrialist and the small-time vigilante in one and the same person. Grace is a quiet, devious, and black reactionary. He achieved national notoriety by paying himself, during the worst years of the depression, a total of almost $4,000,000 in salary and "bonuses." He is the General Franco of Little Steel, busily engaged in whipping up big industry to support a national vigilante movement. After the strike, National Labor Relations Board hearings brought out the fact that he had paid more than $30,000 to the vigilantes in Johnstown alone.

Tom Girdler, the professional tough boy from Cleveland, is Grace's chief-of-staff. Loud, vulgar, and utterly irresponsible in his statements, he is given to shouting obscene opinions of anyone who crosses him. He is in the fortunate position of never needing to warn the press that he is speaking "off the record," for what he says is usually unprintable anyway. To him, Roosevelt, Miss Perkins, John Lewis, Phil Murray, are all "Communists." He poses as an impulsive, plain-spoken, and hard-boiled fellow. And that indeed is true; at least, he is plenty tough. One of the reasons he has great influence with his board of directors, whose sensibilities he constantly offends by his language and behavior, is the fact that he is one of the few men on top in the steel industry who are trained engineers and excellent production men. And he is an effective raider on the business of his competitors. With Weir, he has had the least regard for price agreements in the industry.

The Little Steel satrapies are dismal, isolated, socially backward, the whole community dependent entirely on busy mills. When the mill stops work, the community goes dead. This makes for a comparatively stable working force; there is no way to get another job except to move out of town. In Johnstown, for instance, most of the workers have been with the Cambria Steel for years. The labor turnover is small. Many of them own their homes, such as they are, and the mortgages are held by the local banks. The workers buy things on the installment plan in the local stores. Their families had been on starvation rations during the depression, and the women were not eager for their men to strike. The worker in these little steel towns is half lower-middle-class, half labor. And under the pressure of vigilantism and the prospect of a long-drawn-out fight, the petty bourgeois in him is apt to win out—unless he and his wife have been thoroughly educated and organized by the union. And this the S.W.O.C. had not had time to do. Newspaper men, who were completely sympathetic with the strikers and knew the situation well, told me that the workers in Johnstown would have voted at any time to join the CIO, but would also have voted against the strike. In short, the vigilante terror and the violence of the local authorities were not entirely responsible for the "back-to-work" movement. It was not pure fake;

a good deal of it was authentic. When in the course of three weeks 8000 men out of 13,500 go back to work, as was the case in Johnstown, it is foolish and insulting to call them all scabs by insisting that all of them did it against their conviction. They returned to work because they had been insufficiently organized and prematurely called out, and therefore considered the strike broken early in the struggle.

The weekly payroll of the steel workers in Johnstown fluctuates between $400,000 and $500,000, practically all of it spent among the local merchants. In such a community the business interests are always potentially vigilante, because the merchant is not psychologically identified with the workers, as he is in the coal towns. He is almost forced to join a "citizens' committee" in time of trouble. The church is incredibly backward, the civil authorities are reactionary or corrupt, or both, and the newspapers reflect the whole atmosphere.

In the next chapter I shall describe in detail the whole technique of a new and streamlined vigilantism as it was developed and applied in the Little Steel towns during the strike. In Johnstown, which became the testing-ground of this new vigilantism, civil rights were suspended and the Citizens' Committee really became the local government for the time being. It used the local authorities to break the strike through violence and terror. The same thing happened in Youngstown, Niles, Warren, Canton, Massillon, East and South Chicago, and Indiana Harbor.

These vigilante outfits, under the guise of roused public opinion, were also able to browbeat the State authorities into an "incomplete" martial law, a new way of perverting it to scabbing purposes. In Pennsylvania the State motor police and in Ohio the National Guard were called out soon after the strikes began. The troops were to maintain the status quo, that is, to keep plants shut or open as they found them. But soon Governor Davey of Ohio, and even Governor Earle of Pennsylvania, discovered that the "right to work" is no less "sacred" than the right to strike. The closed plants were allowed to open, and the State police and troops were assigned only to the immediate vicinity of the plants. Otherwise, they "assisted" the local authorities (and therein consisted the "incompleteness" of the martial law), who interpreted the civil rights of the strikers to suit themselves, and simply used the State police power to help them break the strikes. Governor Earle's representative in Johnstown was a Captain William Clark, an old "Cossack" of the Pennsylvania State Police, whose sympathies throughout were obviously on the side of Bethlehem Steel and the Citizens' Committee. Governor Davey of Ohio simply used the National Guard as a strike-breaking agency.

Not the least reason for the loss of the strike was the failure of the S.W.O.C. to gauge the situation in the Little Steel towns. Because it had been able to win in Big Steel diplomatically, it did not quite foresee the Hitler tactics of the Graces and the Girdlers. Also, it was influenced in its optimism by the brilliant campaigns in the automobile and rubber industries. Unfortunately, the situation in Little Steel was very different. For one thing, in the highly automatic belt-line industries, the sitdown is an immediate and paralyzing weapon, whatever its difficulties of control may be in an established union. And for another thing, both in rubber and in automobiles the rank and file is young, enthusiastic, and militant. Thousands of them are hill-billies, many of whom were only recently in the Klan. But once converted to the union, they gave it the same militant allegiance they had formerly given to some Know Nothing movement. Above all, during the last three years they had developed their own leaders right from the belt-line, who knew them and their problems. The workers in Little Steel, on the other hand, never had a chance to develop leaders out of their struggles. In the Pittsburgh district, the heart of Big Steel, the S.W.O.C. had been successful in its organization work partly because it dealt with a class-conscious working mass. The Homestead strike of 1892 is still a great tradition in that area. But in the fastnesses of Little Steel—in Johnstown, Youngstown, Massillon, Warren, Niles, Canton, in East and South Chicago, in Indiana Harbor—there is no real tradition of militant labor.

Finally, the over-enthusiastic reports of the organizers misled the top leadership of the S.W.O.C. This top leadership—Phil Murray, Van Bittner, Clint Golden, John Lewis himself—are extremely able men, but they are also desperately busy men. The incoming reports were glowing. In the earlier days of the S.W.O.C., a good many Stalinists, between seventy and eighty of them, had worked their way into organizing jobs. They padded the attendance figures at meetings, and distorted the entire picture. The Communist Party wanted a strike, because it offered the best chance for entrenchment in the union. The top leadership was also misled by the fact that Big Steel was co-operating beautifully; and that in its wake small firms were signing up right and left. And so the top leaders left the job of organizing Little Steel to the secondary tier of leaders, most of whom were minor officials in the United Mine Workers—who, incidentally, did not know a Stalinist from a Buddhist. In Johnstown the man in charge of the strike was James Mark, president of District 2 of the U.M.W. In Cleveland the two leaders were Bozo Damich and Lee Hall, both Ohio miners. In the Youngstown district, which includes most of the lesser steel towns, the leader was John Mayo, an Illinois miner. Most of their assistants were also miners. In the Chicago area it was pretty much the same story.

Now, the American miner is the most proletarian of all American workers. He has an old and radical tradition of unionism. His union is his whole social life. He does not need to be educated to stick in a strike. The secondary leaders in the United Mine Workers, who were officially in charge of the local areas in the Little Steel strike, had not had to organize anybody these last twenty years in Pennsylvania or Ohio or Illinois. The moment a mine is struck, everybody quits, and that's that. Mark and Damich and Hall and Mayo have had a great deal of experience in adjusting grievances and in signing local agreements. They have had none in coping with the situation they found in Little Steel. I came into Johnstown on July 2. By that time more than 8000 strikers had gone back to work. The atmosphere in the town was like that of a concentration camp. State motor police filled the hotel lobbies, and deputized gunmen were patrolling the streets. I went to see Mark. He is a man of sixty, white-haired, quiet, kindly, honest, and obviously used to running things on a shoe-string. He had no secretary, no publicity man, not even a typewriter.

"We have things pretty well under control," he said. Yet, the Cambria shops were obviously working, though Mark refused to admit it even to himself. Practically the same situation existed in Youngstown, Canton, Warren, Niles, Cleveland. The plants were operating at half or three-quarters normal capacity. The strike was already lost.

A few days later, the S.W.O.C. called off the strikes at the Youngstown Sheet and Tube plant in East Chicago and at the Inland Steel Company in Indiana Harbor. The union claimed victory in both cases, which was absurd. In the case of the Inland Steel Company, both the union and the management wrote letters to Governor Townsend of Indiana, leaving the whole issue to the National Labor Relations Board in case there should be an election. The Inland Steel Company is still unorganized. In the case of the Youngstown Sheet and Tube plant, the claim of victory was even more far-fetched. The company sent a memorandum to the governor, repeating its willingness to recognize "collective bargaining," which, of course, the Wagner Act makes mandatory. But it insisted that its memorandum must by no means be interpreted as a possible recognition of the S.W.O.C. And when the strikers filed back to work, the walls of the plants were plastered with notices to the effect that "we sign no agreements with anybody."

The Little Steel strike was definitely lost. And there can be no doubt that this loss acted, to some degree, as a setback to the CIO drive in general, especially since it was followed soon after by the new depression, which made organization even more difficult.

The S.W.O.C. Goes Ahead

In December 1937, the first national conference of the S.W.O.C. was held in Pittsburgh. By this time the depression had hit the industry so hard that it was working at only 35 per cent capacity. Moreover, a new operating device, the continuous hot-strip process, bound to displace some 85,000 workers, was revolutionizing the industry. But in spite of everything, the organizational success of the S.W.O.C. was so phenomenal that the conference naturally developed into a jubilee. After all, the organization of steel is the greatest success in the history of our labor movement. The S.W.O.C. could boast 450,000 members organized in more than 450 companies. The delegates expressed their complete confidence in the leaders of the S.W.O.C., so much so that no one even thought of reorganizing the Steel Workers Organizing Committee into a national union, writing its own constitution and electing its own officers. The keynote of the conference was the solidarity of labor, skilled and unskilled, white and black, under industrial unionism. And its spirit was thoroughly progressive. It endorsed a vast federal housing and public works program, it came out for federal unemployment payments under the Social Security Act during strikes, and voted for the Ludlow resolution for a popular referendum on war. This last—as we shall see—was a definite slap at the Communist Party, whose program of "collective security" is fundamentally an effort to align us with the Soviet Union in the next war. Phil Murray stated that he would "give the Communists nothing." And, indeed, since then the S.W.O.C. has been quietly laying off the known Stalinist and "fellow-traveling" organizers.

John Lewis received a twenty-five-minute ovation. And his speech expressed eloquently what the union means to the steel workers. "Last night," he said, "as I came again to this city, I passed the great tin plate mills in McKeesport and the great Homestead works and the mills along the Monongahela River, and I rejoiced because I said to myself that that mill, that furnace, that factory, are tended by men who are union men, banded together in a great organization for the first time in the history of America. . . . Today in 1937, as the year draws to a close, we find that the great steel industry of America has for the first time an organization efficient, well administered—a union of workers dedicated to sound policies, to American principles, and to the task of using their collective strength to aid them and all men in industry similarly situated."

On February 9, 1938, the S.W.O.C. renewed its contract with United States Steel. The contract retained the wage scale of $5.00 a day, forty hours a week, time-and-a-half for overtime, paid vacations, the seniority system, and the grievances committees in the mills. The S.W.O.C. tried to retain the provision against wage cuts during the life of the agreement, which lasts a year; and it also tried to gain a closed shop. But the open shop was retained, and the contract provides that either party to it may reopen the question of wages. Even so, Lewis and Murray were quite right in feeling pleased with this agreement. For it showed that Big Steel had decided that Little Steel could not crack the organization of the steel workers.

The real trouble in the S.W.O.C., as is the case in so many CIO unions, is the depression, which cut down on dues almost catastrophically. Thus, in the Chicago steel area, in which there are some 50,000 workers, only 350 members were paid up in their dues in April 1938. To a large degree, the S.W.O.C. still has to be supported by the United Mine Workers. But in steel, the lag in dues-payment is no indication of union collapse. In fact, since its first national conference in December 1937, the S.W.O.C. has signed up practically all the workers in the industry except in Little Steel.

CHAPTER IV

THE NEW VIGILANTISM

ONE WAY in which Big Ownership met the CIO was by diplomacy. The classic example is the recognition of the S.W.O.C. by Big Steel. The other way in which Big Ownership met the CIO was by vigilantism. The classic example is the breaking of the strike in Little Steel.

The Nature of Vigilantism

The average educated American has a certain picture of vigilantism which, like so many of his stereotyped vagaries, he gets from our so-called liberal historians, who know a lot they do not dare to understand.

In this view, vigilantism is a peculiar American phenomenon. It began, the story goes, in California in 1851, when outlawry was in wild and bloody flower, when every adventurer could buy a woman for the asking plus a sack of gold. Naturally, the better elements of the community wouldn't stand for it, and so they started a vigilante movement for law and order. (That, as you can see, was the only thing to do.) During the same eighteen-fifties there also flourished the Know Nothing movement, composed of native white trash, which swept into office a lot of politicians of the Huey Long and Gene Talmadge variety. (That, of course, was a bad thing.) Then came the post-Civil War K.K.K., because such "nigger-lovers" as Thaddeus Stevens and his fellow Northern radicals did not know that the war was over, and that the "best elements" of the South would not be run by a lot of carpetbaggers, scalawags, and too suddenly emancipated Negroes. (That was a bad thing, but quite understandable.) Then came the Molly Maguires—Irish-Catholic and labor—who went around killing mine superintendents. (That was a bad thing; it hurt labor.) Then came a few more Know Nothing movements, until we finally get into our own century, which has been filled with all sorts of violence, frame-ups, judicial assassinations, and labor war. (This is all terrible; it hurts democracy.) And since the World War things have gotten worse. The last decade especially, we have had a veritable plague of new moronic, inverted-populist movements—infantile, illiterate, confused, and vicious. In the nineteen-twenties, there was a revival of the Klan with its mummeries and wizardries. Today there are innumerable shirt organizations, nightgown rackets, the Black Legion, the Friends of New Germany, the Americaneers, the Committees of 100, of 200, of 1,000,000, the Women's National Association for the Preservation of the White Race—a sorority devoted to pure Negrophobia. There are literally hundreds of such outfits. And this spirit reaches into the darker corners of the D.A.R., the R.O.T.C., the American Legion, the Veterans of Foreign Wars, the Chamber of Commerce, the Lions, the Elks, the Eagles, the Moose, and the rest of the zoo of the small-time Babbittry. (It's all very dreadful, and Lord knows where it's leading to.)

Such is the hazy historic panorama of vigilantism that floats in the mind of the average liberal American. And it leads him to one of two conclusions, depending on whether he is a right liberal or a left liberal, whether his respectable perplexity is passive or assertive. If he is a right liberal, he usually decides that, since we have always had the vigilantes with us, they cannot be so very dangerous. If he is a left liberal, he is likely to join some innocent club like the American League for Peace and Democracy, which without any class analysis lumps into a "united front of all democratic forces" everybody from left-wing movie stars and drawing-room communists to steel workers and Georgia sharecroppers.

Now, what's wrong with this liberal conception of American vigilantism? It is not so much the facts. What's wrong with the picture is its complete classlessness. For obviously vigilantism is the most brutally clear of all class phenomena, the most desperate and regressive, and hence, in the last analysis, the most conspicuous expression of class domination. It is no more peculiarly American than is sex or sport, though like them it parades in every country in its own national costume. Vigilantism is as old as anti-Semitism, and as new as the latest Hitler purge. It may be as brutally ignorant as the Black Hundreds under the Tsar, or the Black Legion in Flint, or the Black or Brown Shirts. Or it may be as hoary with sophistication as British imperialism, which is the most distinguished vigilante movement of them all.

Vigilantism is the spirit of permanent counter-revolution, infinitely variegated by place, power, time, culture, and circumstance. In days of peaceful social exploitation it is quiescent. In days of growing social unrest it becomes more articulate and sinister. It may become articulate in the esoteric hokum and pretentious scholarship of a Pareto, or in the slick ignorance of a Thurman Arnold, or in the rabble-economics of a Father Coughlin. But it is always the same, be it sophistical or vulgar, for it fundamentally upholds class spoliation which cannot be upheld without brutality.

The characteristic note in vigilantism is always the mystical defense of class exploitation in the name of the status quo, of "law and order." The appeal is never rational, but always directed to the deepest anti-intellectual and regressive instincts. And the technique of organizing it is invariably the same. Since no movement can beat the masses without a mass base, such a mass base must be created. It is recruited from the most backward layer in the social pyramid. In modern society this is the lower middle class, a true mongrel class, linked to both capital and labor, yet an integral part of neither. Its objective interests are impossible to tell, for the various strains which make up its heterogeneous bulk— farmers, shopkeepers, small professionals, and clerks— are mutually hostile. Yet its fancied interests are with the big bourgeoisie, whose mortgagor it is, and whom it envies. This lower middle class is permanently confused by the split between its ignorance of what it needs and the reveries of what it wants. Incapable of resolving its economic contradictions, it has no political program, and is therefore the tool of every demagogue who plays on its prejudices and resentments. In times of social truce, its perplexities are dormant, but in times of social stress, as in a strike, it can always be enlisted to fight the battles of Big Ownership. For the petty bourgeois is always afraid that the big boys may foreclose on his shaky interests and investments, and force him down into the even greater insecurity of the working class. And his fear of this insecurity turns into hatred of the worker whenever the class war flares up. Then the riffraff in the lower middle class can be inflamed with the lynch spirit. Such is the nature and the mechanism of vigilantism.

To what degree is vigilantism dangerous? Exactly to the degree in which the dominant classes of a society encourage, exploit, and, what is most important, *subsidize* it. The post-Civil War Klan was a dangerous force, which still lives in the lynch law of the South, because it was guided and subsidized, behind the scenes, by the "best elements," the degraded Southern plantocracy, which had made a deal with the Northern conservatives against the Northern radicals. The Klan in the nineteen-twenties was not so dangerous, because Big Industry had decided that it did not need it in defeating a prone labor movement. Today the Klan, under various names, is once more riding in the South, because of the stirrings of the sharecropper and of the textile drive by the CIO.

Small Fry

Just as Mussolini's access to power inspired Hitler and his many lesser imitators, so Hitler's rise encouraged vigilantism from Rumania to California. The Nazi language and technique have been consciously copied by innumerable vigilante adventurers in America. But unless we include in this category the late Huey Long, all of them lack the perverse afflatus of their European models. Today the country swarms with these miscellaneous hick *Führers*, who walk the streets of Big Business, promising it a good time. Often they run scurrilous little sheets, all-moron and half-blackmail.

Some of our vigilantes are free-lance writers, avowedly and philosophically fascist, as some of the group around the new *American Mercury,* most of them former radicals. Another reactionary free-lance writer is George Sokolsky, who sells his thinly disguised reaction in the name of American individualism. He extolled it on Independence Day in 1937 to the workers of Weirton, who were being terrorized by the notorious Hatchet Gang. Mr. Sokolsky is a rather tragi-comic figure, for with his Eastern European Jewish background he ought to know better than to incite the vigilante spirit. Big business enterprises distribute numerous reprints of his articles. Attacking the CIO is Mr. Sokolsky's most lucrative business. He broadcasts against labor for the National Association of Manufacturers, and runs a weekly syndicated column baiting the CIO.

The vigilante entrepreneurs are forever on the lookout for angels to subsidize them until comes *der Tag*. Thus the Reverend Gerald L. K. Smith, who crowds his Committee of 1,000,000 into the ballroom of the Pennsylvania Hotel, is kept going by a New York broker. The

Reverend's main energy goes into labor-baiting, especially of the CIO. Now and then a frightened dowager gives him a check for the good work. In *The Nation* of March 11, 1936, I told how Governor Talmadge of Georgia received from the Georgia textile manufacturers $20,000 for "campaign purposes" in a sure election—and for breaking the textile strike; and how the Liberty League gave him $5000 for his grass-roots convention of all the white trash movements in the South. During the Little Steel strike, local racketeers—in Pennsylvania, Indiana, and especially in Ohio, in Illinois, and in Michigan—did a rush business in plain thuggery and murder. Big industry used them where it found them and paid spot cash for their services.

There are countless such local vigilante nuclei all over the country. In Toledo there are the Young Nationalists, who broadcasted "Americanism" over the radio every Sunday all through 1936 and 1937, when the great strikes in rubber, in automobiles, and in Little Steel took place. In Akron there were the Stahlmate Clubs active during the Goodyear strike. In Warren, Ohio, there is a John Q. Public League. In Columbus, Ohio, the state university has become a regular center of young fascist activities. There are the Student Americaneers, which in 1937 were run by Captain Arden S. Turner of the R.O.T.C. And a Reverend Frank Throop of the Committee of 200 was also very busy among the students. During the Little Steel strike all these groups were active day and night.

In Indiana and in Michigan the Klan can always be

THE NEW VIGILANTISM

resuscitated in times of industrial unrest. The automobile centers reek with vigilantism. In Dearborn, home of the main Ford plant, German Nazi sympathizers and the Veterans of Foreign Wars held joint meetings at the height of the CIO campaigns in 1937. Father Coughlin has a rather insignificant Workers' Council for Social Justice at Ford's. Father Coughlin is lying low, because the Catholic Church is lying low. "My day will come in 1938," he says, which is doubtful. But he still receives a thousand letters daily, and is selling widely an anti-CIO editorial service. At Ford's there are also the Knights of Dearborn, made up of the most vicious elements of the Ford service men. In Lansing, the American Legion and the R.O.T.C. of Michigan State College are very busy against labor, neither of them officially. The worst Red-baiter in town is a Reverend Frank J. Norris, who had a picturesque vigilante record in Texas. The Flint Alliance, which acted as a strike-breaking agency under George E. Boysen during the automobile strike, changed its name to the American Labor League after it was exposed as a racket in the press.

Then there is a multitude of "service" organizations, of which probably the best known is the National Civic Federation. At the height of the Little Steel strike, the Federation circularized the American business community with "confidential" literature and cries of Red Wolf and more money, please! While Matthew Woll, vice-president of the A. F. of L., was acting president of the Civic Federation, it collaborated closely with all the official Nazi agents in this country. It probably still does. Woll was forced to resign from the Civic Federation by John Lewis, at the 1934 convention of the A. F. of L.

"To expedite the creation of a national organization," Ralph M. Easley, secretary of the National Civic Federation, wrote in his confidential circular of July 2, 1937, "the existing membership of local organizations such as the Chamber of Commerce, Kiwanis, Rotary, and Lion Clubs, American Legion and Veterans of Foreign Wars, church, civic, and patriotic chapters will be called upon to personally visit individuals. . . . The individuals to be visited in a city or community are those affiliated with the CIO, on Federal unemployment relief, and WPA workers." "It is safe to assume," Mr. Easley continued, "that the local editor will comply with the requests of local advertisers whom he depends upon for the existence of his paper." Of course, "appropriate literature will be supplied." Mr. Easley enclosed a blueprint of a proposed "sales organization." "The advantage the sales organization created by the National Civic Federation will have over the sales organization conducted by John L. Lewis *et al.*, is that the National Civic Federation organization will consist of respectable citizens. . . ." Mr. Easley's final sentence was a plea for quick money—damned quick. In his business the revolution is always around the corner.

Big Stuff

All these hundreds of scattered vigilante rackets are forever in search of fat cats. But the fat cats, no less than the little Hitlers, have also learned their lesson from across the water. Fascism is the effort to freeze a disintegrating economy through terror. But European experience has shown that the individual capitalist is apt to become the prisoner of the terror. The fact that Herr Thyssen is on an enforced vacation in South America has made quite an impression on that section of Big Industry which is willing to play the fascist game. Therefore it decided on a double strategy. It continued to employ directly various detective agencies, labor spies, thugs, and Service Men, which the La Follette sub-committee exposed in such detail. And it went further. It decided to organize the various local vigilante movements on a national scale *under its own control.* It not only furnished them with funds, but it supplied the leadership, the publicity, and the policies. In other words, it put the vigilante movement under its own management-control. The literature of this more scientific vigilantism is not written by crackpots or illiterates, but by high-powered publicity men in air-conditioned advertising suites in New York and Pittsburgh. And these swank public relations counsels are not hired by the vigilante outfits to help them, but by Big Industry to run them.

A social movement is never a conspiracy. It lives and learns and crystallizes. When the CIO showed every sign of becoming a real mass movement, during the great automobile strikes and in the beginning of the steel campaign, Big Industry gradually moved to meet it. Big Steel decided to recognize the union. But Little

Steel decided to fight. And it went into the fight strategically prepared. It followed the so-called Mohawk Valley Formula.

This formula appeared in the form of an article in the Labor Relations Bulletin of the National Association of Manufacturers soon after the Remington Rand strike at Ilion, New York. It indicated in detail the steps to be taken in a campaign of scientific strike-breaking. It was christened the "Mohawk Valley Formula" by James H. Rand, Jr., who—in the words of the National Labor Relations Board—was "proudly offering it to his fellow-members in the National Association of Manufacturers as an example of modern strike-breaking." It is no doubt the most significant program in the history of American vigilantism. And here is the celebrated Formula, as broken down into nine clauses in a decision by the N.L.R.B., which interpolated its own interpretations:

First: When a strike is threatened, label the union leaders as "agitators" to discredit them with the public and their own followers. In the plant, conduct a forced balloting under the direction of foremen in an attempt to ascertain the strength of the union and to make possible misrepresentation of the strikers as a small minority imposing their will upon the majority. At the same time, disseminate propaganda, by means of press releases, advertisements and the activities of "missionaries," such propaganda falsely stating the issues involved in the strike so that the strikers appear to be making arbitrary demands, and the real issues, such as the employer's refusal to bargain collectively, are obscured. Concurrently with these moves, by exerting economic pressure through threats to move

THE NEW VIGILANTISM 103

the plant, align the influential members of the community into a cohesive group opposed to the strike. Include in this group, usually designated a "Citizens Committee," representatives of the bankers, real estate owners and business men, i.e., those most sensitive to any threat of removal of the plant because of its effect upon property values and purchasing power. flowing from payrolls.

Second: When the strike is called raise high the banner of "law and order," thereby causing the community to mass legal and police weapons against a wholly imagined violence and to forget that those of its members who are employees have equal rights with the other members of the community.

Third: Call a "mass meeting" of the citizens to co-ordinate public sentiment against the strike and to strengthen the power of the Citizens Committee, which organization, thus supported, will both aid the employer in exerting pressure upon the local authorities and itself sponsor vigilante activities.

Fourth: Bring about the formation of a large armed police force to intimidate the strikers and to exert a psychological effect upon the citizens. This force is built up by utilizing local police, State police if the Governor co-operates, vigilantes and special deputies, the deputies being chosen if possible from other neighborhoods, so that there will be no personal relationships to induce sympathy for the strikers. Coach the deputies and vigilantes on the law of unlawful assembly, inciting to riot, disorderly conduct, etc., so that, unhampered by any thought that the strikers may also possess some rights, they will be ready and anxious to use their newly acquired authority to the limit.

Fifth: And perhaps most important, heighten the demoralizing effect of the above measures—all designed to convince the strikers that their cause is hopeless—by a "back to work" movement, operated by a puppet Association of so-called "loyal employees" secretly organized by the employer. Have this Association wage a publicity campaign in its own name and co-ordinate such campaign with the work of the "missionaries" circulating among the strikers and visiting their homes. This "back to work" movement has these results: It causes the public to believe that the strikers are in the minority and that most of the employees desire to return to work, thereby winning sympathy for the employer and an endorsement of his activities to such an extent that the public is willing to pay the huge costs, direct and indirect, resulting from the heavy forces of police. This "back to work" movement also enables the employer, when the plant is later opened, to operate it with strike-breakers if necessary and to continue to refuse to bargain collectively with the strikers. In addition, the "back to work" movement permits the employer to keep a constant check on the strength of the union through the number of applications received from employees ready to break ranks and return to work, such number being kept secret from the public and the other employees, so that the doubts and fears created by such secrecy will in turn induce still others to make applications.

Sixth: When a sufficient number of applications are on hand, fix a date for an opening of the plant through the device of having such opening requested by the "back to work" Association. Together with the Citizens Committee, prepare for such opening by making provision for a peak army of police by roping off the areas surrounding the plant, by securing arms and ammunition, etc. The purpose of the "opening" of the plant is threefold: to see if enough employees are ready to return to work; to induce still others to return as a result of the demoralizing effect produced by the opening of the plant and the return of some of their number; and lastly, even if the maneuver fails to induce a sufficient number of persons to return, to persuade the public through pictures and news releases that the opening was nevertheless successful.

Seventh: Stage the "opening," theatrically throwing open the gates at the propitious moment and having the employees march into the plant grounds in a massed group protected by squads of armed police, so as to give to the opening a dramatic and exaggerated quality and thus heighten its demoralizing effect. Along with the "opening" provide a spectacle—speeches, flag raising, and praises for the employees, citizens, and local authorities, so that, their vanity touched, they will feel responsible for the continued success of the scheme and will increase their efforts to induce additional employees to return to work.

Eighth: Capitalize on the demoralization of the strikers by continuing the show of police force and the pressure of the Citizens Committee, both to insure that those employees who have returned will continue at work and to force the remaining strikers to capitulate. If necessary, turn the locality into a warlike camp through the declaration of a state of emergency tantamount to martial law and barricade it from the outside world so that nothing may interfere with the successful conclusion of the "Formula," thereby driving home to the union leaders the futility of further efforts to hold their ranks intact.

Ninth: Close the publicity barrage, which day by day during the entire period has increased the demoralization worked by all of these measures, on the theme that the plant is in full operation and that the strikers were merely a minority attempting to interfere with the "right to work," thus inducing the public to place a moral stamp of approval upon the above measures. With this, the campaign is over—the employer has broken the strike.

The Mohawk Valley Formula is the chief guide of industrial relations for the National Association of Manufacturers. It was followed faithfully in the Little Steel strike. Half a year later, in December 1937, the National Association of Manufacturers held a Congress of American Industry in New York City. During these six intervening months, the National Labor Relations Board had held a number of hearings in Michigan, Ohio, Missouri, West Virginia, in any number of States. These hearings had brought out the ugly details of industrial violence and suspension of civil liberties provoked by Big Industry. The La Follette Committee had been holding hearings all summer. And its revelations of labor espionage and thuggery by Big Industry shocked the whole country. Senators La Follette and Thomas issued their report at the very time the Congress of American Industry was meeting. Yet all these official exposures had no more effect on the National Association of Manufacturers than to make it phrase more cautiously a new set of anti-labor sentiments. The congress was outraged by the "coercion" to which workers were subjected from bona fide unions, and demanded that the National Labor Relations Act be amended. It expressed the belief that the primary obligation of government is the protection of the "right to work." It insisted on the right of management to deal with its "own" employees. And it came

THE NEW VIGILANTISM 107

out for an amendment to the Byrnes Act (which forbids the interstate transportation of strike-breakers), making it a Federal offense to transport "strike-makers, flying squadrons, and paid pickets." So much for the open deliberations of this Congress of American Industry. In its committee meetings behind closed doors, it not only endorsed the Mohawk Valley Formula, but laid out a completely reactionary scheme of Big Business control for the whole country. In one year the National Association of Manufacturers spent $750,000, more than half its income, on spreading the gospel of company unionism, and on anti-labor propaganda in general. Whether the Association will succeed is another matter. It may under-estimate the democratic traditions in this country and over-estimate the infective power of European fascism. But evidently it is willing.

The Mohawk Formula in Action

During the strike in Little Steel, the scab commandments of the Mohawk Valley Formula were followed with orthodox fidelity. And the thing worked. The strike was broken. There might have been another story to tell if the strike had been carefully prepared and timed. But what actually happened was that the scientific strategy of Big Business vigilantism defeated the poorly planned campaign of the Steel Workers Organizing Committee.

In former days, so-called citizens' committees were merely sub-committees of the local chambers of commerce and other business men's organizations. Under the Mohawk Valley Formula, these citizens' committees became merely the local staffs of Big Business vigilantism. Because of its complete dependence on one big mill and its isolated social structure of sufficient size, Johnstown was chosen as the ideal strike-breaking experimental station. The Johnstown Citizens' Committee was actually organized between June 18 and 22, with Sidney D. Evans and other executives of Bethlehem Steel in the background. It was organized in protest against Governor Earle's declaration of martial law on June 18, when the State authorities disbanded Mayor Shields's 300 deputized vigilantes. The committee's expensive labors were subsidized by the steel companies. This is equally true of the citizens' committees and law-and-order leagues in Massillon, Canton, Youngstown, all through the Mohawk and Mahoning Valleys, where Little Steel is king. The Johnstown Citizens' Committee served as a model for the other centers during the steel strike.

The Johnstown Citizens' Committee is made up of small-time business men and preachers. The chairman is Francis C. Martin, a local banker. The most vociferous member is the Reverend John H. Stanton, a typical Elmer Gantry in his views on labor. His close second is the Reverend George W. Nicely. The official *Führer* is Lawrence W. Campbell, secretary of the local chamber of commerce. Short, fat, bald, chinless, and exophthalmic, Mr. Campbell was forever rushing about during the strike, taking down the names of pickets, urging the authorities to provocative and arbitrary action, calling meetings of various sub-committees of his outfit, and keeping it in fighting trim. But for all his self-importance, he was not his own boss. His local mentor was Mr. Douglas Campbell, who represented the John Price Jones Corporation of New York City, which in real life is Mr. John Price Jones, who was the guiding genius of the Johnstown committee.

John Price Jones is as different from Lawrence Campbell as Tom Lamont is from a small-town banker. Mr. Jones was born in Latrobe, not far from Johnstown. He married a Johnstown girl and has never quite lost touch with his old home section. He is Johnstown's permanent friend in need. He is such a local patriot that he gave up his class reunion at Harvard to put the Johnstown Citizens' Committee on its feet. Since his graduation from college he has made good in a big way. The John Price Jones Corporation is one of the largest publicity and money-raising firms in the country. Mr. Jones raised the money for the Salvation Army, for the Harvey Gibson Committee, which relieved New York City before the government stepped in, for Bishop Manning's sub-Gothic cathedral, for the University of Pennsylvania, for other clients of similar respectability and stature.

Just two days after the hasty organization of the Johnstown Citizens' Committee, on June 24, the committee had sufficient funds "from thousands of real Americans" to run a full-page ad in forty leading American newspapers. The ad protested against the Federal and State authorities for refusing to give protection to the "back-to-work" movement, thus causing violence, chaos, and a breakdown of organized society. The estimated cost of this advertising campaign was $65,000. It was paid for by Little Steel.

The Bethlehem Steel Corporation paid the "expenses" of this whole vigilante campaign in Johnstown, with no questions asked. At subsequent N.L.R.B. hearings, Mr. Francis C. Martin, the chairman of the Citizens' Committee, confessed that he had received from Sidney D. Evans, the local management representative of Bethlehem, $31,456.25 in cash, which he had turned over to Mayor Shields—a former large-scale bootlegger with a Federal penitentiary record. And he admitted that no accounting of the sums obtained from Mr. Evans was made to the Citizens' Committee, of which he was chairman. At the hearings it was also brought out that the company had acted in collusion with the mayor and chief of police to swear in company thugs and "imported gunmen" as special deputies. They interfered with the strikers' right of peaceful picketing, they intimidated them into joining the "back-to-work" movement, and otherwise violated the Wagner Act. This reign of terror lasted from June 24 to July 15.

When the publicity blasts of the Citizens' Committee succeeded in frightening Governor Earle into lifting the effective martial law which had kept the Cambria mills closed for a few days, he left a skeleton force of the State motor police under Captain William A. Clark. Earle, of course, wanted the State police to remain impartial. But Captain Clark had ideas of his own.

On July 3 Captain Clark called in the press with a

grave air. He had big news. At 3 A.M. the Pennsylvania Railroad police had arrested a George Layton, a recent reformatory inmate, for throwing three sticks of dynamite on the tracks of the Cambria carrier, the Conemaugh and Blacklick Railroad. Fortunately the dynamite failed to explode. The prisoner was co-operatively detained by the local, State, and Pennsylvania Railroad police. He had no lawyer. Layton had implicated two railroad workers, Calvin Updyke and George Owens, who had fixed him to do the job. The captain was pleased by this splendid police work. But immediate inquiry at the Brotherhood of Railway Conductors and Trainmen disclosed the fact that Updyke had been a "loyal" company stooge for thirty-five years and Owens for twenty. They had been the ringleaders in the formation of the company union. Obviously somebody had made a bad slip, and Bethlehem Steel was caught framing itself. These tactics may also explain the explosion of a stick of dynamite inside the Gautier gates of the Cambria on June 15, and the dynamiting of the two water mains which feed the Cambria.

Three hours after Updyke and Owens were detained, the company whitewashed them on the ground that some bad mistake must have been made. Some thirty hours later they were released. The police, including Captain Clark, continued to hold Layton incommunicado. Thirty hours later, Layton implicated Louis A. Pegg, the chairman of the striking trainmen on the Conemaugh and Blacklick, who was promptly arrested.

The strike was petering out. And the success of the

new vigilantism gave the citizens' committee movement the idea of organizing itself on a national scale. The Johnstown Citizens' Committee was chosen to call a national convention for July 15. Representatives of various citizens' committees, law-and-order leagues, chambers of commerce, big industries from a dozen States, and a few riffraff vigilante movements met in Johnstown to form a Citizens' National Committee, dedicated to the "inalienable constitutional right to work." Dr. Gustavus W. Dyer, professor of economics at Vanderbilt University, hailed the meeting as "the rising sun for the protection of American liberties." "Thank God for Tom Girdler," shouted J. G. Lester, chairman of the Massillon Citizens' Committee. "I think we ought to send him a telegram congratulating him for smoking out those Communists, John L. Lewis, Madam Perkins, and President Roosevelt." The National Labor Relations Board was attacked viciously. The gist of all the arguments was again that government had "broken down," failing to protect the worker in his right to earn a living. On July 16, another expensive full-page ad was run nationally, again paid for by Little Steel. And this time the ad had a definitely provocative and sinister appeal to vigilantism. The chairman of this newly organized Citizens' National Committee is the Reverend John H. Stanton; the national secretary is Lawrence Campbell. The rest of the committee consists of obscure reactionaries, some of whom, especially those from the South, have long vigilante, anti-Semitic, Negro-hating, and labor-baiting records.

THE NEW VIGILANTISM

The other vigilante movements in the Little Steel towns followed the Johnstown pattern. The Mahoning Valley Citizens' Committee, whose chairman is the Reverend Roland Luhman of Youngstown, ran three characteristic full-page ads in the Youngstown *Daily Vindicator*. The two leading spirits in this Youngstown vigilante outfit were Carl Ullman, president of the Dollar Savings and Trust Company, and Walter O. R. Johnson, a lawyer who is the head of the local American Legion. The actual gang leader during the strike was one of Youngstown's leading machine politicians, Roy Thomas. He is a former district attorney of Mahoning County, who some years ago left office under a cloud. The Youngstown Sheet and Tube Company asked him to serve as the attorney and leader of its company union. "Give me 200 tough armed men," he boasted to me, "and I'll clean up those sons-of-bitches on the picket line in no time." Thomas and a bunch of professional gunmen, whom the company imported and had Sheriff Ralph Elser deputize, provoked a riot in which two workers were killed. On a much smaller scale, the Youngstown story was repeated in Warren, Niles, and Canton.

But on the whole, the Ohio vigilante movements were less well organized and subsidized than the Johnstown Citizens' Committee, partly because this whole development of a national vigilantism under Big Business control is still in an experimental state; and because the steel companies enjoyed the ultra-willing collaboration of Governor Davey, who used the National Guard openly to break the strike. On the other hand, the struggle in Ohio was bloodier precisely because the prostitution of the National Guard created an atmosphere of complete lawlessness. This atmosphere was especially exploited by Tom Girdler of Republic Steel, who deliberately sought to break the strike through terrorism. In Massillon, pressure was brought upon Chief of Police Switter by Carl Myers, district manager of Republic Steel, by the Law and Order League, and by General Marlin of the Ohio National Guard, who had quartered two companies in the Republic plant. Switter was finally forced to swear in forty "loyal" Republic employees as special police. They immediately declared: "We're going to clean the strikers out tonight." And true to their word, by eleven o'clock that night they had provoked a riot among a peaceful crowd of strikers loafing in front of their headquarters, had killed two of them and wounded fifteen. None of the company thugs was even scratched. Then they raided rooming houses in the neighborhood, arresting anybody they suspected of belonging to the union. Those arrested were held two days and then released, after being forced to sign a statement that they would not sue for false arrest.

But the bloodiest outrage provoked by the Republic Steel Corporation was the Memorial Day Massacre in South Chicago. This was perpetrated without the aid of a citizens' vigilante group. On that fateful Sunday afternoon some 2500 men, women, and children attended a mass meeting a few blocks away from the plant. Since Mayor Kelly had granted the strikers permission for peaceful picketing, after the meeting some four hundred of them walked toward the plant across a field. But before the gates were in sight, they were halted by a cordon of two hundred police under the command of Captain Mooney. Mooney is known to Chicago labor as "the Killer." During a parley with the strikers, which lasted some three or four minutes, the captain told them to "get the hell out of here." Then, on a signal, the police charged into the crowd, hitting out savagely to right and left with their clubs. In the subsequent melee, the police began to shoot. Ten people were killed, seven of them shot in the back. Fifty were injured by gunshots, and twenty-five more by clubbing. No officers were shot, and only three were slightly injured. After the La Follette hearings established all these facts, the Cook County authorities and the coroner's jury whitewashed the police as having acted in "self-defense."

The Ford Empire

Henry Ford plays in vigilantism the same independent game he has always played in industry. He has always hated "Wall Street." He still hates it. And today he is our biggest vigilante-independent. The River Rouge plant in Dearborn has its own private underworld to terrorize the workers. No fancy Wall Street public relations counsel for the Ford organization. It simply brought into River Rouge the underworld gangs of Detroit and their leaders, who now control the plant. And the man who did this job is the notorious Harry Bennett.

Harry Bennett is a war product. During the war he was in the navy, where he acquired some reputation as a prize-fighter. Finally he drifted into Michigan and into Ford's. There he got into the personnel department and, being undeniably a gentleman of considerable parts, he gradually came to control it. In time he built up the Ford Service Men, an organization whose backbone is the Down River gang of Detroit under the leadership of one Angelo Caruso.

There are about eight hundred underworld characters in the Ford Service organization. They are the Storm Troops. They make no pretense of working, but are merely "keeping order" in the plant community through terror. Around this nucleus of eight hundred yeggs there are, however, between 8000 and 9000 authentic workers in the organization, a great many of them spies and stool-pigeons and a great many others who have been browbeaten into joining this industrial mafia. There are almost 90,000 workers in River Rouge, and because of this highly organized terror and spy system the fear in the plant is something indescribable. During the lunch hour men shout at the top of their voices about the baseball scores lest they be suspected of talking unionism. Workers seen talking together are taken off the assembly line by Service Men and fired. Every man suspected of union sympathies is immediately discharged, usually under the framed-up charge of "starting a fight," in which he often gets terribly beaten up. Harry Bennett's power extends beyond Dearborn to Detroit. In certain localities in Michigan judges and other State officials cannot run for office without a petition with a specified number of signatures. Bennett simply puts such petitions on the conveyor belt, and in one afternoon the prospective candidate has all the signatures he needs.

In a decision against Ford issued by the National Labor Relations Board on December 23, 1937, the Board states that the Ford Service department has undoubtedly "been vested with the responsibility of maintaining surveillance over Ford employees, not only during their work but even when they are outside the plant, and of crushing at its inception, by force if necessary, any sign of union activity.... The River Rouge plant has taken on many aspects of a community in which martial law has been declared and in which a huge military organization ... has been superimposed upon the regular civil authorities."

Violence by Ford gangsters is chronic, not only within the plants, but outside as well. During the first half of July 1937, the American press carried on its front pages the story of the brutal sluggings of union organizers in front of the River Rouge plant. Richard Frankensteen and Walter Reuther, both important union officials, were badly beaten at that time. In November, more than a score of organizers of the United Automobile Workers were beaten for distributing CIO literature. Dearborn police are arresting men wholesale for handing out such literature. On December 8 there were 60 arrests; on December 16, 208; on January 21, 352.

And this sort of thing has been going on for months.

In October, Ford shut down his Kansas City plant, locking out 3000 workers. On October 13, an automobile carrying three strikers was riddled with shotgun slugs near the plant. After the plant was opened, the police were constantly breaking up the picket line, using tear gas, and making arrests. On December 15, 161 pickets were arrested. Two days later, three men were shot, one was overcome by tear gas, twelve were severely beaten, and more than a hundred arrested. When the plant was reopened, the company supplied the strikebreakers with guns. Since the lockout 1400 men have been discharged for union activities. This system of terrorism is operating in all the Ford plants throughout the country.

The Ford Terror, especially Harry Bennett and his underworldlings, have received widespread unfavorable publicity. And this publicity is increasingly resented by Messrs. Sorenson and Cameron, Ford's production manager and secretary, respectively. They feel that the Ford Service organization hurts the company. In order to undercut Harry Bennett, they tried to push a disguised company union, called the Ford Brotherhood, Incorporated. This "union" was organized in June 1937 by a small lawyer in Detroit named William S. McDowell, who has organized half a dozen other incorporated "unions." But the Ford executives found that they could not get rid of Harry Bennett, whose complete hold on Henry Ford was developed because of the old man's tremendous fear, even before the days of the kidnaping racket, that Edsel or one of his grandchildren might be kidnaped. Bennett developed a regular little garrison to protect the Ford family. And he got himself on Ford's personal payroll in complete independence of the plant executives.

Except for the Ford Terror, vigilantism in Michigan is less efficiently organized, though probably more widespread, than in Pennsylvania and Ohio. In Michigan, as well as in Indiana and Illinois, the vigilante movement is still largely local, disconnected, and erratic, in the hands of illiterates and crackpots. Their literature lacks the polish of the John Price Jones Corporation and their frame-ups are without benefit of high-pressure management.

Espionage

The use of local vigilante outfits and their integration into a national movement is one way in which Big Industry met the CIO drive. The other way, hallowed by tradition, was organized espionage and provocation by professional detectives. The stool-pigeon, whether used by the Tsar, the Gestapo, or by General Motors, after all belongs to the second oldest profession in the world. What's new in the final report of the La Follette Committee is the extent of this espionage in American industry. The list of the companies which availed themselves of the services of various detective agencies, some of them under very high-sounding names, is described in the report as "reading like a blue book of American business." Among the 2500 firms listed, we find practically every well-known corporation in America. General Motors, the largest single industrial client of the commercial stool-pigeon, spent from January 1934 until July 1936 the sum of $994,855.68 for espionage in its sixty plants.

Even more astonishing was the number of spies who had wormed their way into organized labor, mostly into the CIO. Three hundred and four Pinkerton operatives managed to become members in 93 local unions. One hundred of them were elected to office. These offices were distributed as follows: 1 national vice-president, 14 local union presidents, 8 local union vice-presidents, 2 local treasurers, 14 recording secretaries, 14 trustees, 3 business agents, 3 organizers, 3 delegates to central labor bodies, 6 committeemen, 4 financial secretaries, 4 executive board members, 1 division and 2 local chairmen. Undercover agents also managed to fill 20 local union secretaryships, which had charge of the roster of membership. These figures cover only the Pinkerton Detective Agency. Dozens of its competitors, notably Burns and the Corporations Auxiliary, exploited the same field.

General Motors paid 52 Pinkertons to be "members" of the United Automobile Workers. Five such agents were members of the United Mine Workers in Pennsylvania; nine of them were in the United Rubber Workers on the Goodrich payroll; and so on down the list in practically every CIO union. The chart of General Motors expenditures for undercover work in the union shows almost an absolute correlation, month by month, with union activity, until the union was recognized. This espionage system had become as complex as in Comrade Yezhov's G.P.U. Personnel directors would not rely upon reports of spies working directly for plant managers, and employed their own spies to check on these reports. Higher officials of the company had Pinkertons secretly checking up on the Pinkertons of the personnel directors. Finally, General Motors hired special spies to check on other automobile companies. The known number of detective operatives the La Follette investigators unearthed was 3871, almost all of them engaged against the CIO drive. But this figure is far from complete, for some 700 detective agencies refused to furnish the La Follette Committee with any information.

The La Follette report merely gave us a glimpse of the white slugs under the rock of Big Industry. Since Big Steel, General Motors, Chrysler, and the rubber industry have recognized the CIO, they have renounced the use of commercial espionage. In all likelihood the detective agencies have lost considerable business in the industrial field. But it is silly to suppose that union recognition has permanently removed the labor spy. The stoolpigeon in industry cannot be done away with by government research and legislation any more than can the class struggle of which he is the ugliest underworld expression.

But the greatest danger not only to the CIO but also to America is the new vigilantism, experimentally begun in the Little Steel strike. Local in character, it is organized by and for Big Ownership. The efficiency of its national integration will depend on the spread of industrial unrest and the depth of social protest. But the formula for combating an awakening labor movement had been found. American in background, dress, and manner, it points the danger of an American fascism.

CHAPTER V

FACTIONALISM

The Trade Union Movement and the Radical Movement

THERE IS a great deal of talk about the CIO being radical, Red, communist, or whatnot. These labels are tossed about with complete abandon. But fundamentally they are nothing but symbols of hate or faith or plain ignorance. In fact, these words cannot be clearly defined. For social terms have no fixed meanings, at least not until the movements which coined them are long dead. They refer to historic forces in the making; and to yield meaning they must be analyzed in relation to men and events. Thus the word "radical" includes on the one hand Jefferson and Lenin, and on the other General Coxey and Upton Sinclair, who have nothing in common but a spirit of dissidence. The term "Red" is today nothing but a lynch-cry. And "communism" stands for exactly opposite things in the *Communist Manifesto* and the *Daily Worker;* the difference is no less than the difference between social revolution and a socialist form of fascism.

In discussing, therefore, the infiltration of the various radical or pseudo-radical groups into the CIO, we must first clarify two things. We must analyze the historic relation between trade unionism and the radical movement; for though they are closely related, even when mutually hostile, they are not the same. And then we must evaluate what these radical or pseudo-radical groups stand for, and what they want in the CIO.

The simplest example of the relation between organized labor and radicalism we can find in the early A. F. of L. In the days of its growth, from its foundation until about 1910, the A. F. of L. throve, as does every other movement, on its inner struggles against its left-wing opposition. It was the powerful socialist minority, which forever had to be pacified and compromised with, that was the main driving force in the Federation. And it is no exaggeration to say that the A. F. of L. in its heyday was the result of the struggle between Gompers and Daniel De Leon, and then between Gompers and Morris Hillquit and other socialist leaders who influenced the thinking of many trade unionists. For even the most conservative trade union oligarchy flourishes far more on its sound compromises with its own Left than on its necessary compromises with the boss. Forward movements grow on their inner tensions. Hence a trade union movement which crushes all left criticism finally dies from sheer inanition. When soon after the war our socialist movement splintered into various impotent factions, the A. F. of L. lost all vitality, and finally deteriorated into a sort of independent company unionism.

The CIO is an effort on the part of American labor to revitalize itself and to modernize its outdated structure. This it cannot do without the stimulus of political and social radicalism. Mere trade unionism as such, without left agitation, cannot recast its point of view or remodel itself functionally. Only social politics—which, as Aristotle said, is the struggle for power of a whole philosophy of society—can change and advance economic institutions. Trade unionism as such is only the economic organization of labor by and for itself—in crafts, or by industries, or in a mixture of both—within the logic of the economy in which it works and with which it deals. Hence, trade unionism everywhere is a purely practical affair. And being a practical, day-to-day, collective bargaining movement, it has always attracted and developed practical leaders. The average trade union leader the world over, not only in the A. F. of L., is essentially a business unionist. He is the representative and the broker of labor power in the labor market, who is guided primarily by the daily pressures of that market.

Obviously, in long periods of social peace, the purely economic organizations of the workers tend to become opportunistic, far more rapidly than their political parties. And in time this opportunism tends toward spiritual ossification. In every trade union leader, in fact in every leader, there lurks the bureaucrat. And in the long run, the bureaucrat in him is likely to win over the original militant who in his youthful enthusiasm joined the labor movement, almost always as a radical. He becomes a Leipart, a Jouhoux, a Sir Walter Citrine, or a William Green. Gradually his vision shrinks from his original horizon, which never was wider than the existing social order, to the daily needs of his organization; and finally to the needs of the bureaucracy, whose interests he has almost imperceptibly come to identify with the welfare of the workers. In this process, his political interests and his social impulses have become confined to keeping the "Reds" out of his movement, because they criticize his spiritual shrinkage, endanger his position, and create mass unrest. Thus he comes to look down upon all left-wingers of whatever school as Utopians, adventurers, interlopers, saboteurs, or just plain sons-of-bitches. The radicals, on the other hand, whom long social peace has kept out of the dominant labor movement, become—precisely because of their lack of contact with the masses—sectarian, scholastic, factionalist, often embittered by personal disappointment and social maladjustment.

In such prolonged periods of social peace, these two factors—the "practical" sterility of the trade union movement, and the sectarian bitterness of the radical movement—weaken labor both in its economic militancy and in its political and social understanding. And, in turn, this mass lethargy tends to make the trade union leader ever more standpat, and ever more contemptuous of the hair-splitting quarrels of the left critics. Hence few people have less understanding of the radical movement than the trade union leaders. That is why, common opinion to the contrary, men like John Lewis and Philip Murray, or even leaders like David Dubinsky and Sidney Hillman, who have a socialist background, really know very little of the nature of political and social radicalism. They think they know all about it, because they are constantly running into it. But they do not understand its fundamental drives, the history of its factional segmentations, and its contemporary enmities. That is why the trade union leader, no matter how progressive, is almost invariably inept in using the radical movement constructively when he suddenly needs it.

And the progressive union leader needs the "agitator" whenever the masses become restive and demand militant organization. This occurs in periods of economic depression; not at the depth of the depression, but when the business cycle begins to crawl up from the bottom. Then the workers begin to realize that their conservative trade unions were unable to protect them from the ravages of the catastrophe. They begin to gauge the lag between the stationary character of business unionism and the ever-advancing industrial process. That lag has meant to them unemployment and hunger. Their restlessness becomes social awareness. And this class consciousness, no matter how vague and simple, turns to social radicalism for leadership. Then the progressive and alert union leader breaks away from the conservative trade union hierarchy, and puts himself at the head of the forward movement. And he necessarily opens the doors to the radicals, whom he needs as agitators and organizers. But once the various radical groups are in, their first interest is to fight each other. For each school believes that it alone can fashion a class-conscious labor movement, and considers all other schools as reactionary or "counter-revolutionary."

It is absurd to deny that the CIO has admitted radicals into its ranks. If a new and more left orientation had not been the propelling motive of the CIO, it never would have split from the A. F. of L. in the first place.

And once the CIO was on its way, its leaders found it necessary to battle every reactionary force in American life. If the CIO had used only old-fashioned trade union organizers, it could not possibly have organized over 3,000,000 workers in two years. It had to use those who at least in theory had always argued for industrial unionism. Moreover, the CIO should not and did not keep out individuals because of their political beliefs any more than because of their religious beliefs. A worker to whom his union is closed has no choice but to become a scab.

But unfortunately the trade union movement and the radical movement develop unevenly. By the time the CIO started, the various radical schools, which had hitherto lacked all mass support, had already been on the scene for many years and had a long history of internecine bitterness. All these schools are socialist and revolutionary in origin and theory, no matter how rigid or confused or perverted their Marxism may be. Fundamentally they all agree in their *economic* critique of capitalist production. But they differ—and that is far more important—in their *political* means of achieving their end; in their proposed methods of influencing or capturing the labor movement.

These political differences are as old as modern socialism itself, which, like all great social movements, has busily bred sects and heresies. They were exacerbated by the World War and the Russian Revolution. These two overwhelming historical events had in the American radical movement the same splitting effects as everywhere else. In our pre-war Socialist Party the bureaucratization of the leadership had gone on for years, though of course not as obviously as in the trade union movement, for the socialist leader must always pay lip service to the "revolution." But during the war the right wing of the Socialist Party split off and joined Woodrow Wilson's war for democracy, in which it completely disappeared. And after the war what was left of the Socialist Party lost all vitality.

During the 1920's, the party was so weak that all it could do was lift its finger to point with pride at the Weimar Republic *(selig)*, and the British Labor Government *(selig)*, and the various Socialist prime ministers in Belgium, Sweden, or what have you. Every once in a while Morris Hillquit would take a trip abroad and visit all the rich Socialist uncles in the chancellories of Europe. At the same time, like the Second International of which it is a part, our Socialist Party was forever retreating in all directions before the attacks of the Third International. And in this process it got so cracked and fissured that in the 1930's it finally broke into several pieces. The Communist Party, as we shall see, also broke up into factions during the 1920's—into the official party affiliated with the Communist International, the Right Opposition (Lovestoneites) and the Left Opposition (Trotskyites). Accordingly, when the CIO began its drive and opened its doors to left-wing organizers, they carried their mutual antagonisms into the drive.

Political Parties and the CIO

The five conventional socialist and communist groups, which are supposedly playing an active role in the CIO, are the Socialist Workers Party (Trotskyites), the Independent Labor League of America (Lovestoneites), the Socialist Party, the Social Democratic Federation, and the Communist Party. Labor's Nonpartisan League—and its various loose affiliates, such as the Farmer-Labor parties in the Northwest or the American Labor Party in New York—are not directly involved in the factional struggles in the CIO.

The Trotskyites

The Trotskyites in the CIO we may dismiss, with all due apologies to their revolutionary fervor. They are a tiny and isolated sect. They have some influence in Minneapolis. There, the local CIO council, which is Stalinist-influenced, is engaged in a constant and deadly struggle with the Trotskyite Dunne brothers. The Dunnes control the powerful A. F. of L. teamsters' local, and through it much of Minneapolis labor. But the Trotskyites have no one in the national CIO unions. And the half-dozen of them who had been active in the maritime, steel, and automobile industries, were hounded out by the Stalinists.

The main activities of the Trotskyites consist in propagating and printing the views and works of Leon Trotsky, which are consistently brilliant and profound; in defending Trotsky and the other leaders of the October Revolution against the fantastic slanders of the Moscow Inquisition, a task of great historic importance; and finally, in analyzing American labor. In this they have been sectarian, unrealistic, and have amounted to nothing. To be sure, since the middle of 1938 they have been less abstract and more practical in their program to serve the trade union movement. In this purely economic program their position differs rather little from that of the Lovestoneites. Yet these two groups co-operate nowhere in the trade union field. What divides them is not so much a difference in principle as it is their competitive ambition in the labor movement.

The Lovestoneites

The Lovestoneites were expelled from the Communist Party in 1929 for their so-called "right deviation," which served as a blanket indictment of their more realistic attitude on trade unionism. Unlike the Trotskyites, who have always functioned as political propagandists, the Lovestoneites are immersed in trade union activities. They function mainly as research, educational, and organizational assistants in various trade unions, on some of whose leaders they have considerable personal influence.

The Lovestoneites are active mainly in the International Ladies' Garment Workers Union, especially among the 30,000 dressmakers in Local 22. In fact, Charles S. Zimmerman, vice-president of the International, and manager of Local 22, is a member of Lovestone's group, the Independent Labor League of America. Some Lovestoneites are also close to Homer Martin in the United Automobile Workers. There are a number of active rank-and-file Lovestoneites particularly in the Flint and Pontiac locals. The administrative assistant to Martin, Francis A. Henson, and the managing editor of the *United Automobile Worker,* William Munger, are personally followers of Lovestone. Martin listens to these men a good deal in his struggle against the Stalinist faction in the union, simply because they know much better than he does the tactics of the Communist Party. But they do not control him, and he disregards their advice just as often as he takes it. They have no totalitarian "party line" to follow, so they are free to play the game in terms of the needs of the union. They are factional in the sense that they constitute a tight little group under the leadership of Jay Lovestone, who is an able, experienced, and shrewd tactician. But they are not a disruptive force in the labor movement because their success depends entirely on the success of the union.

The Socialists

The Socialist Party has no clear trade union policy in the CIO or elsewhere. Since the 1936 split between the so-called militants under Norman Thomas and the right-wing Socialists under Louis Waldman, in which the militants captured the party apparatus, the Socialist Party has been wobbling all over the lot. Norman Thomas exercises a largely nominal authority over it. Well-meaning and vague, he temperamentally cannot give cohesion to a movement, and since 1936 various wings in the party have been pulling in different directions. There is a right wing, and a left wing calling itself the Clarity group. And there is the venerable good-government machine of Mayor Hoan of Milwaukee, which pays little attention to the national party.

It is impossible to differentiate ideologically between the right and the left wings of the party, for their differences lack all distinction. Both wings are under the influence of earnest young men without much background either in socialism or in labor. In fact, precisely because these fluttering wings cannot carry the party in any direction, its policies are determined in different places by the temperament of local leaders. On the West Coast, for instance, the Socialist Party, under the realistic and shrewd influence of Miss Lillian Symes, has fought the disruptive influence of the Stalinists from the very beginning, and with some success. In Michigan, on the other hand, the party is guided by callow enthusiasts who more or less follow the Communist Party line in the factional struggle of the United Automobile Workers.

What really happened in the U.A.W. was that certain young Socialists in strategic positions used their Socialist membership cards as a screen for Stalinist activities. Finally their disruptive machinations became so conspicuous that Norman Thomas went to Detroit in December 1937 to straighten things out. He supposedly did. And to save their faces, he later endorsed a letter by Ben Fischer, the secretary of the Michigan Socialist Party, in which the Stalinist caucus within the union was described as an ordinary "democratic" opposition, composed of all sorts of "progressives," including Communists. For some time after that, the young Socialists continued to play their double game, though a good deal more carefully. But finally, in May 1938, the Stalinists precipitated a crisis in the union which came near destroying it, as we shall see in the next chapter. For a moment the socialist tyros took such fright that they threw in their lot with Martin. But today they are once more flirting with the Communist Party line.

The Social Democratic Federation

The Social Democratic Federation constitutes the ultra-conservative section of American socialism, which split off from the Socialist Party in 1936. Its leaders, Louis Waldman, Algernon Lee, James Oneal, are old-fashioned socialists of the Vandervelde and Ramsay MacDonald vintage. When the split came, they failed to capture the party apparatus, which was only a blueprint on pink paper anyway. But with the exception of the Hoan machine in Milwaukee, they took with them most of the powerful institutions of our old-fashioned socialism—such as the municipal Socialist administrations of Bridgeport, Connecticut, and Reading, Pennsylvania; the *Jewish Daily Forward*, a wealthy co-operative publishing society; and the *Arbeiter Ring*, a powerful benefit society of Jewish socialist workmen, most of them stanch A. F. of L. members, who formally endorse industrial unionism as required by the socialist liturgy. None of these institutions either has, or cares to have, any influence in the CIO. And they confine themselves to the pious hope that our two dominant labor movements may yet settle their differences. Today the main interest and activity of these Old Guard socialists is not in the economic but in the political field of labor. Their leaders, especially Louis Waldman and B. Charney Vladeck, play a prominent part in the American Labor Party in New York, where Vladeck is the leader of the progressive coalition in the City Council.

The Communist Party

Whatever the attitude of the various parties we have discussed may be toward the CIO, none of them has a disrupting influence on it. The only disintegrating faction is the Communist Party, and its "fellow-travelers." Most of these are no less under party discipline than its members. They merely refrain from membership either for their own or the party's convenience.

One of the main reasons for the influence of the Communist Party is the widespread belief, especially in so-called liberal circles, that it has no influence; that it is a force too alien to play a role in American life. This theory overlooks the simple fact that great social revolutions affect the whole of human society. The October Revolution, like the American and French Revolutions, which determined the course of the entire nineteenth century in every civilized country, has had a tremendous international impact; and particularly, as is always the case, upon the class in whose name the revolution was made. But, unfortunately, great revolutions have a way of being followed by a Thermidor, the new stratification of the victorious revolutionary class into masters and men—though on the new productive level which the revolution has conquered and within the logic of this new order. Since 1923, and especially since 1927, the October Revolution has been perverted into the most violent Thermidorian reaction in history under the dictatorship of Stalin. In the name and under the prestige of October, this reaction has steadily tried to corrupt and to capture for its own uses the working class in every country. The easy theory that Stalinism is an alien force and hence cannot affect American labor, is exactly as bright as the theory that a steel splinter in one's eye is a foreign body and hence cannot affect one's vision.

Now, why does the Soviet bureaucracy need to rule-or-ruin international labor?

The Stalinist International

In order to understand why Stalinism is such a disintegrating force in the CIO, we must look briefly into its history, especially of the past eleven years.

The Communist International was founded in 1919 by Lenin and Trotsky for the purpose of promoting international social revolution. They believed, and rightly, that the October Revolution could not survive without the aid of socialist revolutions in several of the more advanced countries. Hence their theory of "permanent revolution." While the October Revolution lasted, the Communist International was a genuine revolutionary force, though even then it reflected, in the ruthlessness with which it crushed all inner opposition, the revolutionary terror under Lenin and Trotsky who, as we now realize, themselves sowed the dragon's teeth of the Thermidorian Terror.

But by the time of Lenin's death, it had become evident that no other great country was going to follow the Soviet example. The Russian masses became tired of the exalted mood and tempo of October. And the "dictatorship of the proletariat," which after all was a dictatorship of a bureaucracy *over* the proletariat, set about entrenching itself. Under Stalin's leadership, it decided to give up international socialism for "socialism in one country." The Thermidorian reaction in Russia set in, and the negative policy of abandoning international revolution inevitably led to the positive policy of killing revolutionary movements wherever they showed their heads. Gradually the Communist International, which is but the creature of the Russian Communist Party, became a counter-revolutionary force within the international labor movement. And the various sections of the International became the agents of this policy of the Stalin apparatus. Nor could the Stalin regime dispense with the counter-revolutionary functions of the Communist International without endangering its own existence. Just as a German revolution before 1923 would have saved the October Revolution, just so a German revolution—or a revolution in any other advanced country—after 1927 would have endangered the Stalin regime.

This counter-revolutionary development of the Soviet bureaucracy and of the Communist International explains why the International played such a disastrous role in the various labor movements as far back as 1923 —in Bulgaria, Germany, Estonia, Poland. In 1927, when the Thermidor was in full swing, the Communist International betrayed the Chinese Revolution by forcing the Chinese Communist Party into a "united front" with Chiang Kai-shek, who after he had entrenched himself proceeded to massacre the revolutionary workers who had been misled into supporting him.

Again, in the years during Hitler's rise to power— during the so-called Third Period of the Communist International—the German Communist Party systematically confused and divided the German labor movement, which was the only power that could have stopped Hitler. The strategy was to isolate the 7,000,000 German Communist workers from the rest of German labor by making common action impossible. The slogan for this criminal folly was "social fascism." And the term "social fascist" the Stalinists applied to the leaders of more than 8,000,000 Socialist workers. These leaders were supposedly nothing but stooges for the Nazis. Hitler was brought to power by the supineness of the Social Democratic leaders, the Bourbon corruption of the big industrialists and Junkers—and the counter-revolutionary stupidity of the Stalin Thermidor.

Having thus raised up the menace of real German fascism against the Soviet Union, Stalin dropped the theory of "social fascism" and the attempt to build independent Communist trade unions in every country. The Communist International swung way to the right. It not only came out for a "united front" with other working class movements, but launched upon the policy of the "popular front" with the capitalist governments of the western democracies and with every possible middle-class group and trend. When the Spanish civil war broke out, this Stalinist alignment with the Western capitalist governments and the new "Friends of the Soviet Union" was in full swing. Russia even adopted the "most democratic constitution in the world"—written by Bukharin, who was shot without its benefit. In America Earl Browder declared that the Stalinists were the real inheritors of American democracy, and later publicly announced that they would stand for no revolutionary nonsense from any quarter. With France the Soviet Union made a military alliance, and Stalin ordered the French Communist Party to boost French armaments.

When the Spanish civil war broke out, Stalin of course feared the extension of fascism to Spain. But he did not dare to permit the Spanish Communist Party to partake in the rapidly developing Spanish revolution, which was the only force that could have defeated Franco. He was afraid of antagonizing the French and British imperialists. And he bought for the Spanish Communists the power to disrupt the Spanish labor movement in the midst of the civil war, by selling to the Loyalist government insufficient supplies and armaments for cash. In short, the Communist International had its way in Spain through counter-revolutionary blackmail. It accused the P.O.U.M., the strongest revolutionary party in Spain, of being a fascist "column" in the rear. It accused all radical opposition to itself of "Trotskyism" in the pay of Franco. It sent into the country Russian G.P.U. agents, who killed the most militant leaders in the Spanish revolutionary parties and in the dominant Spanish trade union organizations. Even American Socialists in Spain were arrested and kept in jail by Russian agents who could not even speak Spanish. The Spanish revolution was strangled. The Stalin Thermidor is helping to create another fascist state.

"Power corrupts, and absolute power corrupts absolutely," said Lord Acton. And when despotism speaks in the name of the revolution it has murdered, its moral degradation is bottomless. A Thermidor must kill, in the name and under the prestige of the revolution it has betrayed, the ideas and the men who made it. Hence the ghastly spectacle of the Moscow trials, in which leaders of the Revolution are forced to frame themselves into counter-revolutionary spies, and to confess the sins fabricated in the minds of their torturers. Under Stalinism, the very processes of thought must be terrorized. From ballerina to physicist, everyone must follow the "party line," which zigzags with the perturbations of the dictator. And since the dictator must be infallible, history is rewritten to prove him so. Not only contemporary polemics, but the socialist classics are actually changed to follow the changing party line. Even the works of

Lenin are textually falsified, and the revolutionary accomplishments of Trotsky are retroactively attributed to Stalin, the man-God, "who fructifies the earth" of the socialist fatherland.

Such perversion of the October Revolution demands a "counter-revolutionary" scapegoat. October must be rooted out—yet in its own name. Hence the taboo of "Trotskyism," and its absurd extension to include all criticism. Trotsky, who with Lenin made the Revolution, becomes its Banquo's ghost. The psychic mechanism of the Thermidorian guilt is clear: in 1927 Trotsky is a mere oppositionist; in 1936 he is a "fascist spy"; in 1938 he is revealed as having been a "German spy" at the very time when he was leading the defense of the October Revolution in the civil war. The social and political defense of the Thermidor is quite as inevitable: the enemy of Stalinism is the social revolution, hence every potential revolutionary force everywhere, and finally every merely progressive movement in international labor.

Such are the politics and the psychology of Stalinism. And now let us see how it operates in America.[1]

[1] This analysis of the world-wide counter-revolutionary role of the Third International does not mean, of course, that every Communist Party member and "fellow-traveler" is aware of this historic role. The average rank-and-file Stalinist or "sympathizer" in America would be horrified if he were shown a recent copy of *L'Humanité,* official organ of the French Communist Party, which came out for a united front with Italian as against German fascism. To accuse Heywood Broun or Richard Frankensteen, former vice-president of the United Automobile Workers, of being intellectually conscious of the history and strategy of the Stalintern is like accusing a patient in a State hospital of being aware of what is going on in contemporary psychiatry. On the other hand, it is also true that many professional Stalinists, who are consistently playing a disruptive role in the CIO, are adventurers, who must realize the import of their specific activities.

Stalinism in America

In America there is no revolutionary situation. But we are a society of classes. There is a labor movement. In the CIO it is progressive. And Stalinism functions here exactly as it does everywhere else—only in milder form. The Soviet bureaucracy needs American imperialism, just as it needs British and French imperialism, in warding off the fascist menace to itself; or at least it thinks it does. Hence the American Communist Party strives for the Popular Front, an alliance with every middle-class force it can muster. Above all, it must attempt to control American labor. For, just as vigilantism has to have a mass base in the lower middle class, with the more confused working class elements in it, so Stalinism must have its base in the working class, with as many middle-class elements as it can confuse.

Stalinist propaganda among our middle classes has followed its international pattern to a T. Being an "ideological," pseudo-Marxist movement, it appeals to the Know Nothing instincts of the half-baked middle-class intelligentsia. It bewilders them with grotesque theories on Proletarian Literature, the Left Theater, the Revolutionary Dance, and other such arty rackets which exploit the sense of insecurity, maladjustment, and personal failure of the unstable and unformed intellectuals in modern society. It gives them recognition they could never otherwise gain. It gives them the thrill of being "revolutionaries" in perfect safety. It enables the eternal gigolo in the phony highbrow to peddle his revolutionary thrills at Park Avenue and Hollywood cocktail parties. And from the rich ladies and movie stars comes a good deal of the cash to work on the perplexed and well-meaning elements in the middle class. As in every civilized country, the American Communist Party has through this mechanism created literally dozens of "innocent front" organizations—the League for Peace and Democracy, the American Youth Congress, the National Negro Congress, the American Writers Congress, the American Students Union, the International Labor Defense, the American Friends of Spanish Democracy, all of them under hidden Stalinist control. In conventions assembled, these organizations change overnight from the Oxford Pledge of non-resistance to Collective Security, by which the Communist Party means to entangle us in the next war on the side of Russia; from defending all civil liberties and "class war prisoners" to endorsing the Moscow trials and hounding every honest radical in American labor who opposes the "party line"; from any position to its exact opposite—according to the dictates of the Communist Party.

Since 1936 these Innocent Clubs have been used as an entering wedge into the labor movement. Local CIO councils, under Stalinist influence, have been induced to vote exorbitant sums for the American League for Peace and Democracy or the American Youth Congress. The International Labor Defense, a purely Stalinist organization, has virtually become the legal representative of Stalinist-controlled unions. Such unions are even made to "affiliate" with these societies. Stalinist leaders of local unions in the United Automobile Workers have been discovered "siphoning off" union funds for these innocent fronts. The West Coast Firemen and Oilers had over half their strike fund in 1936 thus diverted, which was one of the reasons given by an aroused rank and file when finally, in 1938, they threw their Stalinist leaders out of office. Everywhere, the Communist Party tries to correlate as closely as it can these Stalinoid middle-class organizations with its activities in labor, especially in the CIO.

The moral complexion of Stalinism in America is exactly the same as it is elsewhere. Its press is slanderous beyond belief. The campaign of Red-baiting against all radical and progressive critics of its policies is unceasing. The favorite terms are moral degenerate, rat, fink, stool-pigeon, "Trotskyist" spy, fascist agent. It calls Norman Thomas an ally of fascism, Max Eastman a British agent, Homer Martin a Japanese stooge, the present writer a stool-pigeon and fascist. The Stalinists frame opposition radicals in the labor movement on all sorts of trumped-up charges. Thus, Barney Mayes, editor of the *Voice of the Federation,* was "tried" for irregularities, which, it was proved, he had never committed. Max Federman, the non-Stalinist leader of the Canadian fur workers, was framed on charges of theft, which investigation by his own locals proved to have been invented. The Canadian furriers rallied around him. The Stalinists moved heaven and earth to get Fred Beal extradited from Massachusetts to North Carolina, where he is now serving a twenty-year term as the scapegoat for the violence in

FACTIONALISM 145

the Gastonia strike which he led. Since the strike Beal has written a book indicting the Soviet regime. This sinister aspect of Stalinism is the real index of its menace.

The Communist Party and the CIO

From 1928 until the end of 1934, during the so-called "Third Period" of the Communist International, the Communist parties everywhere were ordered to form their own unions, and to have nothing to do with the mass organizations of the workers in each country, such as the A. F. of L. in the United States. These dominant movements, according to Stalinist theory then, were in the control of "social fascist" leaders, who were to be isolated by forming "a united front from below" with the workers under their leadership. Accordingly, in this country, the Communist Party during this period ran its own paper organizations under such fancy names as the National Miners Union, the Food Workers Industrial Union, the National Textile Workers Union, the Needle Trades Workers Industrial Union, the Building Trades Industrial League, the Metal and Steel Workers Industrial Union, the Marine Workers Industrial League, the Auto Workers Union—all of them federated into the Trade Union Unity League. Unfortunately for the Stalinists, organized labor refused to join these paper organizations, even "from below."

At long last, at a "plenum" of the Central Committee of the Communist Party of the United States in January 1935, the futility of this policy of "building an

Independent Federation of Labor" was confessed. The "plenum" resolved ". . . in view of the changing conditions of trade union work, which demand that the central work be transferred to the A. F. of L., it is not advisable to put the question of an Independent Federation of Labor. Inside independent trade unions, Communists should carry out . . . tactics of struggle for trade union unity and affiliation to the American Federation of Labor . . . the tone used in the press with regard to the A. F. of L. must be changed."

But unofficially the policy of building independent Communist trade unions was given up by the party some time before January 1935, by which time the Trade Union Unity League had been practically wiped out. This reflected a switch in policy by the Communist International after Hitler's accession to power. All through 1934, the petty Communist organizations in coal, in steel, in textiles, in the needle trades and elsewhere had been trying to get into the A. F. of L. without breaking up their groups. They were refused group entrance, and their members had to join as individuals. At last the Trade Union Unity League abolished itself and its Communist affiliates at a convention, called for that purpose, on March 16, 1935. And the Communist Party ordered all its members and followers to get into the A. F. of L. as best they could.

When the next congress of the Communist International met in Moscow in August 1935, Communist dual unionism all over the world was officially prohibited. Orders went out to capture in each country the dominant labor movement by "boring from within," reverting to the policy of the Communist International up to 1923. In America, as elsewhere, this process had already gone on for two years; and now the drive to "capture" the A. F. of L. became even more intense. This strenuous effort to penetrate into the A. F. of L. unions lasted for almost two years longer. By that time, the CIO was a year and a half old. And though the Communist press gave lip service to industrial unionism, the Stalinists actually did most of their organization work for the A. F. of L. until May 1937. This explains, for instance, why Harry Bridges turned over to the A. F. of L. some 6000 retail employees in San Francisco, whom he had helped to organize, as late as April 1937. In later chapters I shall show how those Stalinist-controlled unions which were in the CIO, most of them small and largely on paper, had been knifing the CIO until mid-summer, 1937, by playing with the A. F. of L. behind the scenes.

Long after John L. Lewis had come out for industrial unionism at the San Francisco Convention of the A. F. of L. in 1934, Jack Stachel, member of the Central Committee of the American Communist Party, in charge of its trade union policy, wrote an article on "The Fight of the Steel Workers" in *The Communist* of June 1935. He said:

> The crisis within the A. F. of L. Executive Council is, of course, not over policies for and against the workers. Reflecting the differences in the camp of the bourgeoisie itself, these labor lieutenants of capitalism are fighting over the question

as how best to prevent strikes, how to keep the masses chained to the policies of class collaboration. Moreover, people like John L. Lewis fear that the old craft union policies applied to such industries as auto, rubber, and steel, may well lead to the formation of mass industrial unions outside the A. F. of L.

Furthermore, Lewis believes that through strongly centralized national industrial unions, led by people like himself, he can convince the employers that he can offer the best guarantee against strikes through such model anti-strike agreements as he signed in the name of the coal miners. In this view, John L. Lewis and Major Berry, both of them the most outstanding and infamous strikebreakers in the country, are joined by Hugh Johnson . . . and many other industrialists and bankers. It is clear that the fight for militant industrial class unions is the fight of the masses and will be won not only in the struggle against the Greens and the Wolls but against the Lewises and Berrys as well.

As time went on, this policy of riding both horses—the A. F. of L. and the CIO—became impossible. And in May 1937, the Communist Party decided to work primarily in the CIO. Through its influence on John Brophy and other sympathizers in the CIO, it got Harry Bridges appointed to the directorship of the West Coast CIO. And part of the deal was the promise of the Stalinists to turn over those unions which they controlled in the A. F. of L., which they proceeded to do. The International Fur Workers Union, for instance, switched from the A. F. of L. to the CIO overnight, to the amazement of its rank and file. The policy of capturing the CIO began in earnest.

FACTIONALISM

The Stalinists are obliged to behave themselves with some decorum in those powerful older unions which are under the seasoned leadership of men like Lewis, Dubinsky, and Hillman, all three of whom had licked the Stalinist opposition in their own organizations in the 1920's. And they also have to behave themselves, though far less so, in those new CIO organizations such as the Steel Workers Organizing Committee and the Textile Workers Organizing Committee, which are directly in the charge of these older leaders.

In the new CIO unions, however, the Communist Party and its followers are playing a Machiavellian game for control. In the Automobile Workers Union, in which the Stalinists form an influential opposition to the administration, they cry for "unity and democracy," so that they may sabotage the "dictatorship" of the Martin administration. They have precipitated hundreds of unauthorized sitdowns, merely to embarrass Martin, especially during negotiations with the employers. In the United Electrical, Radio and Machine Workers Union, or in the Fur Workers Union, where the Stalinists and their allies are in power, they term all opposition disruptive, undemocratic, "Trotskyite," silencing all criticism through frame-ups, steam-roller methods, character assassination, and plain hooliganism in meetings.

The whole situation is confused by the violent denial by well-known Stalinists and "fellow-travelers" that they have anything to do with the Communist Party line. To discuss the CIO without mentioning the influence of the Stalinists in it is like writing on the Civil War without referring to the Confederacy. Yet every reference to the "party line" is howled down as so much "Red-baiting." In this new Jesuit order, the greatest insult is to be called a Jesuit. Harry Bridges of the West Coast Longshoremen, Donald Henderson of the Cannery Workers, Joe Curran of the National Maritime Union, Abram Flaxer of the State, County and Municipal Workers, Mervyn Rathborne of the American Communications Association, Lewis Merrill of the Office and Professional Workers, and Heywood Broun of the American Newspaper Guild, are either pseudonymous members of the Communist Party, or "fellow-travelers." Three of these leaders, officially though secretly, represented the party in the CIO-A. F. of L. peace negotiations in December 1937. Yet the slightest reference to their sympathy with the party line is considered a reprehensible attack on the CIO. Thus any criticism of Stalinist disruption in the CIO is twisted into an attack on the whole CIO, and a "sellout" to the reaction. Needless to say, none of the great working-class leaders ever refrained from telling where he stood or what he believed. For it is an eternal platitude that the powers of reaction can never make use of the truth, no matter how frank. "It is never too early to tell the workers the truth about themselves," said Lenin.

Stalinism is a danger in the CIO. For one thing, it is not interested in American labor as such; and for another thing, its violent Red-baiting sabotages all genuine radicalism, without which a progressive trade union movement cannot grow. Yet its extent must not be exaggerated. Two-thirds of the CIO unions are free from Stalinist control. The great founding unions—the United Mine Workers, the Amalgamated, the International—do not suffer from Stalinist factionalism. In the steel and textile drives the Stalinists have lost most of the influence they had in the beginning. Nor do they play a significant role in the United Rubber Workers; the Mine, Mill and Smelter Workers; the Marine and Shipbuilding Workers; the Oil Workers International Union; the Federation of Flat Glass Workers; and the Aluminum Workers. Among the 400,000 automobile workers, the Stalinists have lost out, though they are still a strong force of disruption.

If we exclude some 200,000 workers organized in 500 local industrial unions—that is, by single factories—actual Stalinist control, direct or indirect, extends only to about 500,000 workers in the CIO. Even among these, the rank and file is becoming increasingly resentful of Stalinist sabotage, which by this time they have had a chance to watch for over two years. In the Transport Workers Union, the Newspaper Guild, the Fur Workers Union, the United Electrical Radio and Machine Workers, and to a lesser extent in the International Woodworkers Union—which unions total a membership of some 270,000—some opposition is developing to Stalinist tactics. Only four CIO unions are under the complete control—without any effective opposition—of Stalinist officers. They are the American Communications Association (mostly radio telegraphers); the Federation of Architects, Engineers, Chemists and Technicians; the

United Office and Professional Workers; and the United Cannery, Agriculture, Packing and Allied Workers. These unions give themselves a total membership of some 185,000. In fact they have at most some 60,000 members.

The drift against Stalinism in the CIO began early in 1938. At their last convention the United Mine Workers, representing 600,000 men, reaffirmed an old constitutional provision prohibiting membership in the Communist Party—along with the Ku Klux Klan and the National Civic Federation. Homer Martin of the Automobile Workers and David Dubinsky of the International Ladies' Garment Workers, together heading over 650,000 workers, in January 1938 came out openly and unequivocally in the daily press against Communist Party interference. Seven months later the International Executive Board of the United Automobile Workers expelled three vice-presidents and the secretary-treasurer and suspended one vice-president for three months on charges of Stalinist disruption. Philip Murray and the other leaders of the 450,000 steel workers are discharging, quietly but deliberately, Stalinist organizers. The West Coast Firemen and Oilers have voted their leaders out of office as "Stalinist stooges." In fact, on the West Coast, Harry Bridges and his Stalinist machine are rapidly losing their grip even on those maritime unions which they control. Many locals of the Cooks and Stewards, and even some powerful locals of Bridges's own Longshoremen and Warehousemen, are in opposition to his machine. Almost all the other CIO unions in the Pacific region are up in arms against the Bridges domination. In his efforts to break the opposition among the Office Workers in San Francisco, he ordered them to join the warehousemen's union. This they refused to do and finally returned to the A. F. of L.

But the most telling revolt against Bridges occurred in Los Angeles in August 1938, when four powerful unions decided to withdraw from the CIO Industrial Council. These four unions—the International Ladies' Garment Workers, the United Automobile Workers, the United Rubber Workers, and the United Shoe Workers—represent over 20,000 workers in the Los Angeles area. They founded the Los Angeles Trade Union Conference, stating that they intended to stay within the CIO but meant to be free of Bridges. They declared: "We believe that anyone has a right to be a Communist or a Holy Roller or whatever they choose, but in the trade union movement they must give their first loyalty to their unions and not attempt to use the unions to further the end of any political party." And they charged Bridges with "bringing the Los Angeles Industrial Union Council under Communist control"; with "maintaining this control by fraud and the votes of 'paper' locals"; with "abetting the Communists' attempt to capture and disrupt the auto workers during the recent Ford strike at Long Beach"; with "appointing Communist Party members to executive positions in various unions without regard for their ability and without consulting the rank and file"; with "subordinating the interests of the CIO and trade unionism to Communism"; and with a number of other such offenses.

Then they adopted a new six-point program which calls for peace in organized labor; for "continued organization despite continued depression"; for an end to the Stalinist dictatorship in the trade-union movement; for independent political action; against "raids on existing organizations"; against "anti-labor legislation and 'government interference,' whether through the courts, the National Guard, the police or otherwise."

On the East Coast, Stalinist control of the National Maritime Union was broken in a hotly contested election campaign which ended on August 5, 1938. The progressive opposition won the majority on the National Executive Council and over two-thirds of the minor union officers. In an election in the Fur Workers International Union, the Stalinists saved their control by the most outrageous interference with the ballots. But even there the opposition managed to get more than 2,000 votes out of 7,000 counted. Similar oppositions, though far less organized, are gathering among the office and the transport workers.

This growing opposition to the Stalinists in the CIO comes mainly from rank-and-file pressure. The militant American worker, unlike the liberal "Friends of the Soviet Union," was profoundly stirred by the third Moscow trial. He is beginning to appreciate, from his own experience, that the Communist Party is not a radicalizing but a Red-baiting and reactionary force in American labor. And he is repelled by its immorality and its complete disregard of all union democracy. Anti-Stalinist sentiment is rising throughout the CIO, and the number of anti-Stalinist groups and papers is multiplying. Their common characteristic is a sound proletarian disgust with the moral corruption and the fascist tactics of the "party line."

But in spite of the growing opposition in the CIO to the Stalinist menace, its fate is hard to foretell. Too many imponderables both at home and abroad enter the picture. On these imponderables I shall touch in the last chapter, when I discuss the future of the CIO.

CHAPTER VI

THE AUTOMOBILE WORKERS

AT THE heart of the CIO are the United Automobile Workers.

The automobile industry is the largest all-around customer of the other basic and durable goods industries. It itself is the most mechanized of them all. Ninety per cent of its workers not only need no skill, but must have none. Only industrial unionism could have organized this industry, the archetype of modern automatic production. Here the CIO had its quickest and clearest organizational success. A new strike weapon, inherent in the very processes of the industry, was used with great effect. The sitdown, though it raises many problems of union discipline and factionalism, can, with a dozen men, stop an entire mechanized plant.

Labor unrest had been growing in this industry since before the war. This unrest, according to a governmental report, flowed "from insecurity, low annual earnings, inequitable hiring and rehiring methods, espionage, speed-up, and the displacement of workers at an extremely early age." To prevent union agitation, the great corporations introduced elaborate welfare schemes and company unions. The few skilled crafts in the plants were entirely submissive, and considered the unskilled masses a menace to their organizations. Still, during the war, a semi-industrial union, affiliated with the A. F.

of L., the United Automobile, Aircraft and Vehicle Workers, began to make its way in the industry. And by 1920 it claimed a membership of 45,000. But even the slightest effort to organize automobile labor at once raised the issue of unrestricted industrial unionism, for there just are no craft lines in this industry. And in 1921 the union was expelled from the A. F. of L. for jurisdictional misbehavior. It immediately collapsed, and its membership dwindled to a little over 1000. In the same year the Communists took it over, and within a few months ran its membership down to a couple of hundred.

But all along, unrest among the workers was deepening. And in 1926, at its Detroit convention, the A. F. of L. half-heartedly acknowledged that the seventeen or more trade unions which claimed potential jurisdiction in this field could not very well organize it along craft lines. William Green arranged for a temporary "suspension" of the jurisdictional claims of the various crafts, promising the oligarchy that once the workers were organized they would be divided and "transferred" to the respective trades to which they "belonged." But in spite of their grudging acquiescence in this scheme, the craft leaders immediately began to knife the organization campaign, and a year later the whole idea was given up. At the 1927 convention of the A. F. of L., the Executive Council reported that the campaign "has not developed to the extent we hoped it would." And the auto workers felt just as hopeless about the A. F. of L. bureaucracy. They realized that it was psychologically and structurally incapable of tackling a mass-production industry.

In the early stages of the NRA, several spontaneous campaigns, independent of the A. F. of L. and challenging its craft separatism, arose in the industry. Among these new unions the most successful was the Mechanics Educational Society, which in June 1933 began to organize the tool and die men. In a series of quick strikes, it gained a membership of 25,000, and then decided to take in the production and assembly workers as well. Alarmed by the success of this independent semi-industrial union, the A. F. of L. decided to compete. And by the middle of 1934 it had granted charters to 132 "federal local unions," organized by separate factories on an industrial basis and affiliated directly to the A. F. of L. Again the understanding was that in time these industrial unions in each plant were to be broken up according to imaginary skills and distributed to the various crafts.

The drive was put in charge of William Collins, an old-fashioned A. F. of L. organizer, who could be relied upon not to display too much energy. But the rank and file did respond enthusiastically, and by the end of 1934 these federal locals had a membership of approximately 100,000. Such success made Mr. Green very nervous, for there was always the danger that these industrial local unions might try to amalgamate nationally, which would make their "jurisdictional" reshuffling the more difficult. Under constant pressure from the seventeen to twenty presidents of the crafts theoretically involved in this industry, Green proceeded to treat these local unions like so many baby farms of unwanted foundlings. In fact, early in 1935 he tried to kill the whole movement, and sent instructions to Collins to stop organizing. Green did his best to slow down the drive. At the same time, however, the thing he feared was taking place, and the various industrial local unions were agitating vigorously for some sort of national organization. At the San Francisco convention of the A. F. of L. in 1934, John Lewis and other industrial unionists took up the cudgels for them. And in August 1935, the Executive Council of the A. F. of L. had to grant these locals the right to form a national body—the International Union, United Automobile Workers of America. But as president of this new organization, Green appointed Francis J. Dillon, an archaic A. F. of L. organizer, flat-footed from a long life as walking delegate. The workers protested bitterly against Dillon. They wanted to elect their own leaders. But they were told that it was Dillon or nothing, and for the time being they took Dillon.

Green and Dillon immediately began sabotaging the growth of the new national organization. After one year of Dillonism, 52 of these industrial union locals died from sheer neglect, and membership figures dropped precipitously. But underneath this official sabotage the rank and file, under its own leadership, was organizing feverishly all along. In April 1935, the workers had struck spontaneously the Chevrolet plant in Toledo. And in spite of Dillon's open opposition, the resulting concessions from the management had had a vitalizing effect upon the rest of automobile labor. Finally, in April 1936, some 30,000 workers sent delegates to a national convention in South Bend, Indiana. They promptly threw out Dillon, and a new and vigorous leadership emerged. Homer Martin was elected president, Wyndham Mortimer first vice-president, Ed Hall second vice-president, and George Addes secretary-treasurer. Other leaders—young, alert, enthusiastic—came to the fore. Among them were Richard T. Frankensteen, Robert C. Travis of Flint, and the three Reuther brothers—Walter, Victor, and Roy. Most of these new leaders were around thirty, bright, aggressive, unhampered by sterile tradition and long failure. They had the enthusiastic confidence and complete support of the rank and file. The new union called itself the United Automobile Workers of America. And soon after, it joined the CIO. The union was rarin' to go.

But in the meantime factional difficulties had been developing. No sooner had the United Automobile Workers been established as an unrestricted industrial union than the Communist Party, which had been active in this field for some time, began to concentrate on capturing it. For the very weapon which can so successfully organize labor in an automatic industry—the sitdown—can also be used to sabotage effectively a union administration. And the Stalinist-led opposition to the Homer Martin administration used the unauthorized sitdown as a factional weapon all through 1937.

Homer Martin has become the symbol of the new progressive trade union leader who is interested first and foremost in the building of strong, modern industrial unionism. He has forged ahead in the public mind, partly, of course, because he is leading a labor organization in an industry which ideally demonstrates the advantages of industrial unionism; and partly because he has been fighting Stalinist disruption in this new union from the *left*, with a new attitude and a new vocabulary, completely different from the old Red-baiting stuff of the reactionary A. F. of L. oligarchy. It is impossible to call Homer Martin a reactionary, because there is not a single realistically radical plan to which he does not subscribe, and because he has managed to make it clear that the Stalinists are not a radicalizing but a degenerative force in the CIO. It is largely due to his melodramatic struggle against the Stalinists that the enlightened public is beginning to realize their role in American labor.

Martin, a former hill-billy preacher, was born in 1902 in Missouri. He graduated from William Jewell College, a small but good Baptist School in his native State. For a while he preached, but soon was fired for his active interest in trade union activities. Then he went into a Chevrolet plant, began organizing, and soon again lost his job. But in losing his job on the assembly line, he found his real work. He discovered that he was a natural-born agitator and orator. Next to Lewis, he is the best speaker in American labor. A great many of the automobile workers are also former hill-billies, and no man knows better how to talk to them than Martin. He is quick, intelligent, and absolutely sincere. Unfortunately, he also has some of the faults of the orator in a mass movement. He is a poor administrator, lacking all gift for detail. Though his aim is steady and his courage, especially in a tight situation, is magnificent, his daily tactics are often impulsive and his impromptu statements are likely to be injudicious.

Martin is at his best in critical situations, when his utter fearlessness is released in dramatic action, and is not confused by his rhetorical flights or tempered by his Christian tolerance, for the minister in Martin is still there. This modernist preacher's open-mindedness makes him at times so anxious for peace and harmony within the union that he is likely, against his own better judgment, to play with people he knows will double-cross him. But the moment they do double-cross him, he fights them all the harder for having lost ground. He is winning out against his opponents because, under all these temperamental fluctuations, he is inordinately steadfast and stubborn. This momentary yielding without fundamental budging creates an impression of confusion and inconsistency, which the Stalinists have exploited to the fullest—and to their own grief. It has given them the opportunity to twist his remarks into "wild and irresponsible statements"; and then to develop, through one of the most nauseating whispering campaigns on record, this "mental irresponsibility" into the early stages of insanity, solicitously prescribing a "long rest." Nothing could be more fantastic than these whispers about Martin's failing health, for in his middle thirties he still remains the perfect and exasperating example of the clean-lived and clean-minded young college athlete.

Close to Martin is Vice-President Rolland J. Thomas. Intensely practical, loyal, progressive, and as unexciting as Martin is temperamental, Thomas is a tireless administrator, and utterly reliable both in his word and on his job. A native of Ohio, where he was born in 1900, and a graduate of Wooster College, he worked in the industry from 1921 to 1936. He rose to top leadership during the great strikes when he became president of the Chrysler local, and was elected at the Milwaukee convention in 1937 to the vice-presidency of the International Union. He is a sound negotiator, can sense trickery by sheer character rather than through any shrewdness, and in the factional struggles he has been a tower of strength to the preservation of the union.

Until his expulsion in August 1938, next to Martin the best-known personality in the union was Richard Frankensteen, a rough-and-ready two-hundred-pounder, who had played tackle on the Dayton University football team. In background and outlook, he is the typical lower-middle-class American who might have been a big shot in the local Kiwanis if he had not been swept off the assembly line into the union. His main virtue is great physical courage and the ability to take it on the picket line, a gift which made him one of the heroes in the drive to organize Ford. When he was manhandled in front of the Ford plant at River Rouge in the summer of 1937, the Ford gangsters swung him high above the ground and banged him on the pavement half a dozen times. This murderous treatment scarcely fazed Mr. Frankensteen, who after a few stitches returned to the scrimmage. Unfortunately, his physical courage is not matched either by strength of character, political acumen or social intelligence. It is matched only by an overweening personal ambition and a belief in his capacities as a brilliant and subtle politician. This misplaced self-confidence is rather pathetic, for if there ever was a ham Machiavelli Mr. Frankensteen is it. No doubt he makes a good second lieutenant. But in the spring of 1938 the young man's fancy turned to thoughts of power. And, flattered by the Stalinists, who until then had called him every name under the sun, he attempted to catapult himself into the leading position in the union, with the grandiose idea of ultimately displacing Martin. As we shall see, he met with a quick and humiliating defeat.

The Martin administration is known as the Progressive group. The Stalinist opposition calls itself euphemistically the Unity group. The leader of this Unity group is Wyndham Mortimer, who was also expelled in August 1938 for his disruptive activities in the union. Mortimer is, and has been for many years, a follower of the Communist Party line. He is of a dull, industrious, and clerical disposition, but the Stalinists are forever boosting him as "a real trade unionist and splendid organizer." As an organizer he is uninspired and tenacious. As a "real trade unionist," however, he has been a disrupter all his adult life. He drifted into the automobile industry from mining, and in both industries he has been a Stalinist from the very beginning.

Mortimer's reputation rests on his organizational work in the General Motors shops in Flint, where he was closely associated with Ed Hall and Bob Travis. These two know nothing of either Stalinism or any other ism but are active in the Unity faction because of their disposition for oblique politics. Early in 1938, Hall was tried by the International Executive Board of the union for misuse of funds through lavish expense accounts, and was forced to refund in instalments $800 to the union treasury. The Executive Board also had the books of the Flint local, of which Travis was in charge, audited by public accountants, and discovered grave irregularities. The accounts had been juggled to conceal the diversion of funds for factional purposes.

Then there are the three Reuther brothers—Walter, Roy, and Victor—of whom Walter is the most active. The Reuther boys are all members of the Socialist Party, which they use as a mere blind for their Stalinoid activities. Walter Reuther is president of the powerful West Side Local in Detroit. He has been one of the leading disrupters in the union, and has used his lively sense of publicity to embarrass the Martin administration, especially in its dealings with the employers. He is young, attractive, bright, active, and ambitious. His outlook on life and labor is thoroughly middle class, and his "radicalism" is largely verbal and very naïve. There are a number of such young Socialists in leading positions in the union. Some of them are recent college graduates, totally inexperienced in labor, superficially bright in a sophomoric sense, who think it is great fun to play devious union politics. One of the leaders of these collegiate pseudo-Socialists is one George Edwards, who only recently received his M.B.A. (Master of Business Administration) at Harvard, after graduating from the Southern Methodist University in Texas. Young Mr. Edwards, a typical Socialist boy scout, is the chief lieutenant of Walter Reuther, who made him floor leader of the Unity faction in the Milwaukee convention of the United Automobile Workers in 1937.

The Rise of the Union

The moment the new U.A.W. had organized itself in April 1936, at South Bend, a whirlwind organization campaign was immediately launched. By the end of that year, the 30,000 had grown to 100,000, in spite of the ever-stiffening resistance of the corporations.

The first sitdown strike in the industry, involving 1500 workers, broke out at the Bendix Corporation in South Bend in November 1936. Bendix settled with the recognition of the U.A.W. as the bargaining agent for its own members only. But real industrial war on a huge scale broke out when the union tackled General Motors. The speed-up in the Chevrolet, Buick, Cadillac, and Fisher Body plants had become intolerable, and wages were miserably low. Forty-five per cent of the workers were earning less than $1000 a year, and the average wage had been only $1150 during 1935. In other words, the wage of the workers averaged around $20 a week.

The strike in General Motors began with a walkout of 7000 of the 8000 workers at the Cleveland Fisher Body plant on December 28. By January 1, the strike had spread to the two other huge Fisher Body factories in Flint, which would have been enough to tie up the whole corporation. But the movement spontaneously spread

THE AUTOMOBILE WORKERS 167

like wildfire during the first two weeks of January, and the workers sat down at the Fleetwood, Cadillac, and Buick plants in Detroit and Flint, at the Guide Lamp Company at Anderson, Indiana, and finally tied up practically the entire General Motors Corporation in Ohio, Georgia, and Missouri. By January 11, 113,000 workers were out.

General Motors replied with a double campaign of terror and the run-around. It had long prepared itself for the struggle. Between January 1, 1934, and July 31, 1936, the corporation had spent $994,855.68 on espionage alone. When the strike broke out, the corporation answered with a campaign of violence and intimidation, encouraging the infamous Flint Alliance, a vigilante outfit, which palmed itself off as a union of workers who "wished to go back to work." And it procured a number of injunctions in various parts of the country ordering the sitdowners to evacuate the plants. On January 12, the first violence occurred at the "Battle of Bulls Run." The company ordered the heat turned off in a Flint Fisher Body plant, and attempted to starve out the sitdowners, removing the ladders by which food was passed to them by their friends. The sitdowners surged out of the plant and took possession of the company gates, which had been guarded by company gangsters. The city police partook in the general fight, throwing tear gas bombs both at the sitdowners and at the mass of workers outside the plant gates. The battle lasted for several hours, and the strikers fought the clubs and the riot-guns of the police and the company gangsters with stones and streams of water from the company fire-hose. The strikers won.

In the meantime, efforts were made to mediate the strike, especially by Governor Murphy of Michigan, who was backed up by the Federal administration. But General Motors sabotaged every peace effort until, toward the end of January, the strikers "captured" the strategic Chevrolet plant No. 4 in Flint. By that time, of the 150,000 workers in the plants involved, 140,000 were out. When, early in February, John Lewis arrived in Detroit, General Motors began a series of conferences with the CIO leaders. And on February 11, the corporation capitulated. It recognized the U.A.W. as the bargaining representative for its own members only, but it promised Governor Murphy in writing not to deal with any other labor organization without consulting him. Soon after, it signed an agreement with the union to last until August 11, 1937. The agreement denied the uniform minimum wage scale demanded by the union, and left the problem of wages to negotiation. Through such later negotiations, the union was able to raise pay anywhere from a few cents to twenty cents an hour, depending on the nature of the work. The forty-hour week and time-and-a-half for overtime were retained. The company also granted seniority rights after six months' employment. The speed-up was to be studied, for the purpose of correcting abuses. And an excellent method of handling grievances was laid down in a separate agreement. This system, at least in theory, was both elastic and democratic. It supposedly began at the bottom in each shop, and wound up at the top, drawing into its educational orbit a large number of rank-and-file workers and rank-and-file managers. Unfortunately, both the internal strife in the union and the reactionary attitude of thousands of foremen have to a considerable degree weakened the effectiveness of the grievance machinery.

On March 8, 1937, 60,000 out of the 70,000 workers in the various Chrysler plants struck. And two-thirds of them occupied the Chrysler factories in the greatest of all the sitdown strikes. Chrysler had tried to obviate a strike by raising wages 10 per cent just before the General Motors settlement. But the workers wanted union recognition, and they continued to occupy the plants all through March with a skeleton force of 7500 men. Governor Murphy finally brought Lewis and Chrysler together, and by April 6, Walter Chrysler also capitulated. Though he would not "recognize" the U.A.W. as the sole bargaining agent for the workers, he agreed to refrain from recognizing any dual organization. The final contract he signed with the U.A.W. was pretty much the same as the General Motors agreement.

Thus ended the second great strike in the automobile industry. Except for Ford, unionism had been established in this stronghold of anti-unionism. Among the workers, optimism ran high. They had demonstrated their solidarity and the invincible force of industrial unionism.

Factionalism

With the rise of the union, factionalism became more embittered, and by the time the union became really established, through its successful strikes early in 1937, the inner struggle had become intense enough to endanger its very existence. The Communist Party, which could make no headway in any other basic industry, decided to put every effort into capturing control of the U.A.W. The Stalinist tactics were purely rule-or-ruin tactics, entirely opportunistic, against anything Martin might be for. For there was no difference—there could be none overtly—between the fundamental program of the Martin Progressive group and the Stalinist-controlled Unity caucus. The program was very simple. It called for a renewal of the contracts with General Motors and other corporations on the best possible terms, for the stoppage of unauthorized strikes, and for the organization of Ford.

Finally, in August 1937, the United Automobile Workers held their historic convention in Milwaukee. The General Executive Board reported a membership of almost 400,000, the union having grown more than tenfold in less than a year and a half. The convention assessed each member one dollar to complete the unionization of the industry, which meant Ford. The union no longer had to call for funds or organizers from the national CIO. Strong, young, and self-dependent, it was going places. There was every reason for rejoicing. Yet the convention was in a state of jitters, for everybody knew that the whole future of the union was at stake. Both factions, the Progressives and the Stalinists, had been holding caucuses for months, getting ready to match their strength in Milwaukee. Factionalism was the central issue. The Martin administration accused the Unity group of irresponsibility and disruption, and of having fomented a multitude of unauthorized strikes which were jeopardizing the union's contractual relations with the corporations. Martin therefore demanded that the vice-presidents be entirely subordinated to his authority, as they are in effect in the United Mine Workers. The Unity faction claimed to fight for "democracy" versus dictatorship, which would have been amusing were it less tragic. For the Unity leaders took their orders abjectly from William Weinstone, district organizer of the Communist Party in Detroit, and B. K. Gebert, who had been assigned by the Communist Party as a sort of political commissar to the U.A.W.

The fight in the convention started when the credentials committee, controlled by the Martin administration, refused to seat several phony Unity delegates from Flint. Finally the Unity leaders yielded on this issue. Martin also won when the convention voted a constitutional provision to bar unauthorized strikes and to deprive local unions of the right to call strikes without permission from the International Executive Board. In fact, Martin had it all his way and undoubtedly could have eliminated right there and then the leading Stalinists and their followers. But John L. Lewis insisted on a compromise. Wyndham Mortimer and Ed Hall were retained as vice-presidents, and George Addes, who leaned toward the Unity faction, remained secretary-treasurer. The Progressives got Richard Frankensteen, who at that time was a strong Martin adherent, and R. J. Thomas as new vice-presidents. Moreover, the convention voted to increase the International Executive Board to 24 members, and elected 16 Progressives to it. But in spite of this victory by the Progressives, later events showed how mistaken Lewis's brokerage between the two factions had been. For one year later the union had to be saved from utter inner collapse by the quick and drastic expulsion of the worst disrupters on the Board; and there can be no doubt that this surgical operation weakened the union for the time being.

The convention disbanded with high hopes for real solidarity. But it soon became obvious that the Unity leaders intended to continue in their disruptive course. They were bent on destroying Martin, and on imposing on the union a Stalinist-guided leadership. For some time Walter Reuther, as head of the West Side Local of Detroit, continued to publish a bitter sheet against the national union, the *West Side Conveyor,* and kept as his managing editor Carl Haessler, who at the same time was the Midwest manager of the Federated Press, a labor press service which has been following the "party line" for years. On September 30, three weeks after the "peace" convention, Mr. Haessler, then still on the payroll of the U.A.W., thus described in the Federated Press a certain widely publicized incident of that date:

THE AUTOMOBILE WORKERS 173

The hysterical thrusting of a revolver by President Homer Martin of the U.A.W. into the stomach of Danny Gallagher, a rank-and-file member of the union, is universally regarded by Detroit newspapermen on the labor run as a sensational climax to repeated indications that the union chief is in need of a long rest.

Here is what actually happened:

The opposition leaders knew that Martin was engaged in his hotel room in extremely important negotiations with representatives of one of the largest and most strategic automobile manufacturers. And they decided to embarrass Martin right then and there, because after the recent convention, which had voted for retrenchment, he discharged and demoted a number of organizers and staff members, among whom were several Unity supporters. His haste in doing so was no doubt poor diplomacy. But the Stalinists wanted to show that he lacked the confidence of the "rank and file," which only three weeks before had re-elected him by acclamation. So they rounded up some perfectly honest rank-and-file members from Flint, Pontiac, and Detroit locals, who for good measure were joined by ten or fifteen "rank-and-filers" who had never seen the inside of an automobile factory and were just Detroit Communist Party members. Then they invited the press to witness how the workers were "picketing" the president of the union, whom they allegedly could never get to see, though Martin had given them a later appointment.

When the press arrived, the whole stage-managed affair was executed. The "pickets" rushed through the halls and elevators, pounded at Martin's door, and demanded to see him. Someone who was in the room with Martin thrust a revolver in his hand for fear that he might be harmed. If Martin had had the experience of a Lewis or a Dubinsky or a Hillman, he, of course, never would have opened the door with a gun in his hand, which he pointed downward anyway. The whole idea of Martin, who is a devout pacifist, toting a gun is peculiarly ludicrous. But the opposition immediately spread far and wide the canard that Martin was "irresponsible," in fact quite cracked, that he was a stooge for the companies and what not. And it proceeded to sabotage the Martin administration by provoking a plethora of unauthorized strikes, made to look like "spontaneous" sitdowns. Indeed, the Stalinists had used this provocative method ever since the great sitdown strikes early in 1937, which really established the union. From March to June 1937, they had precipitated the majority of almost 200 such unauthorized sitdowns. Thus, when the Chrysler sitdown ended on April 6, 1937, with an agreement which called for the immediate evacuation of the plants, a Stalinist member of the International Executive Board, who was also on the negotiations committee, sent word down the line—via William Weinstone, district organizer of the Communist Party in Detroit—that the sitdown was to continue. And it did continue for another six hours, almost wrecking the victory of the union. Exactly the same tactics were applied after the convention for the sole purpose of embarrassing Martin in the pending negotiations with General Motors.

Throughout October and November the automobile industry was laying off thousands of workers. John L. Lewis, as indeed everybody in the labor movement, was much worried about the business depression. And he strenuously advised Martin to hurry the renewal of the General Motors agreement, to "take the locals out of the rain," to "take in sail." The idea was to make the best possible agreement quickly. And Lewis sent his old friend and economic adviser, W. Jett Lauck, to help draw up and speed the contract. But the Communist press was howling that there was no business depression; that it was merely a "counter-revolutionary Lovestoneite" invention; and that Martin was betraying the interests of the workers. The negotiations committee of the union had drawn up its demands. These were practically the same as in the old agreement. The only thing really new was a set of suggestions for the fairest and least hurtful way of laying off the smallest possible number of men during the depression.

The Unity opposition immediately began to agitate that Martin was "betraying the workers" and demanded all sorts of "rank and file" ratifications of the contract. In his anxiety for peace, Martin yielded to this absurd and unprecedented demand, which was inspired solely by the desire to discredit his administration. Indeed, he even assumed the leadership of the opposition to the agreement which by that time had been tentatively reached with General Motors, and caused its rejection on

November 14, 1937. Then the Unity faction, playing right into the hands of those provocative elements in General Motors that wanted to show that the union was "irresponsible," started a number of strategic wildcat strikes. On November 17, 1937, an unauthorized sitdown was called in the Fisher Body plant at Pontiac, the third such strike within a few days. General Motors immediately announced that agreements with the union were valueless.

The union declared the strike to be unauthorized. Through his personal representative Martin pleaded with the strikers to evacuate the plant. But George Method, one of the most zealous Communist Party followers, whose dismissal with two other workers had caused the strike, persuaded the men to defy the union. And on the International Executive Board Wyndham Mortimer and Walter Reuther were all for sanctioning this strike.

John L. Lewis stood solidly behind Martin. Finally Martin made a bold move, went out to the plant, and addressed the strikers. They followed him out of the plant, many with tears in their eyes after having had it explained to them how such irresponsible tactics jeopardized the very existence of their organization.

Subsequent investigation brought out several interesting facts. The Unity leaders, in various locals they controlled, had been "siphoning off" union funds for Stalinist activities and publications. They had also been agitating for "splitting up" various large locals where they lacked control, as in some of the Flint locals, while they were for leaving intact such large units as the West

Side Local in Detroit which they already controlled. During the sitdown strikes they had deliberately misinformed the strikers about the attitude of the International Executive Board, and had filled them with tales of how Martin was afraid to meet them face to face. And they tried to make Martin believe that his life was in danger should he visit Pontiac.

The moment the Stalinists were licked by Martin in these wildcat strikes, they turned around and declared themselves for him. The *Daily Worker* and other Communist publications came out for Martin. But not for long. On January 18, 1938, the Communist Party sent a secret memorandum "to all factions in the United Automobile Workers" in the Eastern districts, urging that "efforts should be made everywhere to clean out Red-baiters [that is, Martin adherents], Lovestoneites, and Trotskyites" (by which the Communist Party means radicals who oppose the party tactics), and to elect in the pending local elections "even conservatives" if necessary. Unfortunately for the Stalinists, the elections went against them almost two to one in Flint, which was their main stamping-ground. In the Detroit West Side Local, Walter Reuther and his "Socialist" lieutenants retained control.

Soon after these elections, the rank and file of the automobile workers came out overwhelmingly against Collective Security when the issue was put to a vote by the Martin administration. This was a distinct slap at the Communist Party line, for Collective Security in Stalinist parlance involves America's support of the Soviet

Union in the next war, especially against Japan. Ever since the summer of 1937 this had been the main errand of the Communist Party for Moscow. Martin is vigorously pushing a peace campaign among the auto workers, partly because he profoundly believes in it, and partly as a tactic against the Stalinists. For his efforts, the *Daily Worker* accused him of being a Japanese agent. But since the third Moscow trial, the American workers appear not to be afraid of such "Japanese agents" as Homer Martin.

On March 12, 1938, the contract with General Motors was renewed unchanged, though without a termination date. And a supplementary agreement on grievance procedure replaced the old one. It provided for shop committees of from three to seven men for plants of 2000 men or less, the committeemen to be paid by the corporation for two hours a day. The previous agreement had provided for four hours' pay, for five to nine committeemen per plant, with additional members in plants of more than 3600 workers.

In view of the depression, the new contract was a distinct victory for the union. Out of 517,000 normally employed automobile workers, 320,000 were out of work in March 1938. And the other 197,000 worked so little that more than half of them were eligible for relief. An improvement in the General Motors agreement was out of the question. But the Unity faction began making trouble about the agreement the moment it was signed by the Executive Board. The Stalinists claimed that Martin had sold the workers out once more; and they insisted that the Executive Board had acted "dictatorially" in not submitting the agreement for ratification to "special conferences" called for the purpose. Such "democracy" would practically set up dual bargaining committees to the International Executive Board, and would wreck all union negotiations. Coming from the Stalinists, this demand for "democracy" is peculiarly absurd, for in the unions they control, the rank and file is not permitted even to discuss the decisions of its officers.

Finally, in April and May 1938, the Stalinists attempted to unhorse Martin altogether. For this maneuver they played upon Frankensteen's ambitions and used him as their stalking horse. William Weinstone, B. K. Gebert and Wyndham Mortimer invited him to a conference in which a new scheme for the defeat of the Martin administration was outlined. It called for the "abolition" of all caucuses to save the union from factional dismemberment. Frankensteen was to be the leader of this new "faction to end all factionalism." This strategy was palpably Jesuitical. It would have disarmed only the Progressives, leaving the well-organized Stalinist faction completely intact, for it did not call for the dissolution of the official Communist Party branches among the automobile workers, which would have simply continued as hidden Unity caucuses.

Without consulting anyone in his own Progressive bloc, Frankensteen, with the air of an apostle of peace and harmony in the union, gave this "peace program" to the press. Martin quickly denounced this program and analyzed it exactly for what it was: "Certain forces within the union have failed in their frontal attack against the leadership of the U.A.W. and are now seeking the rear door disguised as a 'faction to end factionalism.'"

Frankensteen became the darling of the Stalinists and their press. Subsequently it developed that the Stalinists had promised Frankensteen, as an immediate earnest, to use their influence in Labor's Non-Partisan League in Michigan for his nomination as Governor Murphy's running-mate. But the whole scheme soon collapsed. Far from splitting the Progressive caucus, it introduced a split into the Unity caucus itself. Frankensteen had always been the pet aversion of the Socialists in the Unity caucus, and his sudden emergence as the shining light among the "lefts" annoyed the Reuther brothers and other Socialists who had been playing the Stalinist game—of late with decreasing relish. And as Frankensteen went over to the Stalinists, the immediate effect was to bring the Socialists closer to the Progressives. They did not join them, however, deluding themselves that they could capture the Unity caucus from Stalinist control and form a truly democratic opposition to the Martin machine. But actually the Unity caucus was completely tied to the Communist Party line which controlled it, for the Unity caucus never had been anything but a technique for Stalinist penetration into the union. Hence by sticking to the Unity caucus, the Reuther brothers quickly lost their momentary and vacillating independence and were quickly brought into line. In fact, ultimately, Walter Reuther was forced to sign the call for a rump convention, which tried to create a new and dual union in the industry.

When the International Executive Board met in May 1938, Martin submitted a twenty-point program which was unanimously adopted. This program once more outlawed all unauthorized strikes and gave the administration the power to take action against irresponsible local leadership. The General Motors agreement and the Ludlow-La Follette resolution for a war referendum were endorsed. At this meeting the members of the Unity caucus did not dare to vote against the twenty-point program. They decided to bide their time.

That time came in June, when a special meeting of the Executive Board was called in Washington to consider a group insurance plan. After the meeting, some of the Progressives left town, whereupon the Stalinists called a rump meeting of the Board which only they attended. They intended to remove Martin on charges that the proposed insurance plan was a huge swindle, a charge which they themselves had to drop a few days later for its obvious absurdity. The rump board sat only for one day. Martin, deeming that an emergency had arisen, called together the full International Executive Board, which suspended Frankensteen, Mortimer, Walter Welles and Addes for violating the officially adopted twenty-point program. In a letter to the membership, Martin explained the reasons for these suspensions.

As you know [the letter read], for months the International Union has been in the midst of factional strife which has threatened its very existence. I have pointed out time and time again that the administration of the union must carry forward in such a way as to gain the respect of our members, the employers with whom we have contracts, and the general public. Our union has been dragged in the dust, its name has been blasphemed, its prestige irreparably injured by the factional attitude and the factional action of those in opposition to the administration. But, despite all these things, the May meeting of the International Executive Board came forth with a 20-point program which was unanimously adopted and voluntarily signed by every member of the International Executive Board. I and the majority of the I.E.B. members have kept this program to the letter, never once deviating from it; and we were of the opinion that all was well and that the union was headed forward, united at last on the basis of this program.

To our great dismay and disappointment, certain International officers and Executive Board members on last Wednesday afternoon, June 8, 1938, in Detroit, repudiated the whole program by seeking, arbitrarily, without consultation, to overthrow the whole action of the Executive Board which had ended two weeks previous. Mr. Frankensteen announced in a press conference: "Martin will be surprised to find that his majority has dwindled to a minority."

This group, thinking themselves in power at last, not only repudiated the 20-point program but violated their oath of office and acted in such a manner as to prove that they were not only irresponsible but that their whole action was that of men who were determined to place their own personal and political ambitions above the needs of the membership which they were elected to serve.

The five suspended officials immediately went to the local unions and tried to force through resolutions in their defense. They called all sorts of rump and illegal meetings, but on the whole the membership failed to respond. The Stalinists also tried to engineer a special convention to take up the issue of their suspension, but soon gave up the effort for lack of support among the rank and file. Then they went to Washington to urge Lewis to intervene, insisting that they would not stand trial on the ground that such a trial would be unconstitutional, although the Constitution of the union clearly provides both for the suspension and the expulsion of any member or officer by a majority of the International Executive Board.

Next, a group of non-Stalinist Unity officials appealed to Lewis, again asking for his intervention. In this second appeal the Socialists participated, as did thirteen union presidents who claimed to represent the sentiments of hundreds of thousands of workers. But they represented largely themselves, for when they returned to their locals they found that the rank and file opposed any interference by the national CIO. The majority of the workers are sick and frightened of Stalinist disruption and are desperate for real internal peace, which they have come to realize is impossible as long as the Unity caucus is tied up with the party line.

Not only the Martin administration, but also a group of no less than 155 local presidents asked John L. Lewis to permit the U.A.W. to clean house. These men represented almost three-quarters of the union membership.[1]

Meanwhile, George Addes, the suspended secretary-treasurer of the union, was tried on July 8. The charges against him were presented by John Schiefelbein, president of Local 283 at West Allis, Wisconsin. After his suspension, Addes had sent out two letters to the general membership, in one of which he had urged the members to send their dues directly to him. "You have undoubtedly been advised," he wrote, "to forward funds belonging to the International Union, United Automobile Workers of America, to Delmond Garst. This is to advise you that the sending of any funds belonging to the International in this manner is illegal. . . ." He also notified the banks not to honor union withdrawals unless authorized by him. The Executive Board found Addes guilty and expelled him.

The trials of the four vice-presidents—Mortimer, Frankensteen, Hall and Welles—dragged on until July 29, when the defense dramatically produced documents and letters which, alas, were almost immediately proved to have been stolen from the home of Jay Lovestone. They were presented as evidence of Lovestoneite control

---

[1] Since then Lewis has stepped in with a peace proposal, calling for reinstatement of the ousted officers, adherence to the 20-point program, and arbitration of all internal differences by the national CIO. The expelled officers eagerly accepted this scheme. Martin, of course, rejected it, partly because he believes in union autonomy and partly because he has with him the overwhelming majority both on his Board and in the local unions. If, none the less, Lewis should insist on this plan, it may lead to dual unionism. For the International Executive Board may well decide to call a special convention to determine whether the union is to leave the CIO rather than face reinvigorated Stalinist disruption.

of the Martin administration. For one day the *Daily Worker* ran some of this correspondence, which, though printed completely out of context, showed nothing incriminating anyway. The correspondence did show that the Lovestoneites had done their utmost to check the Stalinists—which was not news. And some of these letters were critical of Martin and other Progressives in a way which showed how little they controlled them. Lovestone immediately secured counsel to prosecute those responsible for the burglary. The *Daily Worker* stopped its much advertised "exposé" of this supposedly incriminating literature, and the suspended officers avoided all further reference to it during the trial.

On August 8, the International Executive Board voted to suspend Walter Welles for three months; and it expelled from the union Richard Frankensteen, Wyndham Mortimer and Ed Hall. They were charged with "trying to starve the union by withholding finances"; with "violating and disregarding the discipline of the union"; with "pretending to speak in the name of the union"; with "slandering the union, [and] trying to create the impression that the union was against the CIO and John L. Lewis"; and, finally, with "calling numerous local regional state conferences and a national conference without authorization."

The Unity caucus called a special meeting for August 13 in Toledo, at which it was decided to call a rump convention to reorganize the U.A.W. But only thirty-five heads of local unions were present out of almost 600 locals in the U.A.W. The expelled officers will, I believe, stay expelled. The back of Stalinist factionalism in the union has probably been broken. However, there can be no doubt that factionalism will continue in the U.A.W. for some time to come and that the union has been tremendously weakened by this inner upheaval, especially in its drive to organize Ford. Today the U.A.W. is in the position of an invalid recovering from a major operation.

Yet there is every hope that the invalid will recover. It is inconceivable that, after their victories, the workers in this basic industry will ever give up their union and return to the old days. The U.A.W. is one of the great triumphs in the history of American labor. Moreover, industrial unionism as against craft unionism is not merely an economic organization of labor. It is a social movement in the widest sense, and derives its strength from a new outlook on life which it gives the workers. The United Automobile Workers is today the strongest progressive force in the State of Michigan and in the city of Detroit, civilly and politically no less than economically. The union has gone into political action, it is extremely active in behalf of adequate relief, it is fighting for American neutrality in the next war. Though defeated, Judge O'Brien, the labor candidate for mayor of Detroit in November 1937, polled 35 per cent of the total vote. The United Automobile Workers Union has been the main driving force in securing increased Federal relief for Detroit. In short, the union is more than a mere collective bargaining agency for the automobile workers. It has become their form of life. It is for this reason that the U.A.W. is here to stay.

CHAPTER VII

THE MARITIME WORKERS

No INDUSTRY is more complex than the maritime industry. The shipyards, the docks, and the ships constitute a miniature of our industrial society as a whole. A ship is built by thirty-seven different crafts. The docks are run by half-a-dozen others. And a ship is manned by nine crafts more. Almost half of the unions in the A. F. of L. in one way or another claim jurisdiction in this mosaic field. Accordingly, the drive for industrial unionism hit the A. F. of L. in the center of its jurisdictional plexus.

The Shipbuilders

Slowly and painfully the shipyard workers began to build an industrial union during the NRA. This new organization—the Industrial Union of Marine and Shipbuilding Workers—grew by defections from eighteen A. F. of L. crafts working in the yards, such as machinists, chippers, boilermakers, carpenters, and electricians. The union really became established when in 1934 it won recognition and a 14.8 per cent wage increase at the New York Shipyards in Camden, New Jersey, after a strike of seven weeks. In the fall of 1936 it joined the CIO.

John Green and Philip Van Gelder, the leaders of this union, used to be in the Socialist Party. Green had been a shipyard worker, always a progressive, for many years. Van Gelder had been an instructor of philosophy at Brown University. They are both simple, honest, intelligent, and plodding men, who have managed to keep their union out of suicidal factional difficulties. In 1936 and 1937 the union fought eight major strikes. It won only one, at the United States Steel plant at Kearny, New Jersey, where it signed up some 2500 men. It was badly beaten by the powerful Todd-Robins Dry Dock Company at Brooklyn in 1937, where 14,000 men walked out. The strike was prematurely forced by Stalinist agitators, was sabotaged by Joseph Ryan, the Tammany brave who is president of the International Longshoremen's Association, and was broken with the aid of the mounted police. The union did no better on the West Coast. But in spite of all these setbacks it is making headway. In 1938 it was able to renew its contracts in the New York harbor area. These contracts call for a closed shop, for time-and-a-half for overtime, and for a wage scale ranging from 85 cents an hour for helpers to $1.45 for skilled mechanics. Today the union has some 20,000, not quite one-third of the industry.

West Coast

The most strategic and picturesque unions, around which the other maritime trades group themselves magnetically, are the longshoremen and the sailors. Both these unions have a long and stormy history. But under the leadership of Joseph Ryan, the International Longshoremen's Association has become one of the most reactionary outfits in the A. F. of L., and on the East Coast a mere annex to Tammany Hall. The International Seamen's Union had deteriorated in the course of years, especially since 1920, from a militant and thriving organization into a corrupt nothing, until finally in 1938 it was dissolved by the A. F. of L. altogether.

On the West Coast the longshoremen and the sailors came into their own in the great maritime strike of 1934. They both remained in the A. F. of L.—the sailors until 1935 and the longshoremen until 1937. But the 1934 strike made both West Coast unions practically autonomous. It was this strike which brought forth two leaders on the Pacific, as unlike each other as can be. One of them is Harry Bridges of the longshoremen, and the other is Harry Lundeberg of the sailors.

Harry Bridges is an Australian who had longshored for many years on the Pacific Coast. He came up in the 1934 strike in a meteoric, ultra-militant career and acquired a mythical halo as a revolutionary leader. But soon thereafter he came under the influence of the Communist Party. Today he is distinguished by his violent Red-baiting of every radical and progressive critic of the Stalinists. For over three years, he has been playing a furtive and completely opportunistic game, under the cloak of a purely verbal radicalism, being as much responsible as anybody else for breaking up every shred of unity in West Coast labor. His one and only aim, as we have seen in the chapter on factionalism, is to bring the American labor movement under the control of the Communist Party.

Harry Lundeberg is a Norwegian, and an I.W.W. in his entire outlook, though he never was a member of the Wobblies. He shares the old I.W.W. obsession for the strictest rank-and-file democracy, which makes all administration a slow-motion picture. "In our union even the buying of stamps is supervised by the finance committee," he proudly assured me. Slow, stubborn, fanatically honest, and suspicious, Lundeberg is the idol of the 8,000 sailors in the Sailors Union of the Pacific, which controls every port on the West Coast.

While Harry Bridges, following the Communist Party line, played with the A. F. of L. until May 1937, Harry Lundeberg welcomed the CIO from the very start. As a syndicalist, he had always believed in industrial unionism. But in time, especially after Bridges's appointment in June 1937 as director of the West Coast CIO, Lundeberg became bitterly opposed to the CIO. For one thing, he was convinced that in the maritime industry the CIO was completely under the thumb of the Stalinists; and for another thing, he believed that John Lewis double-crossed him by appointing Harry Bridges to the CIO leadership on the West Coast.

Early in June 1937, Lundeberg went to Washington to talk to Lewis. According to Lundeberg, Lewis asked him to organize the sailors on a national scale, and to take them into the CIO. Lundeberg, with his orthodox belief in rank-and-file democracy, replied that he would have to go home and consult his people. What really happened at the meeting of these two men, no one can tell. But there is little doubt that Lewis was impatient with Lundeberg's uncompromising rank-and-file democracy, his failure to appreciate that organization drives cannot be determined by referendums and initiated in conventions. Be that as it may, before the month was up Lewis suddenly appointed Bridges as director of the West Coast CIO. John Brophy, who by that time was entirely under the influence of the Stalinists, was strong for Bridges and just as strong against Lundeberg. In fact, Brophy went west to see to it that Bridges got the job. In the meantime, the sailors had had a referendum on whether or not to join the CIO. There is no doubt that they had voted for it. But when it became clear that Lewis and Brophy meant to put Harry Bridges at the head of it, the sailors' unions in the various ports quickly voted to seal the ballot boxes.

The 1934 strike had established the seven West Coast maritime unions, both on the shore and on the ships. The three key unions were the longshoremen, the sailors, and the firemen and oilers, about seven, eight, and five thousand strong respectively. These three unions really won the strike. The four other unions were the marine engineers, the mates and pilots, the radio telegraphers, and the cooks and stewards.

Ever since 1934 the shipowners had been trying to smash these seven unions and had been chiseling on the agreements. They were especially bent on weakening union control over the hiring halls. In 1936 they demanded drastic modifications of the agreements. The newly created United States Maritime Commission tried to mediate by proposing the extension of the existing contracts. But neither side would give in, and the men answered with a strike which involved 37,000 workers and tied up the whole shipping industry on the Pacific Coast. The tie-up, known as the "99-Day Strike," began on October 29, 1936, and ended on February 4, 1937.

Unlike the strike of 1934, the 99-Day Strike was comparatively peaceful. The unions won. The longshoremen retained the six-hour day and the thirty-hour week, and a minimum wage of 95 cents an hour. The other unions made positive gains. Their wages were increased on an average of $10 a month. The new pay for sailors began with $55 for ordinary seamen and $72.50 for able seamen. Wages for the steward service ranged from $55 for messboys to $125 for stewards; for firemen and oilers, from $60 to $82.50 a month on deep-sea vessels; and for radio operators from $112.50 to $175.00 a month. Labor remained in control of the hiring halls.

Unfortunately, a bitter feud, instigated by the Stalinists, developed during the strike. The Sailors Union of the Pacific had reached a tentative agreement with the shipowners, subject to ratification by its rank and file, before the other unions. Harry Lundeberg made it amply clear that the sailors had no intention of signing up separately. But Bridges accused him of running out on the rest of maritime labor, and made tremendous capital out of the incident.

As we have seen, the policy of the Communist Party, from the formation of the CIO in November 1935 until May 1937, was to talk more or less pro-CIO, but to play with the A. F. of L. In this game of playing both ends against the middle, Bridges had been especially devious, and completely callous to its destructive effects. Thus, as late as March 1937, he threw a picket line around the Matson docks in San Francisco against a local of the CIO shipbuilding workers, claiming that the job of scraping and painting the boats belonged to a scalers' local of his A. F. of L. longshoremen. At that time even Brophy protested by wire against Bridges's tactics. The resulting bitterness had an enormously disruptive influence on the whole West Coast labor situation. This situation has been complicated by the fact that, since Bridges joined the CIO, he naturally got into a deadly struggle with his former buddy, Dave Beck, boss of the Seattle teamsters and the most powerful personality in the A. F. of L. on the West Coast. Back in 1935, the longshoremen had taken in the warehousemen in the Bay District and in the course of two years practically doubled the union membership. And now Beck suddenly announced that the teamsters had jurisdiction over the warehousemen. After a spectacular and bloody fight, Beck lost.

But the struggle between Bridges and Lundeberg in the Maritime Federation of the Pacific went on and deepened. The scapegoat of this struggle was Barney Mayes, editor of the *Voice of the Federation,* which he had made into one of the best labor papers in the country. Mayes was a bitter opponent of the Communist Party line, and the party decided to get rid of him. Accordingly, Bridges, right in the middle of the 99-Day Strike, forced a trial of Mayes, on trumped-up charges, by the editorial board of the *Voice of the Federation*. He accused Mayes of furnishing Lundeberg's sailors with 500 extra copies of the paper every week; later on, it turned out that it was the Stalinist business manager of the paper who had oversupplied the sailors' union. Bridges also accused Mayes of obtaining the editorship with forged references, which was proven to be untrue. And he objected to Mayes's fight on Senator Copeland's Continuous Discharge Book, called by the maritime workers the Fink Book, for it really amounted to a blacklist. Mayes believed in agitating among the workers against the Fink Book, which he did very effectively in the *Voice of the Federation*. The Stalinists, on the other hand, wanted to exercise merely polite legislative pressure against it in Washington. And the reason was that by that time the Stalinists were interested primarily in Collective Security, and avoided all propaganda which might even remotely render the marine workers less amenable to government supervision in the next war. (Indeed, the attitude of the Stalinists on the Fink Book on both coasts became ever more supine, and was one of the main reasons for their increasing loss of support among the rank and file.)

The trial lasted for weeks. The editorial board cleared Mayes of every charge. But Mayes quit, because his usefulness had been ended. The whole wretched struggle acted like so much gasoline on the inflammatory factional situation in the Maritime Federation. But the trial did serve to stimulate the crystallization of democratic sentiment in the rank and file against Stalinist totalitarianism, and in time this opposition found the requisite militant leadership. In January 1938 the West Coast Marine Firemen, Oilers, Water Tenders and Wipers Association kicked out its Stalinist administration and elected a progressive slate. Progressive sentiment against Stalinist control is growing among the Cooks and Stewards. And even among Bridges's longshoremen the rebellion against his dictatorial control is rife. The Seattle, San Pedro and Portland locals are in the control of anti-Bridges progressives. In Tacoma, the longshoremen preferred to stay in the A. F. of L., not from reactionary motives but because they refused to knuckle down to Stalinist dictation.

The Sailors Union of the Pacific started a drive early in 1938 to amalgamate the whole unlicensed personnel on the West Coast into an International Maritime Union, a proposal which has been endorsed all up and down the Pacific Coast by every local of the Firemen and Oilers, except in San Francisco, and by 50 per cent of the Cooks and Stewards. The S.U.P. also founded a Seafarers' Federation to displace the factionally torn Maritime Federation. This new organization, under Lundeberg's leadership, includes both the licensed and the unlicensed personnel.

The paradoxical effect of the Stalinist wrecking tactics has been to drive progressive West Coast maritime labor more and more into the arms of the A. F. of L. In its bitter enmity to the CIO, the Executive Council of the A. F. of L. dissolved the atrophied and corrupt International Seamen's Union in order to clear the way for the affiliation of the Sailors Union of the Pacific. Green told Lundeberg to "write his own ticket." Moreover, he announced a tentative plan for one international union of sailors on all American and Canadian ships, with the idea, of course, that the S.U.P. would be in charge of the drive. Since the S.U.P. is committed to industrial unionism, and through the new Seafarers' Federation is making a drive for it on the Pacific Coast, Green's invitation to Lundeberg implies the recognition of the principle of industrial unionism in the maritime industry.

In the summer of 1938, the S.U.P. polled its members on every ship on the issue of reaffiliation with the A. F. of L. The rank and file voted overwhelmingly for it, for the liquidation of the I.S.U. assured them that the A. F. of L. would not interfere with their program. All this does not mean that the Executive Council of the A. F. of L. has seen the light on industrial unionism. Its main objective is of course to fight the CIO. And therein lies the tragedy of Stalinist disruption—it deepens the division in the working class.

East Coast

The labor situation on the East Coast, the Gulf, and the Great Lakes presented until 1936 a very different picture. For all its internal struggles, maritime labor on the West Coast had established itself in the strike of 1934. In the East, the maritime unions were still represented by Ryan of the International Longshoremen's Association, and by the now extinct International Seamen's Union. Finally, the CIO decided to organize maritime labor on a national scale, realizing that the drive would have to be concentrated in the East. In July 1937, John L. Lewis appointed a committee of seven to organize the maritime workers. As chairman of this committee he chose John Brophy. And the three other important figures on it were Harry Bridges, Mervyn Rathborne of the radio telegraphers, and Joe Curran of the sailors. Brophy follows the Communist Party line in effect, while the other three follow it without deviation on anything that really matters.

When Curran began his agitation among the East Coast sailors, he of course ran into the bitter opposition of the old-line A. F. of L. unions. In March 1936, he managed to get some 2400 seamen to engage in a fugitive strike, really against the A. F. of L. International Seamen's Union, to enforce union contracts. The strike accomplished nothing. But finally, toward the end of 1936, a group of insurgent sailors in the old I.S.U. organized a Seamen's Defense Council, and called a strike on November 6, 1936. On November 23, they were joined by the mates and pilots, and on November 30 by the radio operators. This strike was called on a national scale, in sympathy with the strike on the West Coast. But on January 24, 1937, the strike was called off, for on the East Coast the Stalinists secretly urged the sailors to ship out with the Fink Book whenever the shipowners insisted that they carry it. The effect of the strike, however, was that the men began to break away, finally in a rout, from the old-line A. F. of L. unions. And they joined in flocks the N.M.U., which includes all the unlicensed seafaring crafts—sailors, firemen and oilers, cooks and stewards. In the East, the Firemen, Oilers, Water Tenders and Wipers, who had been in a separate division in the I.S.U., joined the N.M.U., not as a separate section but as individuals.

Toward the end of 1937, the N.M.U. was able to report a membership of 51,500 on the Atlantic seacoast, the Gulf, and the Great Lakes. It had 15,200 men on deck (sailors), 15,100 in the engine rooms (firemen, oilers, water tenders and wipers), and 17,200 cooks and stewards. The union also had more than 4000 men on the Great Lakes in the subsidiary Inland Boatmen's Union. The radio telegraphers and the licensed personnel were by that time practically all in the CIO in separate unions. Only the longshoremen were still largely in the International Longshoremen's Association of the A. F. of L., though hundreds of them were joining Bridges's followers, who have a skeleton organization in the East.

Considerable trouble broke out between the new CIO unions and the old A. F. of L. crafts when the National Labor Relations Board began to supervise elections on the docks and ships. David Grange, of the Cooks and Stewards in the International Seamen's Union, had his strong-arm men on the boats, and Joe Ryan's "goons" used their baling-hooks on the docks. But these tactics could not stop the overwhelming sentiment of the men for the N.M.U. Violence was kept down to a minimum by the courageous impartiality of Mrs. Elinore Herrick, regional director of the N.L.R.B. She would appear on the docks or board a ship in the middle of the night to see that elections were held fairly. She also prevented patently illegal collusions between the companies and the old-line unions, which would sign contracts before the vote was taken. By March 27, 1938, the votes on most of the Eastern lines were in. Of the men who voted, 14,108 were for the N.M.U. (CIO), and only 2974 for the I.S.U. (A. F. of L.). Obviously, maritime labor was pro-CIO.

The agreements which the N.M.U. has been able to sign are on the whole fair, certainly better than the old A. F. of L. contracts. Wages have been increased, especially in the deck department, where the average monthly pay for seamen rose from $37.83 in 1936 to $60.00 in 1938. Increases for the cooks and stewards were a good deal less, but their hours were reduced considerably. Unfortunately, the National Maritime Union, no more than the Sailors Union of the Pacific, could get more than straight pay for overtime. But, unlike the S.U.P., the N.M.U. has been so lax in its supervision of overtime (and most sailors make their money through overtime) that the income of the Eastern sailor is still about $10 a month less than on the Pacific Coast.

In May 1938, the N.M.U. was able to come to an agreement with the American Merchant Marine Institute, which represents most of the steamship lines on the East Coast and the Gulf. This was the first time that these shipowners dealt as an organized group with organized labor. The union lost on several of its major demands, notably its demand for wage increases, and for a contract which would expire in 1938 simultaneously with the West Coast agreements. Wages remained the same; and the new agreement is to remain in effect until September 1939. Union members received preferential hiring rights, though the owners retained the privilege to select those satisfactory to themselves. The contract also included arbitration and grievance clauses and prohibited all strikes and lockouts.

A serious threat faces the N.M.U., and maritime labor in general, in the attitude of the United States Maritime Commission. In its strenuous efforts to build a strong merchant marine by subsidizing private enterprise, the Commission is apt to see entirely too much the side of the shipowners. On the West Coast, the militant Sailors Union of the Pacific has its own union hiring halls, an institution which no one dares to challenge. But on the East Coast the Maritime Commission established federal hiring halls, known to the men as Fink Halls. Moreover, a recent amendment to the Merchant Marine Act provides for a training school for seamen under government auspices. "You're in the navy now," seems to be the attitude of the Commission toward the merchant sailors. The rank and file is bitterly opposed to this growing control of maritime labor by the government, a tendency which was drastically illustrated in 1937 by the conviction of fourteen striking seamen on the government-owned *Algic*. They were found guilty of "mutiny," under a statute of 1790, for a sitdown strike in a foreign port.

The Stalinist officialdom in the N.M.U. has accepted

this increasing control of maritime labor by the federal authorities. The reason is that the Communist Party today is primarily interested in Collective Security, and hence not at all averse to government domination of marine labor in case of war. It is particularly the covert but none the less obvious co-operation of the Stalinists with the Maritime Commission hiring halls which brought about the final revolt of the militant rank and file against their leadership in August 1938.

Until this defeat the Stalinists were in complete control of the N.M.U. The Communist Party had assigned to it a "political commissar" in the person of Roy Hudson, who is the secretary of the National Maritime Fraction of the party. As president of the union, Joe Curran was merely the front for such Stalinist politicians as Jack Lawrenson, Tom Ray, Moe Byne, and Blackie Myers. In the very beginning the Stalinists had captured this union, which is the focal organization in eastern marine labor, by exactly the same methods by which they had originally captured many of the West Coast maritime unions. A lot of them got into the union as "one-trippers," making a single trip merely to get hold of a union card. Then these mariners religiously attended every union meeting, while the opposition membership, which had no such "sailors," was in and out of port. They organized the famous "booing squads," which howled down every criticism in union meetings, and "lying squads," created for the sole purpose of spreading slanderous whispering campaigns against the radicals and progressives who objected to the Communist Party line.

Another effective way of silencing all opposition was the constant and irrelevant introduction at every meeting of the so-called "debating society resolutions," such as those in favor of Collective Security, or in defense of China and Loyalist Spain, or for Peace and Democracy, and so on and on. Whenever a serious issue arose on which the progressives objected to the Stalinist steamroller, the proletarian duty of supporting Loyalist Spain or of boycotting Japanese goods was somehow tied up with the issue in question, and the critic of the "party line" was smeared as a dirty fascist, "Trotskyite spy," Japanese agent, stool-pigeon for the shipowners, fink, or what have you. The more insistent militants were handled more roughly and "purged" with a 99-year "suspension."

This sort of terrorism continued to flourish until the election campaign of 1938, during which the progressive opposition began to crystallize. In the beginning, this opposition was quite unorganized. It was inexperienced, resentful, inarticulate. But as the campaign went on, it gathered remarkable momentum and developed a new rank-and-file leadership of amazing strategic acumen. The outstanding personality in this rebellion was Jerome King. King has a long and irreproachable record as a left-winger in the old International Seamen's Union. He is a rank-and-filer, very similar to Lundeberg both in his personal background and in his passion for union democracy. Close to him is Fred Phillips, another rank-and-filer, with a well-known radical background in marine labor and great moral authority among the men. The Stalinists found it rather hard to make the sailors believe that Jerry King and Fred Phillips were "stoolpigeons" and "wreckers."

The National Executive Council of the N.M.U. consists of nine officers. During the campaign, the opposition did not quite realize its developing strength and did not oppose the re-election of Joe Curran for the presidency and of Ferdinand Smith for the vice-presidency, though it was later discovered that Smith had been a strikebreaker in the 1934 struggle. They put up only seven opposition candidates. During the campaign, which lasted for six weeks, the Stalinists outdid themselves in character assassination and in every sort of snide and highhanded persecution of the opposition candidates. They branded their paper, the *Rank and File Pilot*, as a "fink sheet," claiming that it was being financed by all sorts of labor-baiting agencies.

As a reaction to these tactics, there were several outbreaks of violence. The average left-wing sailor is inclined to "direct action" when sufficiently aroused. Jack Lawrenson, the Stalinist candidate to succeed himself as secretary-treasurer, was chased out of his office and down the fire-escape by a crowd of rank-and-filers. On the same day, the oppositionists raided the office of the Maritime Fraction of the Communist Party and wrecked the place. Finally the opposition succeeded in swinging the New York membership in a general meeting. The meeting voted to clear the national office staff of some forty-odd Communist Party members and followers. Even Curran's sentimental plea to save his private secretary was of no avail.

The election returns were announced on August 5. Jerry King received 8417 votes for secretary-treasurer against 6788 votes for Lawrenson. In addition to King, the following rank-and-file candidates were elected: Fred Phillips, George H. Hearn, Arthur Thomas, and Charles Torres. The final tabulation showed that the rank-and-filers had captured the Atlantic District Committee by two to one, and the Gulf District Committee by five to one. And they won the great majority of the minor union offices all along the East Coast and the Gulf.

The progressives lost no time in living up to their election promises. The moment the returns came in, a group of sailors made for the print shop where the *Pilot* was being set up and substituted an editorial of their own for one which had been prepared by the Stalinists. But in strict accord with their democratic program, they left in a long and violent letter by Curran attacking the opposition. Jerry King announced that a new office staff, loyal only to the interests of the union, would immediately replace the old staff in the national office. Most of the new office workers were promptly recruited from Socialist Party ranks.

Of course, the victory of the progressives does not mean that the union has been rescued entirely from Stalinist disruption. The progressives control only five out of the nine members on the National Executive

Council, and past experience has shown that a strong Stalinist minority, as in the United Automobile Workers, can do a great deal of damage. This would be especially true in the N.M.U., which the Communist Party had permeated for so long. On the other hand, experience has also shown that once the rank and file becomes conscious of Stalinist disruption, the Communist Party has little chance of re-entrenching itself in key positions. It is most unlikely that Joe Curran will be re-elected to the presidency next year.

Another tower of strength to the progressives in the N.M.U. is the fraternal attitude of Harry Lundeberg and the Sailors Union of the Pacific. To be sure, since the S.U.P. has reaffiliated with the A. F. of L. it has also taken over the A. F. of L. Seamen's Union, a federal local on the East Coast. But the S.U.P. has no intention of competing with the N.M.U. On the contrary, it is helping the new leadership all it can. And there is every hope that in time the S.U.P. and the N.M.U. will unite and start a real drive, without factional strife, for industrial unionism in the maritime industry.

CHAPTER VIII

NEW UNIONS IN NEW FIELDS

So far we have dealt with two groups of CIO organizations. We have traced the history of the charter unions, especially of the miners and the tailors. These unions gave the CIO its impetus, its vitality, and to some degree its character. And we discussed in detail the campaigns in the steel, the automobile, and the maritime industries. These three drives, each in its own way, presented significantly and dramatically the major problems of industrial organization at this critical period of national and world affairs. And we have seen the way in which the CIO faced or shirked these problems. It has done both in a big way.

The CIO has more or less kept out of those highly skilled crafts in which the A. F. of L. is entrenched. But the rest of American industry was an open field. Unorganized labor was eager to be organized. Committees of workers from every conceivable industry besieged the CIO, clamoring for industrial unionism. The CIO responded, though during the first two years it naturally tried to concentrate on mass production industries. But it turned nobody away. Today it ramifies throughout our industrial society.

In this chapter we shall deal with the new unions of manual workers, among which we shall include the furriers and the shoe workers, who have a longer history and who joined the CIO in 1937. We shall deal with each of these eleven unions separately, for they fall into no groups.

The Textile Workers

The United Textile Workers of America had been for many years one of the most venerable, decent, and extinct organizations in the A. F. of L. Its officers were notoriously honest, and notoriously never did a thing. Tom McMahon, president of the union from 1921 to NRA days, was in many ways a counterpart of old Mike Tighe of the scrapped Amalgamated Association of Iron, Steel and Tin Workers. He was an Owl and a Hibernian, and a sound pinochle player, and spent all his spare time keeping his small machine in order. The big idea was to let well enough alone, and not to agitate the 1,250,000 textile workers in the country into swamping the 65,000 members of the United Textile Workers. Of these 65,000, incidentally, between 35,000 and 40,000 had always been in the completely independent section of the United Hosiery Workers, who ran their own conventions, elected their own officers, and did very well for themselves.

Every few years, some "outside agitators" would organize thousands of workers—in Lawrence and Paterson in 1912, in Passaic in 1927, in Gastonia in 1929—and try to hand them over to the United Textile Workers. But no go. McMahon's little retail business union could not handle such wholesale labor problems. The U.T.W.

would take these new workers in—and a year later somehow there would be no trace of them.

During the first half of the NRA, the union couldn't help itself, and grew to tremendous proportions. For one thing, the Southern mill workers, after their tragic losses of the Gastonia and Marion strikes, saw their chance. And for another thing, Mr. and Mrs. Roosevelt were bent on abolishing child labor, which infested the Southern textile fields, and were especially interested in the organization of the textile workers. Francis J. Gorman, the new president of the U.T.W., led the great national textile strike in September 1934, as a result of which tens of thousands of workers flocked into the union. Gorman became for a while one of the Messiahs of American labor. Actually he is an incompetent and ineffective man, whose ambition merely serves to emphasize his weaknesses. He failed to get any agreements, and under his leadership the union gradually went back from 350,000 after the 1934 strike to its original 65,000 by the beginning of 1937. The rest of it had ebbed back again into the industrial swamps of the South. Before the NRA expired, this fiasco was hastened by the Textile Labor Relations Board under Robert Bruère, for many years one of the earnest editors of the *Survey*, the national gazette for social workers. Mr. Bruère divided his time between "handling grievances" (of which there were none officially, because no contracts had been signed after the strike) and "studying" the stretch-out system to which the workers had been driven back.

Then came the CIO. But nothing happened in the textile industry for a whole year and a half. The reason is quite understandable. The CIO wanted to get established before it tackled this "sickest" of all our industries. The textile industry is disorganized not only in its labor end, but financially, productively, geographically, as well as in its management and marketing ends. It would take a Dickens to do it justice. It is not so much an industry as a species of industrial confusion. This confusion is extraordinarily far-flung, extending from the New England States way down to the South, to which some of the New England plants have migrated in search of cheap and illiterate and hence supposedly docile labor. The industry consists of several large corporations on the one hand, and of thousands of tiny "family" shops, where the worst sweat-shop conditions prevail. In many places in the South I have seen the weekly pay envelopes of mill-workers marked anywhere from $2.50 to $6.00 a week, especially for women and children. The industry includes silk, rayon, woolens, knit goods, cotton, and literally dozens of other products, from thread to hatbands. And all these products have a "seasonal" market, not by necessity but because of the prevailing merchandising methods. For the industry is at the mercy of the independent "factors," the sales agents who control it. And by their cut-throat competition, they keep the industry in a sort of manic-depressive dementia, in which wild over-production is followed by a complete slump.

Obviously, the CIO wanted to be sufficiently organized itself before it tackled the textile chaos. Finally in April 1937, it set up the Textile Workers Organizing Committee, and appointed to its board Sidney Hillman and Charles Weinstein of the Amalgamated, Charles S. Zimmerman of the International, Francis J. Gorman of the United Textile Workers, and Emil Rieve of the Hosiery Workers. The T.W.O.C. is really run by the big needle trades, especially the Amalgamated. The chairman is Sidney Hillman. As in the case of the old steel union, the United Textile Workers Union was immediately shelved. Frank Gorman became a pensioner of the T.W.O.C. In the summer of 1938, he resigned from the T.W.O.C. altogether and began a fight against it by trying to revive the machine of the old United Textile Workers Union. Today he is a disgruntled reactionary, and is not likely to do much damage to the T.W.O.C. outside of his own stronghold in Rhode Island.

Mr. Hillman, being an Industrial Statesman rather than a labor leader, saw a great opportunity of bringing order into the chaos of the textile world. He started off with a bang. In no time at all the T.W.O.C. had organized "99 regional offices with a staff of over 600." By March 1938, it claimed to have signed some 600 agreements, covering almost 1000 companies employing over 280,000 workers. Unfortunately, these spectacular figures do not reflect actual conditions in the field. When the T.W.O.C. speaks of having 280,000 workers "under agreements," it generously includes non-members as well as members in the shops which it has signed up. Thus, in a shop which employs 500 workers, the T.W.O.C. may have only 80 members. To be sure, the other 420 benefit equally by the agreement, but that does not justify the exorbitant claims which Mr. Hillman makes for the textile drive. Nobody knows just how many members the T.W.O.C. really has. In March 1938, the best opinion gave to it 125,000 members nationally. Anything above this figure is sheer optimism. Even this, of course, is an excellent showing. For it means that—if we except the Hosiery Workers—the T.W.O.C. has increased the organization of textile workers fourfold in about one year.

Mr. Hillman brought to the textile drive his celebrated Amalgamated technique of viewing "the industry as a whole," rather than simply organizing the workers. "A new line of strategy has been developed," his committee boasted. "T.W.O.C. is here to save labor and industry from itself." It has not succeeded in saving the industry from itself, but it has almost succeeded in saving labor from itself. We have seen how this technique has, in the course of years, weakened the Amalgamated Clothing Workers. But after all, the Amalgamated is an old and well-established union, with many comparatively skilled workers in large shops. In the textile drive, this strategy has been singularly inappropriate. Hillman has tried, first of all, to put on their feet the various manufacturers' associations in the industry—such as the Hatband Group, the Master Weavers Institute, the Textile Converters' Association, and others—in order to be able to deal with them in a "responsible" fashion. But, alas, these various organizations have neither the will nor the wit to rationalize the industry even for their own benefit. All Mr. Hillman's method accomplished was to half-organize the workers as quickly as possible, without any real union agitation, for the purpose of signing them up wholesale with the various manufacturers' associations. The result is that the T.W.O.C. has hastily signed any agreement it could get, and it couldn't get much. Having no militancy or cohesion, which alone can obtain favorable contracts, the T.W.O.C. could gain nothing but Pyrrhic victories. For the T.W.O.C. is a rope of sand. But Mr. Hillman wanted victories—Phil Murray and Homer Martin were getting them.

So far, the best type of agreement the T.W.O.C. has been able to achieve grew out of the general silk strike in August and September 1937. It was one of the few strikes the T.W.O.C. has called. It was all above the Mason and Dixon Line. The T.W.O.C. succeeded in getting a forty-hour week, a closed shop in a number of smaller firms, and a theoretical $15-a-week minimum, which is really a $13 week's wage for the vast majority. This miserable wage is the high-water mark in the drive so far. This was hailed as a great triumph because even in the North the great majority of workers was getting a good deal less. But experience has shown time and again that a really well-organized and militant campaign in *sweated* industries can raise wages anywhere from 50 to 100 per cent. So far the T.W.O.C. has increased the annual textile wage by $65 a year. Unfortunately, the depression has hit the industry very hard, and early in 1938 it was working only one-third of normal. The effect of such a catastrophe on the morale of hurriedly organized workers, with no trade union experience, can be imagined. And indeed the T.W.O.C. has had the largest turnover in membership of any CIO union, in spite of the fact that it has been winning most N.L.R.B. elections.

Yet paradoxically the T.W.O.C. *is* a success, though not in Mr. Hillman's Brain Trust sense. In one way or another, it has touched 450,000 textile workers, and that is permanently significant. Its sweep, for all its superficiality, has been for the first time on a national scale. And it has given the workers in this industry as a whole the idea of unionism. Not much more. But the idea is there, the curse is broken. That is why everybody senses that, though the drive in textiles cannot be compared to the drive in steel or in automobiles, it has none the less set textile labor on a new road. That the A. F. of L. could never have done. The CIO has done it in one year.

The Rubber Workers

The history of the United Rubber Workers offers a striking parallel to that of the United Automobile Workers, except that the rubber workers have escaped practically all factionalism.

The rubber workers first began to organize under the A. F. of L. in the summer of 1933. The federation organized about 4000 of them into 39 federal local unions. These locals grew by leaps and bounds, especially at

Goodyear. But as they grew, the A. F. of L. began to sabotage them, and sixteen crafts wrangled over their "jurisdiction." Within a year, the Goodyear local had shrunk to a few hundred members.

Like the automobile workers, the rubber workers are comparatively new to industry, and unspoiled by a long A. F. of L. tradition of sterility. A great many of them are hill-billies, and some of them had belonged to the Klan and other Know Nothing organizations. But their motive had always been a restless militancy against intolerable conditions. When they became converted to unionism, they gave it an almost religious devotion. All along, since the beginning of the NRA, they had been organizing under their own rank-and-file leadership. They insisted that the A. F. of L. grant them an industrial union charter, which was finally given to them in September 1935. But the charter was so restricted that all the semi-skilled and skilled workers were left out, and the organization drive was stymied.

Finally, in January 1936, 800 workers sat down in the Goodyear Akron plant, quickly closing down the plant, and drawing 14,000 workers into the strike. It was the first great sitdown strike in America. The country was fascinated by this new spectacle. The workers invited John L. Lewis to address them under the auspices of the United Rubber Workers, which officially was still in the A. F. of L. He assured them that the CIO would back them unstintingly, and invited them to join it. Lewis, as good as his word, sent in money and experienced organizers, and put the whole strength of the CIO behind them. On March 31 the strike was settled. The company recognized the union as the bargaining agent for its members, granted the thirty-six-hour week in the tire and tube division, corrected its indiscriminate layoff policy, and reinstated every striker. Wages were to be left to arbitration, and shop committees were set up in the various plants. Soon after, 10,000 workers struck at the Firestone Company. The strike was settled on April 18, with a verbal recognition of the union as the bargaining agency for its own members. The workers were granted a thirty-six-hour standard week, and time-and-a-half for all work above forty hours. No worker was to be discharged without a stipulated notice. Wages, as in the Goodyear settlement, were to be fixed by arbitration. After these two victorious strikes, the union considered itself really established. And in July 1936 it joined the CIO.

One of the reasons for the success of the United Rubber Workers is the progressive though uninspiring leadership of President S. H. Dalrymple. Dalrymple is himself a hill-billy, slow, honest, and painfully cautious. He faces factional quarrels with an air of not knowing what it's all about, which is largely true; and he judges each situation as it comes up entirely on its trade union merits, and with considerable common sense. He is extremely democratic, and his authority derives entirely from his popularity. The union has grown steadily and rapidly. Just before the Goodyear strike, it had a little more than 3000 members; in September 1936, it had 25,000; and in November 1937, it had 75,000 out of a possible 125,000.

Through 1937 it increased the number of its local unions from 47 to 135. Of these, 70 per cent had signed agreements in their plants, while the other 30 per cent had only verbal contracts. Wages have been raised substantially throughout the industry to an average of over one dollar an hour for men, and about 75 cents an hour for women.

In March 1938, the Goodrich Akron plant, which had only a verbal agreement with the union, proposed a $17\frac{1}{2}$ per cent wage cut, under the threat of moving part of the plant out of town. The union rejected the proposal, staged enormous mass demonstrations, and entered a complaint with the National Labor Relations Board that the company was using coercion to intimidate the workers before the pending election. The company immediately backed out, but a month later cynically flouted its commitments. It engaged in a series of violations of seniority rights and in other breaches of the agreement. Finally, in May 1938, 9000 workers went on strike. The strike was brief, for the company gave in. In the same month, the union renewed its agreement with Firestone, which called for paid vacations, seniority rights, reduction of work to a 24-hour week before layoffs, and retention of the old grievance machinery. Solicitation of membership by any other union on company time or property was forbidden. During the same period a strike of 3000 workers took place at Goodyear. It lasted only four days, but was marked by some violence and vigilante outbreaks. It was called off on May 30, and the union agreed to accept the verbal promise of the firm that the abuses of the grievance procedure, which had brought about the strike, would stop, and that a written agreement would be negotiated later.

The great task ahead is to organize the remaining 50,000 workers in the industry, who are scattered throughout the country. And the only way to accomplish this is to get the large corporations to sign national, rather than plant, agreements. The union has already succeeded in getting Firestone to deal on a national basis.

The Radio and Electrical Workers

As indicated by its name, the United Electrical, Radio and Machine Workers Union has grown through accretions in three vaguely related fields. It began with the radio workers in 1933, when the company union at the Philadelphia Storage Battery Company (Philco radio) converted itself, with the aid of the NRA, into an authentic local union which became the nucleus of organized labor in the field of radio and radio appliance manufacture. In 1937 this union of radio workers extended itself to include labor in the public utilities and in the electrical manufacturing corporations. And it also branched out to take in the workers in the light machine shops, which make minor electrical equipment, small machine tools, light machinery, and domestic gadgets of all kinds.

This illogical proliferation raises new and interesting problems of jurisdiction in industrial unionism. Industrial unionism is the organization of all the workers in one given industry. In theory, industrial unionism leads to vertical unionism, which is the amalgamation of all the industrial unions in allied fields. To illustrate: If all the workers on all the railroads were in one union, that would be an industrial union; if all the workers in every field of transportation—the sailors, the taxi and truck drivers, the subway and streetcar workers, the air pilots, the railroad workers—were in one union, that would be a vertical union. The United illustrates the folly of plunging into vertical unionism indiscriminately, without having first established a sound base in its own industry, of running off into ill-defined "allied" fields, in short, of running off in all directions. Such confusion raises a new type of jurisdictional difficulty. Just as the A. F. of L. is jurisdictionally too tight, so the United is jurisdictionally too loose. The reason for this jurisdictional dysentery was, as we shall see, purely political. The Stalinists, who control this union, wanted to get a foothold as quickly as they could in as many places as possible. Thus, the United organized, for no intrinsic industrial reason, the Mergenthaler Linotype Company, claiming it as a "light machine shop." After having won a majority of the thousand workers in this plant, the union came near destroying this local, because the organizers who were sent in were far more familiar with the Stalinist theory that Trotsky is a Japanese spy than with the problems of the linotype manufacturing industry. The situation got so bad that the workers in the Mergenthaler local requested the national CIO to deliver them from the bungling Stalinist politicians.

Under Stalinist direction, the United also forced the

gas workers in the Consolidated Edison Company to join District 50 of the United Mine Workers, solely because the Communist Party wanted to get a foothold in the miners' union. Among these "gas workers" there were a number of meter-readers, office workers, repair men, and others who felt that they were decidedly not miners. But they were not consulted. They found themselves juggled into the United Mine Workers. Articulate objectors were not notified of the union meetings in which this transfer was decided, and these meetings were packed with Stalinist sympathizers. This policy of the United to spread out beyond its normal jurisdiction led it into such far-off fields as toys, combs and brushes, pencils, almost anything. The excuse for all this was that as soon as unions in these industries were established, they would be turned over to their proper prospective organizations in the CIO.

After the workers in the Philco radio plant were recognized in 1933, nothing dramatic happened for the next two years. The movement spread to the Emerson Electric Manufacturing Company (Emerson radio), and gathered members here and there in radio shops all over the country. When a number of such local unions had been thus established, James P. Carey, the youthful leader of the Philco workers, appeared before the Executive Council of the A. F. of L. in January 1936, pleading for a national charter. The Council, with characteristic contempt for all self-organized labor, wanted these workers to join the International Brotherhood of Electrical Workers, as a Class B group without voting powers. The radio workers rejected this insulting offer in February 1936, and formed their own national organization. And in November they joined the CIO.

As is usually the case, the radio workers became really established through a series of strikes during the first half of 1937. After a 68-day strike of 2000 workers at the Emerson plant, ending on March 14, the union was recognized as the bargaining agency for its own members. It got a 5 per cent wage increase, and a minimum of 35 cents an hour. The next great strike took place at Philco. It lasted four weeks, involved 8500 workers, and ended on June 1. The union gained no official recognition, but a thirty-six-hour week was established, and the union clearly became a force to reckon with. Finally, the United conducted a four weeks' strike, ending on July 21, at the Radio Corporation of America in Camden, New Jersey, and won recognition as the bargaining agent for its own members. The contract provided that the wages were to be as high and the hours as few as in the industry in general, that the strikers were to be rehired without discrimination, and that a National Labor Relations Board election should determine whether the union was to represent all the workers. In the subsequent election, the United failed to get a majority, and had to be satisfied with representing only its own members. But here again, as at Philco and at Emerson, unionism has come to stay. Even a serious lockout by Philco in May 1938 could not shake it.

The union has also cracked the big electrical manufacturing plants. In April 1938, the General Electric Company signed a national agreement for one year, recognizing the United as the sole bargaining agent for its workers in all the plants in which it has a majority, and barring company unions. The contract, which covered 30,000 workers in six of the ten major plants of the corporation, provided for a forty-hour, five-day week, time-and-a-half for overtime, and wages equal to the prevailing rate in the industry. A conciliation clause forbade strikes and lockouts pending adjustment of disputes.

As I have indicated, the story of the United in the public utility field is a good deal more confused. The union branched out into this field in March 1937, when it was joined by Local B-752 of the International Brotherhood of Electrical Workers. This local union, while still in the A. F. of L., had conducted a drive in the Consolidated Edison Company in New York City. The local received a great deal of encouragement and help from the CIO. For this fraternizing with the CIO, the International took disciplinary action against Martin A. Wersing, the president, and Albert Stonkus, the business manager, of the local. Whereupon the local left the International and joined the United as Local 1212. The United found itself in the public utility field.

Early in 1938 it claimed almost 60 local unions with 15,000 members in 26 companies. These locals are scattered all the way from Wyoming to New York, and in some instances have won signed contracts, even closed shop agreements. But the organization drives of the United in this field are erratic and irresponsible. The director of its public utility division is Albert Stonkus, one of the most unscrupulous of the Stalinist politicians. During the drive to organize the Consolidated Edison, the Communist Party was working actively for a "united front" with the Catholic Church. The party distributed leaflets in which "Catholic workers" were exhorted "to join America's progressive front for peace and freedom against war and fascism," for Collective Security, and for the whole party program. This, the literature proclaimed, is in line with the views of "His Holiness Pope Leo XIII," and even of the present Pope, and is "good Catholic doctrine." The leaflet was printed in very fancy ecclesiastical type, including the final exhortation, "Join the Communist Party of America." The devout Catholic workers of course could not be snared by such tricks; among the more bigoted Protestant workers, the effect was to deepen their old religious antagonism to the Catholic Church; and the rest were either confused, or deeply outraged, by the nonsensical theory that the Catholic Church is a progressive force in the labor movement. The president of the union local in the Consolidated Edison is Martin A. Wersing, who is also at the head of the Association of Catholic Trade Unions, which publishes *The Catholic Worker*. This sheet is full of the most ignorant diatribes against Communism, real and Stalinist. But the Stalinists by no means object to it since their discovery that the Catholic Church is a

NEW UNIONS IN NEW FIELDS 223

"progressive" force in the labor movement. And Messrs. Stonkus and Wersing work together very nicely.

Even more confusing are the activities of the Stalinists in Michigan. Early in 1937 the United Automobile Workers undertook to organize for the CIO the Consumers Power Company in the Saginaw Valley. The campaign was directed by Bob Travis, then one of the leading members of the Unity faction of the U.A.W. But the real leader in this campaign was one Kempton Williams, who behind the scenes caused part of the power to be cut off in the Saginaw Valley on May 19 and on June 12. These shut-downs affected a population of over 400,000 people in more than 180 communities. Industries, hospitals, and private homes were without electric light or power, and thousands of workers were made idle. The union had demanded a wage increase of ten cents an hour, while the company would grant only five. The rest of the demands seemed arbitrable. John L. Lewis and Homer Martin were almost driven out of their minds by this performance. The sole purpose of the strike had been to embarrass the Martin administration of the U.A.W. The strikes were, of course, extremely brief, and the matter was finally settled by the union accepting the five cent increase. The agreement was to last till April 1, 1938.

Meanwhile, the CIO had appointed a Utility Workers Organizing Committee, with the idea of ultimately forming a separate industrial union in the utility field. And John Brophy maneuvered Albert Stonkus into the national directorship of this new committee. For seven weeks before the expiration of the agreement with the Consumers Power Company, Stonkus negotiated for a renewal of the contract for one year, with a guarantee of no wage reduction. The company offered a renewal for three months without wage cuts. But once again the Stalinists began an agitation for the seizure of the power stations, and on April 1 the union seized all plants, sub-stations, and construction bases in the Saginaw Valley area, threatening to cut off the power for nearly a thousand communities. Where there is no revolutionary situation, such tactics are inspired only by disruptive motives. And that was exactly the motive of the Stalinists in this case. Their only reason for this performance was the fact that they were being licked by the healthy forces of the CIO, especially among the automobile workers in Michigan. The main purpose of the whole maneuver, ordered directly by the Communist Party, was to stir up trouble in order to discredit the progressives in the Michigan CIO, who objected to such tactics. Lewis publicly reprimanded Stonkus for his irresponsibility. The strike was settled three days later, with the aid of Governor Murphy. The contract was renewed unaltered for four months, and both sides agreed to an N.L.R.B. election to determine whether the CIO, the A. F. of L., or a disguised company union was to represent the workers.

At its convention in September 1937, the United branched out to include labor in the light metal industry. The director of this new division was James Matles, for many years a leading Stalinist. Mr. Matles appointed a number of organizers whose only credentials were their loyalty to the Communist Party, and they invaded the light metal field. They didn't have the slightest idea of the problems in this variegated industry, and the campaign was pretty much a flop, causing a great deal of confusion among these workers. During the first half of 1938 the union signed forty-five renewals and ten new contracts covering some 25,000 workers, and gaining almost 2500 new members. It could effect no improvements, but it did defeat a series of concerted and dangerous lockouts by the employers. And it won ten out of eleven Labor Board elections.

The bitter and bizarre factionalism, created by the Stalinists, keeps the United in constant turmoil. The union has an arrangement with the *People's Press,* by which special editions of the paper are put out, with a few pages of general news and the rest of it devoted to being the official organ of the organization. The *People's Press* is one of the most rabid "innocent fronts" of the Communist Party. And in its vulgar sensationalism it outdoes the late *Graphic* of Mr. Macfadden. In November 1937, the United claimed a membership of 137,000, which it may well have.

The Transport Workers

The Transport Workers Union was first organized, mostly among the subway workers in New York City, in 1934. In 1936 the International Association of Machinists admitted it as Lodge No. 1547. The vast majority of subway workers are not, of course, machinists.

And from its foundation until early in 1936, the union tried to get into the Amalgamated Association of Street, Electric Railway and Motor Coach Employees, the old street car union in the A. F. of L. under the reactionary leadership of William B. Mahon, who has been losing street car strikes all over the country since 1893. But Mahon, in spite of the obvious and constant growth of the new union, would have nothing to do with it, on the ground that "New York can't be organized." Then suddenly, in the spring of 1937, when the A. F. of L. discovered that the union had several thousand members, it ordered its officers to turn their organization over to the A. F. of L. for proper "jurisdictional" dissection among some twenty crafts. The machinists and their helpers in the union were to remain as a local in the International Association of Machinists. In answer to this outrageous proposal, President Michael J. Quill took the Transport Workers into the CIO on May 10, 1937.

Quill, who in November 1937 was elected councilman in New York City on the American Labor Party ticket, is a militant Irishman. He is a successful organizer, and is largely responsible for the growth of the union. But ever since the union was founded he appears to have been a devout follower of the "party line," although he denies it. His predecessor as president of the union, Thomas O'Shea, who was a member of the Communist Party Fraction in the Transport Workers Union until January 1935, was ordered by the party to step aside for Quill, which he did. Opposition leaders in the union, who were part of this Fraction before they broke with the party, have stated in affidavit that at that time Quill, John Santo, the secretary-treasurer of the union, and Austin Hogan, president of the New York local, were all active members of Unit 19-S, Section 2, of the New York District of the Communist Party. Quill is a contributor to the *Daily Worker,* and his denial of any Stalinist entanglements is considerably discounted by the New York labor world. Be that as it may, in this union the Stalinists have played their least disruptive role, indeed have done a good deal of constructive work—partly because they controlled it from its very inception, and partly because the vast majority of the union are Irish Catholics, whom Quill understands thoroughly.

Within the short span of three years, the union has achieved closed shop agreements with the Interborough Rapid Transit Company, the Brooklyn-Manhattan Transit Company, the Third Avenue Railway Company, the New York City Omnibus Company, and the Fifth Avenue Coach Company, all in New York City. It has been refused recognition by New York City's independent subway system. To have gained mere union recognition from the New York transport companies is in itself no mean feat. And the contracts obtained for the various classes of subway workers have been, on the whole, quite fair. They provide for a 10 per cent wage increase, for a basic forty-four-hour week, and for a paid two weeks' vacation, which in this industry is a godsend to the men.

The union also signed up the five large taxi fleets in New York City—the Parmelee, Terminal, Bell, Atlas-Liberty, and Sunshine systems. There the agreements signed are miserable, though it is hard to conceive of any agreement in the New York taxi business which might help the men in the immediate future. Everybody in this field agrees that there are almost 10,000 too many cabs cruising the streets of the city. The contract abolished commission earnings and substituted a flat $15 a week for day drivers and $18 a week for night drivers—*provided* the men worked six full days a week. At Parmelee's union dues of $1.25 are checked off by the company. Unfortunately these wages are only drawing accounts, for they were computed on the basis of former percentage earnings; and if the take-in of a driver fails to justify his wage, the company is free to fire him. In August 1938 an authentic anti-union strike broke out at Parmelee's. This curious strike was quickly settled when the company agreed to abolish the check-off. The married drivers simply cannot spare $1.25 a month for dues.

Outside of New York the union has a number of agreements with various trolley and bus lines throughout the country. It claims a national membership of 80,000, of which 34,000 are in the New York subway system. The latter figure is indisputable. But the most objective estimate gives a national membership of 55,000 at most.

Of late there is considerable progressive opposition stirring to the Stalinist leadership. The main demand of the opposition is the ousting of the "party line" and the introduction of strict trade union democracy.

The Shoe Workers

The shoe industry has always been cursed with a multiplicity of competing and fratricidal unions. The old Boot and Shoe Workers Union of the A. F. of L., known as the Boot and Shoe, was universally hated by the rank and file, for in time it became literally a strike-breaking agency. It got control of the various New England shoe centers by stepping in on strikes of competing unions, and signing up with the employers. The workers referred to it always as the "label union." For the racket of the Boot and Shoe was to sell to the boss the A. F. of L. union label, over which it had sole control, and then let him run the shop as he pleased behind it.

The result was that there constantly were break-away movements from the Boot and Shoe, which explains why there were so many petty and weak shoe workers' organizations in the old shoe centers of New England. The more stable of them were the Shoe Workers Protective Association, the Brockton Brotherhood, and the National Shoe and Leather Workers Union. In New York City most of the shoe workers had been in the Shoe Workers Industrial Union, an affiliate of the Trade Union Unity League. And some time after the T.U.U.L. had dissolved, they joined the Boot and Shoe.

When the CIO came on the scene, unionism in the shoe industry was at a very low ebb and in utter confusion, both in New England and in New York. In the new shoe centers in the South and in the Middle West there was no organization of any kind. And the CIO formed a Shoe Workers Organizing Committee under the chairmanship of Powers Hapgood. Hapgood is a member of the Socialist Party, a Harvard graduate, who for years had been associated with John Brophy in the United Mine Workers in opposition to John Lewis. He is a member of the happy Hapgood family—Hutchins, William, and Norman—who for three decades have enlivened American middle-class radicalism with their Utopian views, with which they have had the sincerity to experiment in many fields. The most desperately sincere of them is William's son, Powers Hapgood. Powers is utterly naïve, generously confused, and as selfless as he is courageous.

The Shoe Workers Organizing Committee gathered about 16,000 workers in the various shoe districts into one union, and in March 1937 established the United Shoe Workers Union. In August 1937, most of the 10,000 shoe workers in New York City voted, under an N.L.R.B. election, to join the new union, and left the Boot and Shoe. Since then, the United Shoe Workers has grown by thousands more, mainly through a series of heroic strikes in the corrupt and vigilante-ridden New England shoe towns. In these strikes, Hapgood and the other leaders were jailed and beaten and "ridden out of town." But when it was all over, the union could claim over 50,000 members. The agreements signed managed to clinch, with slight improvements, the prevailing conditions in the industry, and that was quite a feat, for the new depression was playing havoc in the shoe centers.

At its first annual convention in November 1937 in

Milwaukee, Powers Hapgood was elected president. But four Stalinists, representing the four important locals in New York City, got on the General Executive Board. The slate was a compromise; and the Stalinists voted for Hapgood on the theory that they could manage him. And indeed, Hapgood is very strong when facing the boss, but completely ingenuous when dealing with "revolutionaries"; for the one thing he can't stand is to have anyone claim that there is space to the "left" of him. Since the convention, the Stalinists have been hounding all progressives who oppose them, and have kept the union in a perpetual state of upheaval. The locals in New York, which more or less dominate the union nationally, are completely Stalinist-controlled. The Los Angeles shoe workers, on the other hand, have officially joined the opposition to Bridges on the West Coast, leaving the bewildered Powers Hapgood in the center.

The Fur Workers

While in the other needle trades the progressive administrations had triumphed over the Stalinists in the factional struggles which shook these unions in the 1920's, the Stalinists were victorious in the Fur Workers Union at that time. And they have kept control of it ever since. Ben Gold is the only avowed Communist Party member in the presidency of an established international union. One of the reasons for the Stalinist victory in the Fur Workers Union was that the leading export-import firms in the industry, which control the market, have large Soviet contracts, and they used their influence with the manufacturers to get them to recognize the Stalinist faction in the union.

The Fur Workers Union is the classic example of how cynically anti-democratic a union can be under Stalinist control. Anybody who fails to jump at the crack of the whip is immediately attacked as a sell-out, stool-pigeon, and "Trotskyite," and sometimes even framed and expelled. Thus, in 1937, one of the leading progressives in Local 70 in New York City, Charles Soulounias, was framed on charges of accepting "bribes" in the form of checks from the employers, and was expelled from the union, though his local staunchly defended him. For everybody knew very well that Soulounias, who for a time ran a job printing shop, had received the checks for printing work done for various fur jobbers. The fight split the local wide open. Finally Soulounias was reinstated by court action.

An even more serious disruption occurred in Toronto. There the Gold administration accused Max Federman, manager of the two powerful locals 40 and 100, of the theft of $2000 from the unemployment fund of the union. Federman was expelled. A committee elected by the two local unions completely exonerated him. Federman is a leader of long and unblemished reputation, and his members knew exactly why this $2000 had been withdrawn from the treasury without appearing on the books. Now and then a union has to use its funds quietly in all sorts of emergencies—obtaining police neutrality during a strike, for instance. The upshot of it all was that the union had to kick out, along with Federman, Locals 40 and 100. Federman, too, has since been exonerated in court. And the Toronto furriers have joined the A. F. of L. They did not want to go back to the A. F. of L., but they felt they had no choice.

When the Communist Party decided to switch the unions under its influence from the A. F. of L. to the CIO, the Fur Workers Union switched accordingly overnight at its convention in Chicago in May 1937. Most of the delegates were for the change. But they could not help but be bewildered because until the day of the switch they had been assured that the A. F. of L. was their permanent home. And the rank and file resented bitterly the undemocratic procedure on this vital issue. Nobody outside the Gold clique had an inkling of what was afoot.

In July 1938 the union had a national election. By that time the opposition had become so strong that the Gold machine could afford to take no chances. Elections in the needle trades always last one day, so that nobody can take the ballots "home to sleep with." This time the Stalinists decided to run the elections for three days, and they refused to grant watchers to the opposition. For three days a minor civil war raged around the polls. The United Progressive Furriers issued a statement which was distributed by the thousands in the fur district. They charged that "members of the Communist party have carried on a campaign of terror among the polling places. The noise, the chaos, the wild persecution of every suspicious-looking member . . . all helped to create a repulsive and disgusting atmosphere about the elections. . . . Paid officers [filled] the air with vile epithets flung at opposition candidates." The Stalinists took "the ballots from members and [voted] for the administration slate at a table in the open."

The New York press reported all these doings in considerable detail, and the entire fur market was in an uproar. Out of some 7000 votes, the opposition writes, "the bureaucrats were forced to grant more than 2000 votes to the opposition, which is the best proof that the expression of protest by the workers against the Administration was very strong."

The union today has some 35,000 members, which means that it has practically the entire fur industry organized. As in the case of the other needle trades, relations with the employers are of long standing, and the agreements signed are usually renewals. Strikes and lockouts are often considered as almost inevitable periodic shut-downs during negotiations. But early in 1938 a serious strike broke out which lasted for fifteen weeks.

This strike, which began as a lockout, was brought about by the refusal of the Stalinists to renew the contract with the employers, who had agreed to various changes. Dubinsky, Zimmerman, and other leaders in the big needle trades—who, in spite of their critical attitude toward the Gold administration, always play the part of Big Brothers to the Fur Workers Union—advised them that the depression made their new demands impracticable. But they would not listen. The strike dragged on for almost four months, and finally was settled in July. The workers received an increase of from one to two dollars a week, which increase the employers had been willing to take up in the very beginning. Moreover, this increase is available only to the "permanent" workers, who constitute a small minority, for it includes only those who had steady employment in May 1938.

The issue of "permanent" as against "temporary" work always was, and still is, the central and most vital issue for labor in this industry. The old agreement provided that during six months of the year work had to be equally divided between permanent workers and all available union members. Workers hired during this period, which more or less coincided with the busy season, could be fired after six weeks. The furriers employed during the other six months had a contractual right to their job. The new agreement extends the period of work-division to eight months. All this means that the employers will in future concentrate on hiring their permanent labor during the other four months of the year. For the union it is a purely arithmetical gain on paper.

The rank and file appreciates that the new agreement was a setback, certainly not a "victory" worth a strike of fifteen weeks' duration. They had gone into the strike primarily to win the right to their jobs, as it is enjoyed by labor in the men's and women's clothing industries. They really lost, and they are well aware of it. And they are especially annoyed by the demagogic claims of "victory" by the Stalinist administration—an annoyance which the opposition is exploiting to the utmost. Today the Stalinists, though still on top, are rapidly losing control over the rank and file in this union which they had dominated for a dozen years.

The Aluminum Workers

The aluminum workers were organized into six Federal union locals by the A. F. of L. in 1933. These locals were being continually raided by the various crafts, each of them claiming jurisdiction over some of the members. And all their efforts to obtain an industrial charter from the A. F. of L. were in vain.

Finally, the largest of these local unions, in New Kensington, Pennsylvania, came into open conflict with the A. F. of L. It refused to turn over $27,000 which it had in its treasury for organizing purposes. And in March 1937 it called a conference of the other aluminum locals in order to form an international union, and to join the CIO. William Green took the New Kensington local to court, but fortunately lost the case.

On April 13, 1937, the national convention met, and organized the Aluminum Workers of America. Thirty-one delegates representing ten plants and 12,000 workers elected N. A. Zonorich as president of the new union, which immediately joined the CIO. Zonorich is slow, steady, and cautious, but a real progressive with socialist leanings. On May 10, 1937, the new union called a strike at the plant of the Aluminum Company of America at

Alcoa, Tennessee, which employs 5200 workers. Nominally, the local union of this plant was still affiliated with the A. F. of L. But more than 3000 workers responded, and stayed out until July 11. The A. F. of L. did everything in its power to break the strike. It expelled Fred Wetmore, the leader of the strike, and it approved the reopening of the plant on July 8, which precipitated a fight in which two men were killed.

Under the leadership of Zonorich, the union has been steadily increasing its membership. It even has a few local contracts. The main problem of the union is to crack the Aluminum Company of America, which is owned by the Mellon family. The Mellon monopoly pays no attention to labor, to the N.L.R.B., to hell or high water. Many of its plants in small God-forsaken communities have local company unions. Union organizers are put on the first train out of town. Zonorich has tried to meet the problem by asking the N.L.R.B. to certify the Aluminum Workers Union as the collective bargaining agency in the industry, either by investigation or through elections. But in spite of all these difficulties, the workers are joining the union, not in a rush, but surely and steadily; and out of the 40,000 workers in the industry, 15,000 are dues-paying members of the CIO.

The Flat Glass Workers

The Federation of Flat Glass Workers was organized in 1934, as an independent industrial union. Later in the year, the A. F. of L. took it in, and forgot about it.

And in February 1937 this union found its right place in the CIO.

The glass industry is controlled by two monopolies, the Pittsburgh Plate Glass Company and the Libby-Owens-Ford Glass Company. These two companies supply almost all the glass for the automobile industry, and during the great sitdown strike at General Motors 14,000 glass workers saw their chance and walked out. They returned to work before the General Motors strike was settled, because the CIO wanted them to supply glass to Chrysler and other competitors of General Motors, in order to bring the latter to terms. The glass workers gained a wage increase of eight cents an hour and other concessions, and virtual recognition in the individual plants. But they were not strong enough to sign national agreements with the two monopolies until early in 1938. These national agreements, covering 20,000 workers, provided for the maintenance of existing wage rates with upward adjustments in certain classifications, a six-hour day, a thirty-six-hour week, and machinery for settling grievances.

During the summer of 1937 a serious crisis developed in the union. President Glen W. McCabe was accused by his General Executive Board of using the union publication for personal publicity and of appropriating union funds for personal use. McCabe refused to call a meeting of the board, which was bent on ousting him, and began collecting dues directly from the various locals. Two conventions held within a short space of time failed to adjust the conflict. At last the CIO sent an investigating committee, which induced McCabe to withdraw from the union in the interests of peace. The CIO then appointed Paul Fuller, its regional director in Cincinnati, as provisional president. Fuller is a worker who for many years has devoted himself to workers' education. Plodding and progressive, he is giving the union his best, which is a steady and unexciting administration.

The Woodworkers

The International Woodworkers of America is composed of lumberjacks, loggers, and saw-mill workers, who for a number of years had been in the Brotherhood of Carpenters, where they had no voting privileges. This caste arrangement made it impossible for them to buck the Hutcheson machine, though they greatly outnumbered the carpenters. Finally in July 1937, they broke away from the A. F. of L. and joined the CIO. In revenge for this defection, the carpenters declared a boycott on all the wood cut and prepared by CIO labor.

The president of the union is Harold Pritchett, with headquarters in Seattle. He is completely under the sway of Harry Bridges, and follows the Communist Party line, without knowing much about it. The largest local of the union in the East, Local 105 in New York, is led by Sam Nessin, who spends most of his time playing the Communist Party game. Under party direction, he attempted to organize packing-box workers, smoking-pipe makers, piano builders, and other such "woodworkers."

The Stalinist disruption within the union, the A. F. of L. boycott, the reactionary attitude of some of the northwestern State governments, and the incompetence of the Pritchett crowd are keeping the union weak and in constant hot water. It has signed no contracts of any significance. Pritchett claims 100,000 members. According to the best opinion available, this union has approximately 25,000 members.

The American Communications Association

The American Communications Association is an outgrowth of the American Radio Telegraphists' Association, the latter still forming a separate section in the union. The A.C.A. has jurisdiction over the workers in the Western Union, the Postal Telegraph, the non-manufacturing end of the American Telephone and Telegraph Company, the operators in the Radio Corporation of America, and of course over the radio operators on the ships.

Mervyn Rathborne, president of the union, had been an organizer way back in 1931 for the Commercial Telegraphers Union of the A. F. of L., from which he was dropped in 1932. He then founded the West Coast Commercial Radio Men's Protective Association, a purely personal paper organization, which he merged into the American Radio Telegraphists' Association, then also a paper union affiliated with the Communist Trade Union Unity League. He became the head of the new A.R.T.A., but was ordered by the Communist Party to remain on the West Coast as the right-hand man of Harry Bridges.

The A.R.T.A. joined the CIO in April 1937; and at its convention in August it expanded into the American Communications Association. Mervyn Rathborne, whose entire time is devoted to trouble-shooting for the Communist Party in the maritime industry, was ordered East. And today he is one of the leading Stalinists in the maritime unions on the East Coast.

Outside of the marine telegraphers, the main strength of the A.C.A. is in the Postal Telegraph Company, with which it signed a national agreement, with a slight increase in wages, in March 1938. It also has an agreement with the Radio Corporation of America, covering more than 1000 workers in the United States and in Hawaii, with the Globe Wireless Corporation, with the French Cable and Telegraph Company, and the Mackay Cable Corporation. The A.C.A. announces its agreements with great bombast, but on analysis they boil down to very little. At the national CIO conference in November 1937, the union claimed 10,000 members, though it certainly had no more than 6000 or 7000. At its own convention in June 1938, the A.C.A. claimed a membership of 15,000, which expert opinion boils down to about 12,000.

Farm and Cannery Workers

The very name of the United Cannery, Agricultural, Packing and Allied Workers of America is the best index to its utter confusion in a welter of unrelated fields. From its very foundation in Denver on July 9, 1937, its leadership has been nothing but an "innocent front" for the Communist Party. The Denver convention was financed by the CIO, and Lewis was persuaded by John Brophy and other Stalinist sympathizers to start this mongrel organization with a large initial subsidy.

The Stalinists claimed that 56 organizations representing 100,000 workers met at Denver. The most important bodies were the Southern Tenant Farmers Union, the Sharecroppers Union of Alabama, the Federal Agricultural Workers (a group of locals in the A. F. of L.), and various independent farmers' organizations. The Southern Tenant Farmers Union had been formed some time before in the Southwest, under the leadership of Norman Thomas and other Socialists; it was progressive, militant, and realistic. The Sharecroppers Union of Alabama, organized by the Stalinists, had also done some splendid work among the sharecroppers in the deep South, who didn't know Stalinism from any other ism. These two organizations had finally come together in 1936, and have been co-operating since. On the other hand, the Federal Agricultural Workers, largely Stalinist-led, were scattered and ineffective groups. As for the various farm organizations which joined the Denver convention, most of them were typical granges whose radicalism goes up and down with the price of wheat.

This mélange of groups at the convention was run by one Donald Henderson, who was elected president of the new union. Henderson is a former instructor in economics at Columbia College, where his contract was not renewed by Professor Tugwell, because he neglected his own work and his classes in order to devote his time to various Stalinist activities. This affront to his "academic freedom" made him a great hero to the Communist Party, and the Trade Union Unity League put him in charge of the strike at Seabrook Farms at Bridgton, New Jersey. During June and July 1934, Comrade Henderson ran the strike into the ground. And that made him in Stalinist eyes the great expert in organizing agricultural labor.

The new mongrel union has conducted a number of strikes, almost all of which were failures. It has a few casual farm laborers here and there, a few sharecroppers elsewhere, and a number of Mexican and Filipino workers in the Southwest. The Southern Tenant Farmers Union, which fortunately has kept its organization intact, is still doing excellent work among the Southwestern sharecroppers, but entirely on its own, paying no attention to the Stalinist clique.

This clique has developed into a positive danger to agricultural labor, especially in California. Once a group of progressives in Congress, all stanch friends of the CIO, warned John Lewis of this danger. Wherever the union tries to organize farm workers, whose conditions are just plain barbarous, it arouses every vigilante force against these workers, whom it takes into a strike without the least organization. Every experienced and progressive organizer in this field has been either ignored or hounded out of the union. As the editor of a California labor paper, devoted to the problems of agricultural labor, stated: "The following represents the sum total of the past year's efforts in the CIO's drive to unionize upwards of 250,000 farm workers in California." The "following" consists of a large blank space.

In the canning industry, the union has done even less, if possible. Henderson claims to have 120,000 members. The claim is utterly fantastic. The best opinion is that the union has somewhere around 20,000.

CHAPTER IX

WHITE COLLAR AND PROFESSIONAL WORKERS

The Newspaper Guild

FOR YEARS newspaper work to everybody in it, from cub to editor, was a romantic "game." And part of that attitude was that wages, hours, and conditions did not really matter. What mattered was the high adventure. The bosses shared this attitude, and exploited it to the limit.

Until the American Newspaper Guild came on the scene, this high adventure paid on an average of $38 for a week of 48 to 50 hours; and 25 per cent of the reporters made less than $20. No job was less secure. The reporter was fired, or he quit, as befits an adventurous spirit, at the drop of a hat. The boss, "a newspaper man himself," told him to get out; and the reporter usually told the boss just what he thought of him. Of course, such a temperamental mutual relation did not lend itself particularly to contractual dealings.

In time, however, the "game" became too obviously a business, and on the big papers a mass production industry. Even before Section 7A of the NRA, there had been sporadic efforts to organize the editorial workers. The A. F. of L. assigned them to the International Typographical Union. And for years the I.T.U. used to raise its own wages by threatening to organize the city room. Finally the editorial workers organized themselves.

The idea of a newspapermen's union was born at the copy desk of the Cleveland *Press* late one afternoon in the midsummer of 1933. The moving spirits were two reporters, Lloyd White and Garland Ashcraft. Ashcraft suggested that a telegram be sent to President Roosevelt, outlining the deplorable condition of the editorial workers throughout the country, and asking that something be done to better their lot under the New Deal. The crowd chipped in, and the telegram was sent. By inadvertence a carbon copy of the wire, signed by Ashcraft, reached the front office. Ashcraft was called in, and rumors of dire consequences spread through the city room. But Ashcraft was told: "Never mind." The scare, however, made White and Ashcraft realize that the newspapermen had better organize to protect themselves. And soon a nucleus of newspapermen from the *Press,* the *Plain Dealer,* and the *News* was formed. The question immediately arose whether the new organization was to be a professional club or a regular trade union. It was decided to make it a union, which precipitated the first division in the Guild. Within the next few months, 34 *Plain Dealer* members were to withdraw on the ground that trade union membership might interfere with their objectivity as editorial writers and reporters.

The Cleveland Guild was organized on August 3. A constitution was adopted, and officers elected, with Lloyd White as president. In the meantime, Heywood

Broun had written a column advocating the organization of all editorial workers. The Cleveland Guild sent him a telegram saying that they were already organized, and nominated him as president of what they hoped would be a national organization. They immediately started a heavy mail campaign throughout the country. Cleveland helped to found chapters in Minneapolis-St. Paul, in Toledo, Columbus, Cincinnati, Detroit, and Rockford, Illinois. On December 15, twelve guilds met at Washington for their first national convention. Broun was elected president, and White first vice-president.

In those early days, Broun served mainly as a social front for the new organization. He never could be made to do the hard digging in organizing work, to take a hand in preparing reports or drafts or statistical material, while the industry was being codified under the NRA or after. But he functioned well and naturally in the limelight. He was extremely valuable in publicizing the new union. And for this job as semi-fashionable public relations counsel he had just the right temper and talents.

Mr. Broun has been for years a journalistic Broadway character, a sort of left-wing man about town, who knows all the right people with the left touch. He has that skin-deep charm of the middle-aged *enfant terrible,* who can make the Upper Classes take the "class struggle" as a canapé with their cocktails, and titillate the middle-class intelligentsia into a sense of "proletarian" boldness. With real labor Mr. Broun has little contact.

But real labor understands him quite well. "He has prayed in so many churches in the past dozen years," says the official organ of the International Ladies' Garment Workers Union, "that his innocuous dilettantism neither shocks nor offends any longer. One gets to anticipate balderdash from Mr. Broun, when he picks the labor movement as a topic for entertainment."

In the course of years, Mr. Broun has become the living embodiment of his daily column. As one of his friends put it: "He has no private intellectual life." He thinks and talks in pieces of 1200 words. And if the idea is too long, you can just cut out a paragraph or two anywhere you like. Like his column, he is mellow without being wise, critical without the least gift for analysis or knowledge of social forces, and for all his felicity he is oddly lacking in either form or content. Mr. Broun is the natural victim of the national vaudeville of the daily column. Only his daily song and dance is executed on the "left" side of the stage.

For over a decade, Mr. Broun has been the amateur weathervane for all the winds of liberal doctrine. Successively, he has drunk toasts to birth control, Lucy Stoneism, socialism, Farmer-Laborism, what-have-youism, and finally Stalinism. And he was always a strong defender of civil liberties, until Stalinism became the most fashionable form of revolutionary bohemianism. He is given to periodic crushes on strong men and movements. And so he fell head over heels for John L. Lewis and the CIO—which is splendid, though the CIO is not a college play but our most important social movement since the Civil War.

He also fell for the cocktail communism of our literary and pseudo-literary world during the past three years, an intellectual fashion which the Moscow murders have considerably shaken. These two hobbies made him feel good and hard, which is his great ambition—though what really happened was that he merely became unfair to all opponents in the best style of our literary "proletarians." Since 1935 he has been the journalistic troubleshooter for the Stalinists in his daily column, as much as possible; and in the liberal weeklies, first in the *Nation*, and then in the *New Republic*, all the way. Every time the Communist Party press is after somebody in a big way, Mr. Broun is certain to make the same attack, point by point, in one of his columns.

Broun's personality gave the tone to the New York Guild, and through it to the national organization, at least until the St. Louis convention of the Guild in July 1937. In the beginning, the publishers were under the vague impression that the Guild was a sort of newspapermen's club. But all along the rank and file of newspapermen were flocking into the Guild in all seriousness. To them, the Guild was a labor union. And when the National Association of Newspaper Publishers woke up to that fact, it got all excited about this new danger to the "freedom of the press." Of all men, Colonel R. R. McCormick, owner of the Chicago *Tribune*, one of the most reactionary papers in America, became violently agitated on that issue. Other Bourbon publishers, to whom freedom of the press had always meant the unabridged right to hire and fire, and to color all the news from their own Tory point of view, became all hot and bothered for fear the union would rob the reporter of his sacred prerogative of writing as he pleased.

But the Guild was getting on. It won strikes at the Newark *Ledger* in 1934, at the *Amsterdam News* and the *Jewish Daily Bulletin* in 1935, at the Seattle *Post-Intelligencer* and the Milwaukee *Wisconsin News* in 1936, at the Long Island *Daily Press* and the Brooklyn *Daily Eagle* in 1937. In almost every case it won signed agreements, which usually, however, recognized not the national Guild but the local chapter. On the whole, the Guild won even better agreements where no strike was necessary, especially in New York City. It signed contracts with the New York *Daily News,* the *World-Telegram,* and the *Post.* Through the country it has agreements with the Scripps-Howard newspapers, the Cleveland *News,* the Hearst papers in Chicago and Milwaukee, and a number of other papers. The agreements have a certain basic pattern. They provide for a five-day week and an eight-hour day, for paid vacations, and for a graduated severance pay upon dismissal. Practically all agreements provide for minimum wages and wage increases. The minimums range, depending on the length of service and the nature of the work, from $25 to $40 a week; and the increases are also graded, the lower brackets receiving the largest raises. On the whole, the increase that the Guild has been able to obtain for its more poorly paid members is about 10 per cent.

As the Guild grew, however, the emergence of the Stalinist party line became ever more visible in the national leadership. Heywood Broun, Jonathan Eddy, the executive vice-president of the Guild, and Carl Randau, president of the New York Guild—known as the Broun clique—follow the party line with that peculiar fidelity with which the "fellow-travelers" cling to it. And what is especially exasperating to the radicals and progressives who oppose them is their cynical denial that there is such a thing as the "party line." Yet the Broun outfit, and his claque throughout the country, display toward all progressive opposition an undemocratic and high-handed scorn. Leading progressives who are critical of the machine are told to stay away from national headquarters. "We don't like you," said Mr. Eddy to a reporter who had organized an important guild, for which activity he had lost his job, and who is equally active now in the Guild chapter on his new job.

Needless to say, there was never anything more "revolutionary" or "communist" about the Broun clique than about the Stork Club, the Algonquin, or the Astor bar, where they hang out. But in the last two years their tactics have served to split the union. In the smaller towns and on the country papers, where the majority of our newspapermen still work, they frightened away a great many prospective members. In the metropolitan centers, all critical opposition was stifled. And since reporters are a pretty independent lot, a good many of them quietly dropped out. Dozens of such unobtrusive resignations by stanch union men have taken place all over the country—on the New York *Times* and *Herald Tribune,* various Scripps-Howard papers, other great newspapers throughout the country.

The whole factional issue finally broke out in the Guild convention in St. Louis in July 1937. The national officers came with a cut and dried program, on which no one beyond the inner circle had been consulted. Quite rightly, the administration wanted the Guild to shift from its recent A. F. of L. affiliation to the CIO. But as part of this shift, it insisted, in the name of "industrial unionism," that the Guild take in the commercial departments, not as affiliates but as an integral part of the union. To be sure, industrial unionism holds that all workers in one industry should be in a single union. But at the same time industrial unionism does not require a strategy which would weaken a young organization. Thus even Broun did not demand the fusion of the editorial workers with the printing crafts because the typographical workers just wouldn't join. The opposition under Robert M. Buck, president of the Washington Guild, was not against organizing the business and advertising departments. It was for helping them to organize in some kind of association with the Guild. In fact, progressive opponents of the Broun machine had organized chapters of non-editorial workers in several cities. But they justly feared that if all newspaper workers, editorial and business, went into one organization, the editorial workers would be swamped by the workers in the business offices, whose problems were very different.

But the Broun clique insisted that the two resolutions —the resolution in favor of joining the CIO and that for taking in the commercial workers—could be no more separated than "corned beef and cabbage." This steamroller policy had been decided upon and worked out by Broun, John Brophy, and Len De Caux in the national headquarters of the CIO. And the impression was conveyed that John L. Lewis backed this program to the utmost. When Lewis was asked about it later by a member of the opposition, he sensibly replied that he felt the two issues should really have been dealt with separately.

To force the issue through the convention, the Broun followers introduced the usual "debating society" resolutions so dear to the party line. Resolutions were introduced against fascism in Spain, for labor's independent political action, for greater support of the WPA, and for the reformation of the Supreme Court, which at that time was the most controversial issue in the country. The majority of the delegates were personally for the principles expressed in these resolutions. But many of them felt that a growing and still vulnerable union of news-writers should not commit its membership officially on such controversial issues, especially since these issues were introduced as a political red herring. Yet anyone who objected to the dragging in of these "debating society" resolutions was immediately labeled as a reactionary, an emissary of the boss, and practically a buddy of General Franco. The very idea that Bob Buck, who has been an indefatigable worker in the radical and labor movement all his life, is on the right of Heywood Broun, is downright comical to those who know the careers of both men.

The Broun-Eddy-Randau machine rejected all proposals for a referendum on the various issues, though it was demanded by the delegations from Washington, Columbus, Minneapolis-St. Paul, and other chapters. But after the convention, the opposition enlisted enough chapters to use its right under the Guild constitution to force a referendum. In the meantime, the Broun clique used the *Guild Reporter* to present the administration's side of the case without the least regard for fair play.

Seven thousand members did not vote at all. Of the others, 3392, as against 1691, voted for joining the CIO, while only 3013 as against 2054 voted for taking in the commercial and advertising departments. The resolution against fascism in Spain was actually lost by 2592 to 2409, though I dare say that over 95 per cent of Guild members are anti-fascist. The vote on the fascist issue simply expressed the outrage of many rank-and-file members against the Stalinoid assumption that a vote against Messrs. Broun, Eddy, and Randau on a union issue meant that they were in favor of fascism. The vote for labor's independent political action was 2774 to 2202. And 2815 voted for greater support of the WPA, as against 2178; while 2685 to 2271 voted for Roosevelt's court reform. The closeness of the vote is the measure of the revolt against the Broun administration. For, obviously, a great many people voted for the administration lest they endanger the union as a whole.

Some members of the opposition were also against the "Guild shop," a slightly modified form of the closed shop. In a closed shop, none but union workers can be hired; the Guild shop provides that non-members can be hired, but must join the Guild after a certain time. Again, those who opposed the Guild shop were not against it on principle. But they knew that the Guild shop could not be enforced on the vast majority of papers, and felt that it was poor tactics to demand it, and then be forced to compromise. The fact is, that the union has hardly any Guild shop agreements. In almost every contract, it has had to waive this demand.

At its fifth annual convention in Toronto in June 1938, the Guild was able to report a membership of 16,797, of which 3292 were in the commercial departments of the industry. It had contracts with eighty-two newspapers and various news and photo services. Forty of these contracts had been signed since the last convention. The officers of the union were re-elected without much opposition. In fact, the opposition in the Newspaper Guild has lost out considerably since the St. Louis convention. The administration was even able to put through a resolution which will make it more difficult for a dissident group to call for a referendum against the will of the leadership, as was done after the St. Louis convention in 1937. Henceforth, ten locals in five states will not be sufficient to call for a national referendum. To initiate one, it will be necessary to have at least eleven local chapters in five states, comprising at least five per cent of the national membership. This last provision was a compromise, for Heywood Broun had demanded that ten per cent of the membership be the minimum requisite for a referendum.

The opposition in the Guild has lost, at least for the time being, because it is fighting primarily for the principle of trade union democracy, and little more. In the United Automobile Workers, in the National Maritime Union, in the Fur Workers, the Communist Party line was wrecking the unions in the *economic* field, which accounts for the growing revolt of the rank and file against Stalinist control. The Guild, on the other hand, has been amazingly successful in improving the lot of the editorial writer. It has given him more money, greater security, more leisure, and greater dignity as a human being. But it has achieved all this in spite of the tactics of its national officers. It has achieved all this partly because of the loyal aid of other unions, the A. F. of L. printing unions no less than the CIO; and mainly because the newspaper men are probably the most intelligent crowd in American labor. Behind their hard-boiled attitude they hide a great devotion to their ideals, which comes from their unique experience in observing every facet of our social life. And they have used their knowledge of publicity with great acumen in enlisting public sympathy.

The Office Workers

In 1926 the A. F. of L. expelled a number of left-wing groups from the old Bookkeepers, Stenographers and Accountants Union. These groups reorganized themselves, and in 1928 joined the Communist Trade Union Unity League. After that both the A. F. of L. and the Communist unions languished until the NRA, which did very little to revive them.

When in 1935 the Communist Party decided to dissolve the T.U.U.L., it told the office workers to go back into the A. F. of L., and most of them joined the B. S. & A. U. as individuals, and soon they dominated it. And like all Stalinist-controlled unions not organized directly by the CIO, it did not join the CIO until 1937. As late as April of that year, it was calling conferences all over the country to organize the office workers into the A. F. of L., and it would not permit the question of joining the CIO to be raised even in whispers. "Certainly no A. F. of L. union of white collar and professional workers," read the official call, "can refuse to seriously consider the possible assistance it may render towards increasing the prestige and strength of the A. F. of L. among other white collar and professional workers."

When the Communist Party line changed on the CIO question, this union shifted almost overnight, joined the CIO in May 1937, and called a national convention of white-collar unions which constituted itself the United Office and Professional Workers of America. In November of that year it claimed 25,000 members, and in March 1938 it raised the claim to 45,000. In fact the union has about 16,000 members, a good many of whom have joined since it entered the CIO. This figure had been checked in various ways for purposes of representation at the last convention. About half of the new members, around 4000, are insurance agents, organized in Local 30, which so far has no contracts with the insurance companies.

The international union has done fairly well where one might expect, in the offices of various CIO and other labor unions, and in liberal and radical organizations which are committed to the principle of unionism. There the minimum union wage for a stenographer is $21 a week, and for unskilled office workers, $18. But in most of these offices both the wage-rate and the working conditions are above the minimal standards. The union is also making good progress in the book and magazine publishing fields, where it has a practically independent subsidiary, the Book and Magazine Guild. The Guild has agreements with such publishing houses as the Viking Press, Modern Age Books, Random House (Modern Library), the Vanguard Press; and with *Asia*, the *New Republic*, the *Nation*, and a few other magazines. Its contracts provide for a closed or preferential shop, a $21-a-week minimum, and a five-day week of thirty-five hours, time-and-a-half for overtime, vacations with pay, and a grievance machinery.

Unfortunately the international union has made no dent whatever on the big corporations employing thousands of office workers, for which it can hardly be blamed. The job of organizing the white collar masses is extremely difficult. For one thing, clerical workers, unlike manual labor, are lower middle class in background and in outlook. For another, the middle class, in its desire to have its children rise above manual work, overproduces stenographers and typists and other white collar practitioners of petty skills easily acquired. Finally, white collar labor is diffused through thousands of small enterprises and therefore lacks cohesion; and the few large employers of office help, such as life insurance companies, carefully select workers who are safely petty bourgeois in their psychology. But the union can be blamed for signing "green agreements" in some of the offices it has been able to organize—such as the various "letter shops" and miscellaneous small concerns. These agreements, even where they provide for the closed shop, have largely embodied the miserable wage scales and poor conditions previously obtaining.

Moreover, the Stalinist leadership has called a number of chaotic strikes, all of which have been lost. Thus a strike was called on December 10, 1937, at the Howard Clothing Company, in New York City. Two days later it was suddenly called off and "settled." Only 21 of the 42 workers involved got their jobs back. The only change in wages was an eight-dollar-a-week reduction for one worker. This is the characteristically brilliant strike strategy of the union leadership.

The president of the international union is Lewis Merrill, one of the most devout followers of the Communist Party line. The Merrill clique is a closed corporation which, until forced by a growing opposition, rendered no accounting to the membership of union policy, finances, enrollment, or anything else. The progressive opposition is also critical of the fact that Merrill has turned down hundreds of WPA office workers who applied for admission to the union. He has done so at the insistence of the Communist Party that the WPA office workers must belong to the City Projects Council and the Workers Alliance, both of which are "innocent fronts" of the party. These criticisms of the Merrill policies are met with characteristic Stalinist hounding and abuse, with booing and hissing in union meetings, and a fantastic misuse of parliamentary procedure.

In San Francisco, where control was wrested from the Merrill machine by a group of progressive Socialists, the union conducted early in 1938 a well-prepared strike of the office workers in the Safeway Stores, the largest grocery chain in the West. The strike was won and the agreement provided for a closed shop, two weeks' vacation, time-and-a-half for overtime, sick leave and dismissal pay, and raised wages from 10 to 45 per cent. By January 1938, this San Francisco Local 34 had twelve similar contracts, which shows what the union can do when it is free to function.

But subsequently Harry Bridges tried to force the progressives out of office, accusing them of being "agents" of the San Francisco Industrial Association, one of the most reactionary organizations of employers in America. He even demanded that these officers be tried, stating that he "knew in advance that all the defendants were guilty" of being stool-pigeons. These progressives were all well-known militants of long standing, who had just won a series of brilliant strikes, and of course the rank and file howled down this calumny. Bridges then tried to break up the office workers' union by insisting that it merge with the warehousemen's local of the International Longshoremen's and Warehousemen's Association, which he controls. After this amazing proposal, Local 34 left the CIO altogether and rejoined the A. F. of L. There was no other place to go.

The Salespeople

The Retail Clerks International Protective Association had been moldering for years in the A. F. of L. Even the NRA could not revive it. But in 1935 and 1936 the clerks themselves began to organize, especially in New York City. The Protective considered this campaign a form of insurgency, and on April 30, 1937, it kicked out the five so-called New Era locals in New York City, which were leading in the organizing drive. But these locals continued to function lustily, attracting more and more members from the Protective. In May 1937, the new union, 15,000 strong, joined the CIO. Toward the end of the year, it extended its jurisdiction to include wholesale clerks, and called itself the United Retail and Wholesale Employees of America. The president is Samuel Wolchok, a Socialist, who has long been active among the grocery clerks.

Beginning in 1935, the union conducted a number of strikes in New York department stores and large women's wear establishments. In 1935, Local 1250 ran spectacular strikes at Ohrbach's and at May's department store. Ohrbach's settled without a wage increase, but with some improvement in conditions. Soon after, however, the store began firing the girls who had been active in the strike. At May's the strike was lost. Through 1937 the union called sitdown strikes in several of the Woolworth stores in New York City. The final agreement recognized the union for its own members only, and established a $15.60 minimum wage and a forty-hour week.

During this period Local 1250 had been under Stalinist leadership, and was in chronic upheaval, partly because its strikes were more dramatic than effective, and the agreements it was able to sign were not enforced. Accordingly, in December 1937, the CIO set up a Department Store Organizing Committee under the chairmanship of Sidney Hillman, to operate within the national union.

During the first few months of 1938, the Wolchok leadership, with the aid of Sidney Hillman, reasserted itself in the campaign to organize the big stores. The Amalgamated Clothing Workers aided the union in signing up the salesmen at the Crawford Clothing Stores, which run their own manufacturing plants, where the Amalgamated has a closed shop. In quick succession, the union signed agreements at Macy's, Hearn's, and Gimbel's, all in New York City. The contract with Macy's covers 2000 workers in the delivery, warehouse, and manufacturing departments. It recognizes the union for the workers involved, and provides wage increases, time-and-a-third for overtime, a five-day week for drivers, and vacation with pay. At Hearn's the union won its first closed shop agreement with a three-year contract for 2000 workers, providing for annual negotiations on wages, hours, and conditions. At Gimbel's it signed an agreement for more than 2200 employees. Wages were increased from $1 to $2 a week, a forty-five-hour week was established with time-and-a-third for overtime, and a seniority system and a grievance machinery were set up. But after this organizational spurt in the big department stores, the campaign petered out. After all, it is the salespeople and not the warehouse and delivery men and skilled craftsmen who are the vast majority in the merchandising field. And the union made very little effort to organize the salesgirls, notably at Macy's. In time, even the warehouse and delivery men lost their enthusiasm for the union because it failed to make a concerted drive for all the workers in the stores.

Even more confused is the picture in Local 1199, which consists of drug clerks. Thirteen out of the fifteen members of its Executive Board are Stalinists, who fight all opposition with their usual methods, and even call strikes without consulting the membership. Early in 1938 this local struck the Whelan Drug Stores in New York City. After several weeks the men went back on the terms offered them on the first day of the strike, that is, those who got back. This sort of irresponsibility has created enormous disaffection among the rank and file of the local, in which a sound progressive opposition is growing.

The union has had considerable success in New England, where it has organized almost 100 small department and dry-goods stores. The agreements usually provide for a 10 per cent wage increase for those receiving $15 a week or less, 7½ per cent for those receiving $15 to $20 a week, and 5 per cent for those getting more than $20.

Today the union has about 30,000 members through the country. It faces a double problem. For one thing, the administration, which is progressive but weak, has to contend with a strong Stalinist opposition. And for another thing, it has to deal with thousands of establishments, large and small, throughout the country. It's one thing to sign an agreement with a little storekeeper, it's another thing to make it stick. And in grocery business the union is not yet strong enough to tackle the powerful chain trusts, which select their workers from the most socially backward layers of the lower middle class.

The Technicians

The Federation of Architects, Engineers, Chemists and Technicians was organized in 1934, mainly from among the technical staffs in the WPA. It is as much a professional association as a trade union. And until recently it has been both chiefly on paper. Most of its members are technicians in industrial and medical and dental laboratories. Among the architects and engineers they are chiefly draughtsmen; and among the chemists they are in the cosmetic and other commercial trades. From the very beginning the Federation has been under Stalinist leadership, and its rank and file have been chiefly Communist Party followers. When the Stalinist-controlled unions trooped into the CIO in the middle of 1937, this union was among them. Ever since, its main strategy has been to follow in the wake of the industrial unions, and to try to sign up technical workers in those plants where the industrial union drive was successful.

In November 1937, the Federation reported a membership of 7000, though it no doubt had considerably less. But in the spring of 1938 it gained almost 2000 members when the Society of Designing Engineers in the automobile industry joined it in a body, after John Lewis had got the United Automobile Workers to waive jurisdiction over them.

Government Workers

There are three unions of general jurisdiction over federal workers outside the Post Office Department. The largest of these, the National Federation of Federal Employees, is an independent organization of 50,000 members which for two decades has been primarily interested in the enforcement of civil service regulations, and in protective legislation for federal workers. It is usually called the government's company union. The second is the American Federation of Government Employees,. which was formed during the NRA. Its members are bureaucrats in the higher brackets and its leadership is so thoroughly reactionary that in 1937 a number of Washington lodges broke away and formed the United Federal Workers of America, which joined the CIO in June of that year. The United Federal Workers have a constitutional provision which makes the uniformed personnel of the fighting forces and the post office workers ineligible, and also forbids strikes and picketing. The union is active in its progressive social legislative program. It demands a five-day week, a minimum annual salary, the extension of civil service to all government workers, and it also fights against racial and other kinds of discrimination within the various government departments. Most of its members come from the newer services such as the Social Security Board and the TVA. And it is doing surprisingly well outside Washington, among the civilian workers in the army bases, the navy yards, and the immigration service. Early in 1938 the union had between 6000 and 7000 members.

John L. Lewis appointed as president of the new union Jacob Baker, who had been Harry Hopkins's right-hand man. Baker is extremely intelligent and progressive, with more than a touch of philosophical anarchism in his outlook. He is handling the factional situation in the Washington locals, where the Stalinists are active, with considerable skill. And the union is slowly establishing itself under his leadership.

The State, County and Municipal Workers of America was set up by the CIO in July 1937. In New York City this organization consists mainly of investigators, supervisors, and clerical workers in the Home Relief Division of the Department of Welfare, and it also has some strength among social workers and office clerks in various city and State agencies and institutions. Outside of New York City the membership includes also a considerable number of manual laborers on state highways and in other construction work. This union is completely at the mercy of its Stalinist oligarchy. Abram Flaxer, the president, and his crowd conduct the union with utter disregard of all union democracy and run things by the caucus method. Instead of membership meetings they usually call "mass meetings," which are open to the public, and are not subject to the nuisance of parliamentary procedure. In the spring of 1938 the union claimed 50,000 members. According to the best available information it has just under 30,000.

CHAPTER X

WHAT'S AHEAD?

To PROPHESY about the distant future of the CIO is to indulge in star-gazing. Even its immediate future is in many ways imponderable. Its effect on our economy is so profound that its fate is bound up not only with our national life, but through it with all the major forces of international chaos and construction.

What if there is war? And if there is war within five years, will we be in it—in time to save the British Empire for another breathing-spell? Will international war bring social revolution to the fascist countries? If so, one thing is certain. Stalinism will no longer be able to parade as Communism, even if the Stalin apparatus survived such a war. For social revolution, especially in advanced countries, can be achieved only through a mortal struggle with the Communist International.

Should we get into the war by way of Collective Security—the phrase which is paving the way for another catastrophe to Save the World for Democracy—will the CIO fall for it? Its leaders very well may. To be indispensable, to have jobs at high wages for everybody, to be recognized overnight by the most recalcitrant employers—these are great temptations. If the CIO goes in for war, it will suffer the fate of the A. F. of L. after the last war. It is an axiom that labor has nothing to gain and everything to lose in every international war. Finally, the future of the whole of American Labor of course depends on our internal economic situation. Will the American economy after the next great crash, which some economists place in the first half of the 1940's, go into a permanent decline? If so, all organized labor will suffer and weaken. For American imperialism still has plenty of will and power to maintain its privileged position through intensified reaction. And in that case the New Deal, all blah to the contrary notwithstanding, will fulfill its historic liberal function of "saving capitalism from itself" by first saving it from labor.

It is obviously safer to predict the near future of the CIO on the assumption that for the next three or four years we shall continue to drift in all directions.

On that assumption, the CIO presents four major questions. First, will the CIO grow during these next few years; will it organize at least ten or twelve millions out of more than fifty million American wage-earners? Second, will the CIO go in for independent political action, or will it continue to be the political left wing of the New Deal? Third, what of the factional struggles within the CIO? And fourth, can there be peace between the CIO and the A. F. of L.?

I

By the end of 1937, the CIO had organized over 3,000,000 workers. It has done a lot for them. It has improved their wages, hours, and conditions. Above all, it has enriched their lives by giving them a new sense of solidarity, of human dignity and social purpose. It is turning American labor from primitive craft separatism to modern industrial unionism. And industrial unionism is here to stay. Only a reaction of fascist violence could break it up.

But for the time being, the drive of the CIO has slowed down. The loss in Little Steel in the summer of 1937 was a set-back. At about the same time, the new depression was on its way. The consumer-goods industries began to lag in June, and by October the heavy industries were in full decline. If we take January 1937 as our norm, then in January 1938 steel production was only 37.3 per cent of normal; automobiles 54.2 per cent; rubber tires and tubes 53.7 per cent; textiles 60.8 per cent. Thirteen million men and women were out of work. And in the absence of government statistics on unemployment, no one knows just how many millions more were working only two or three days a week. Naturally, this "recession"—our latest euphemism for catastrophe—has seriously affected the CIO. The income of the national office in March 1938 was only $60,000, of which half was contributed by the United Mine Workers, who kept up their full dues. This means that of more than 3,000,000 members in the CIO, only 1,200,000 could keep up their assessments, of which five cents a month goes to national headquarters. Of course it must be remembered that workers in the process of being organized often have to be excused from paying dues; and even at its financial peak the CIO did not collect from more than about 1,600,000 members. Needless to say, the loss of a fourth of its monthly income is a serious matter. Hundreds of organizers have had to be laid off. Constituent unions could no longer draw freely on the national treasury. The CIO has had to take in sail.

But the CIO has been hurt by Stalinist disruption far more than by the depression. It has been hurt in its spirit. In a united and enthusiastic labor movement there is little correlation between dues-payment and union membership in good standing. The miners and needle workers pay their dues through years of unemployment, many of them even after they have left the industry. A worker who participates in his union is a member of organized labor, whether he pays dues or is excused from it. But during the last half year many a member of the CIO who fell behind in his dues dropped out of the movement. Most workers in the CIO are new to organized labor. They are revolted by Stalinist tactics and they cannot understand why Lewis and Brophy and Murray seem to do nothing about it. Brophy, in fact, is obviously encouraging the Stalinists and is rapidly becoming discredited among the rank and file, especially on the West coast. The publicity department of the CIO, which is under Stalinist influence, is quite unreliable in its membership figures; and so, of course, are the unions under Stalinist domination. It is impossible to tell just how many members the CIO has as it approaches its fourth year. I would not venture a guess. But in the opinion of those leaders in the CIO who prefer not to fool themselves, it is considerably below 3,000,000.

The enmity of the A. F. of L. is also beginning to

tell. Since the CIO drive began, the A. F. of L. has picked up almost 800,000 members. In the beginning it has done so by offering its "conservative" services to the employer. Time and again it has signed collective bargaining agreements before the workers had a chance to vote in an N.L.R.B. election; and on a few occasions it has actually tried to break CIO organizing strikes. But of late the A. F. of L. has been more careful. Green has concluded that factionalism in the CIO is bound to play into the hands of the A. F. of L. And, indeed, the office workers in San Francisco and the furriers in Canada have rejoined the A. F. of L. to save themselves from factional extinction. We have seen how four powerful unions in Los Angeles have rebelled against the leadership of Harry Bridges and have founded their own CIO council. The International Ladies' Garment Workers, next to the miners the richest and best-disciplined union in the CIO, has definitely decided not to attend the first convention of the CIO, where it means to reorganize itself from a committee into a permanent rival federation to the A. F. of L. There are other such straws in the wind. And this drift from the CIO toward the A. F. of L. may grow, unless the CIO eliminates factional disruption. In 1935 Green and Company thought that industrial unionism was endangering their power. If they should discover that they can increase their power by admitting even militant unions from the CIO, they will quickly forget that industrial unionism is "dual unionism."

If the CIO holds its own in the immediate future, it

will be because the rank and file in the National Maritime Union, in the United Automobile Workers, in the West Coast Firemen has been driving the factionalists from office and has elected progressives in their stead. This rebellion against Stalinist domination is growing in the CIO and revitalizing it. Should John Lewis give way to Stalinist pressure and try to force "peace" with the Stalinists on the victorious progressives, the CIO will decline rapidly and perceptibly within the next year.

II

The CIO is not getting ready for independent political action in 1940. It functions politically through Labor's Non-Partisan League, of which the various local and State-wide labor and farmer-labor parties are autonomous parts.

The non-partisanship of the CIO is not in the least like the old-fashioned A. F. of L. brand. It is militantly, not passively, opportunistic. In the New York City elections in 1937, the American Labor Party polled 25 per cent of the vote, re-electing La Guardia and electing five out of twenty-six councilmen. In Detroit the labor candidate for mayor polled 35 per cent of the total vote, though he was defeated. In Akron labor's candidate got 30,000 votes to his rival's 35,000. In the cities and towns of Western Pennsylvania, the CIO endorsed the Democratic ticket and swung the elections. In Pittsburgh and in every one of the surrounding steel towns, all municipal offices, from mayor down, went to the Democratic-Labor fusion. Whether or not labor, by its differential vote, re-elected Roosevelt, it demonstrably elected Governors Earle and Murphy, which is one of the reasons why they were so sympathetic to it in the steel and automobile strikes.

The CIO puts its strength behind every State farmer-labor party, the local left Republican organizations, the Progressive Party in Wisconsin, and the left wing of the Democratic. In short, the CIO plays in with the most progressive local parties which have a chance to win. For it needs, especially during strikes, pro-labor or sympathetic governments in local and State power. Labor's Non-Partisan League, which practically means the CIO, intends to continue in this piecemeal non-partisan program until it feels there are enough such pieces to give real strength to a third party movement.

There are three factors which threaten to spoil this optimistic theory. For one thing, the A. F. of L. has come out against Labor's Non-Partisan League and its affiliates all over the country. Green accuses the League of being the political "stooge" for the CIO, which—if we ignore the invidious touch—is quite true. For only a progressive unionism can stimulate labor to act politically; if the League depended on Bill Green for inspiration, it could not elect a dog-catcher. The League is, as much as the CIO, an outgrowth of the drive for industrial unionism. But since the A. F. of L. has more members than the CIO, the prospects for a strong and united political labor movement are not as bright as the campaigns of 1936 and 1937 appeared to indicate. It was the A. F. of L. which defeated Maury Maverick of

Texas for re-election to Congress, and Green's only reason was Maverick's enthusiastic endorsement by the CIO.

The second difficulty is presented by the Stalinists, who are losing out in the CIO unions, but are gaining in influence in the various labor and farmer-labor parties. The rank and file of industrial unionists are beginning to appreciate the disruptive influence of the "party line." But labor parties have a large admixture of left-middle-class elements, sufficiently confused in their "liberalism" to fall for a "united front" with the Communist Party. In Minnesota, there is a working alliance between the Stalinists and the Farmer-Labor Party under Governor Benson. This united front, now admitted, now denied, is splitting the Farmer-Labor Party, for the Communist Party is trying to run it behind the scenes. The Minneapolis Central Labor Union, dominated by Trotskyites, together with the teamsters, printers, and building trades, held a mass meeting on April 11, 1938, to oppose the program of a united front with the Stalinists. A similar factional situation has developed in the Commonwealth Federation in the State of Washington; in fact, throughout the farmer-labor movements of the Northwest. The American Labor Party in New York City has on its Executive Committee three Stalinists and one Stalinoid, who represent non-Stalinist organizations. The Stalinists have also captured a large number of Assembly District Clubs, using the American Labor Party as a front. And Labor's Non-Partisan League, too, is innocently but busily playing with Stalinist stooges.

The third difficulty with the non-partisan policy of the CIO in tying up with the progressive political machines as it finds them, is that it is apt to become "progressively" confused. Fundamentally all these progressive parties are so many tails to the New Deal kite. And as the chaos of the New Deal increases, they too become increasingly disoriented. The Stalinists abet this tendency of the various labor parties to fuse with the New Deal. For their main political interest is in Collective Security. And since Roosevelt has come out for it, the New Deal is to the Stalinists almost as infallible as the Kremlin.

III

The basic program of the CIO is simplicity itself. Modern industrial labor must organize in industrial unions. There can be no honest factional disagreement on this point; and there is none. Factionalism in the CIO, therefore, is not programmatic but artificial. And as we have seen time and again, it is confined to the line of the Communist Party, rigidly followed by its members and its sympathizers. It is idle to predict the contortions of this line, for they will be determined by the struggle of the Stalin regime to maintain its power in the U.S.S.R. The zigzags of the Communist International have and can have no relation to the interests of American labor. Of late the rank and file in the CIO is realizing this mortal danger, and their pressure will in time no doubt influence even those of the top leaders who minimize it. But it will take time and great determination to get rid of it.

IV

After conferences lasting for two months, the effort to heal the breach between the A. F. of L. and the CIO ended in failure on December 21, 1937. Both sides "agreed to disagree," and blamed each other for the failure.

The conference had been called partly through pressure from the Roosevelt administration; partly because some powerful leaders in both camps really wanted peace, fearing that continued war would endanger the entire labor movement; and partly because both the A. F. of L. and the CIO oligarchies wanted to satisfy the deep desire for unity of the masses by at least attempting to make peace.

The CIO proposed that all its organizations should enter the A. F. of L. as a special department, to be known as the CIO, without prejudice to their character as industrial unions. The A. F. of L. proposed that the CIO immediately disband, that its charter unions return to the fold under the old status, and that the new CIO organizations be made the subject of special conferences. In short, the A. F. of L. demanded that the CIO commit suicide in return for the privilege of being buried in the ancestral mausoleum.

After the conference broke up, David Dubinsky, whose union is a charter member of the CIO, accused the CIO of having cut short the peace negotiations. He felt that if negotiations had been continued, the A. F. of L. would have given in on all essential issues. Philip Murray and Charles P. Howard took issue with him, and blamed the A. F. of L. Be that as it may, there was no peace. And now peace is more remote than ever. Of late Green has come to believe that the A. F. of L. might gain from CIO defections, due to the factional struggles within the latter. But, in his mind, such accretions would have to be a retail process. The A. F. of L. oligarchy cannot afford to welcome suddenly three dozen industrial unions, for they would endanger the craft structure of the Federation and the sinecures of its officials. And conversely, the CIO unions cannot afford to enter the craft-jealous atmosphere of the A. F. of L., which would tend to disrupt both their morale and their industrial form of organization. Moreover, the CIO too has become a vested interest for its leaders; all successful organizations do. John L. Lewis wants peace with the A. F. of L. on his own terms. He is scarcely anxious to be once more just the president of the United Mine Workers.

It is a major tragedy for American labor that its two dominant movements should be at war. And even though fusion seems for the present impossible, co-operation in various fields should be perfectly feasible. There is no reason why they should not collaborate on essential labor legislation, such as a sound wages and hours bill, and on other questions of public policy such as relief, housing, social security. Unfortunately, mutual bitterness has gone so deep, and mutual recrimination has been so violent and so public, that such collaboration seems as much out of the question as amalgamation.

The founders of the CIO had no choice but to leave the A. F. of L.; there was no other way of organizing the unorganized masses. But John L. Lewis has not only fought the A. F. of L. tactically when necessary; he has also fought Green emotionally when unnecessary. It must have given him a kick to heave "Benedict Arnold" Green out of the United Mine Workers. But the result was that Green was forced to retaliate by expelling the United Mine Workers. To be sure the position of both gentlemen in one another's organizations had become uncomfortable and ambiguous. But the status quo was advantageous to the CIO, not to the A. F. of L. For a great number of State federations of labor and of local A. F. of L. bodies have, quite illogically but with excellent effect, been helping the CIO. They refused to expel CIO unions, and in a number of cases they actually helped the CIO in its organization drive. Green tried to ignore this fraternizing, as much as the reactionaries on the Executive Council of the A. F. of L. would permit. But as the bitterness between Lewis and Green increased, and spread through both hierarchies, the A. F. of L. increasingly expelled regional bodies sympathetic to the CIO. And having expelled them, it automatically had to set up dual organizations in their stead. Early in 1938, for instance, it expelled the Colorado and the Pennsylvania Federations of Labor. The expulsions have done the CIO no good because these bodies had already been extremely helpful to it. And the dual organizations set up in their stead, no matter how ineffective, are bound to give it trouble.

Finally the CIO called a convention for the fall of 1938, when it will change its form of organization from a committee to a federation, adopt a constitution, and elect officers. This is theoretically a great step forward in union democracy. But it will also mean that the CIO must set up its own regional and local bodies; and this will mean that it will not be able to exploit the weakness of the A. F. of L. as effectively as it could if it remained for a time in its present ambiguous position as a mere organizing committee.

If we escape war, the CIO will succeed to the degree in which it follows, through the maze of its innumerable problems, certain basic policies.

First, it must permit radical and revolutionary criticism. But it must stamp out artificial and Jesuitical factionalism. The CIO must not exclude any worker for his political beliefs, no matter what they are. But it must rid itself of Stalinist officials, staff members, and organizers. This appears to raise the issue of representation, but in reality it does not. Democracy does not demand the democratic toleration of its destroyers. If Hitler has not taught us that, then we have learned nothing. Besides, if the worker is made to understand that Stalinism is neither Red nor communist nor labor, and that the effort to get rid of it is not Red-baiting but on the contrary an effort to get rid of Red-baiters and union wreckers, he will elect no Stalinists to office. The rank and file is already defeating them for office throughout the CIO.

Second, the CIO must go into political action under the banner of a labor party. The elder La Follette got more than 5,000,000 votes 'way back in 1924. In his economic views he was behind his time; as a third-party candidate, before his time; and he had no organized mass base. The CIO is both timely and has an organized mass base. It is better to elect twenty Congressmen on a straight labor ticket than to ride herd on five hundred La Guardias, big and little, all over the country.

Third, though the A. F. of L. hierarchy is hopelessly reactionary, it still has a mass following. The theory of capturing masses of workers "from below," through abuse of their leaders, has never worked. The working class, like every other historically rising class, can be gained only through education. Good propaganda is nothing but simplified education. The CIO can get the masses of American labor by its services to labor.

And finally the CIO must continue to organize without let-up; and it must concentrate its energies in the great mass production, distribution, and public service fields.

If the CIO goes on organizing energetically; if it permits complete trade union democracy everywhere and autonomy to its national and international affiliates; if it tolerates every kind of radical or revolutionary dissent except political disruption; if it goes in for a labor party sooner rather than later; and if it plays a shrewd game of peace as against an indiscriminate game of war against the A. F. of L.—then It Can't Happen Here. Otherwise —anything may happen.

INDEX

INDEX

Addams, Jane, 50
Addes, George, 160, 172, 181, 184
Aluminum Company of America, 236, 237
Aluminum Workers of America, 151, 236, 237
Amalgamated Association of Iron, Steel and Tin Workers, 23, 66–71, 78, 207
Amalgamated Clothing Workers of America, 13, 14, 16, 18, 27, 49–56, 59, 151, 210, 211, 262
Amalgamated Street, Electric Railway and Motor Coach Employees, 226
American Chamber of Commerce, 93, 100
American Communications Association, 150, 151, 240, 241
Americaneers, 93
American Federation of Government Employees, 265
American Federation of Labor, history 5–18; San Francisco convention, 19–22; Atlantic City convention, 22–6; relations with CIO, 29–31; relations with steel workers, 26–70; and factionalism, 23–130; and automobile workers, 156–9; and maritime workers, 187–204; and new unions, 206–44; and what's ahead, 271–82
American Federation of Teachers, 19
American Friends of Spanish Democracy, 143
American Iron and Steel Institute, 71
American Labor League, 99
American Labor Party, 60, 130, 135, 273, 275

American League for Peace and Democracy, 94, 143
American Legion, 93, 99, 100
American Liberty League, 77, 98
American Merchant Marine Institute, 199
American Mercury, 97
American Newspaper Guild, 150–1, 245, 249, 250–6
American Radio Telegraphists' Association, 240, 241
American Smelting and Refining Company, 62, 63
American Students Union, 143
American Writers Congress, 143
American Youth Congress, 143
Amsterdam News, 250
Anaconda Copper Company, 63
Anderson, Judge Albert B., 40
Arbeiter Ring, 134
Architects, Engineers, Chemists and Technicians, Federation of, *see* Federation
Arnold, Thurman, 95
Ashcraft, Garland, 246
Asia, 258
Association of Catholic Trade Unions, 222
Atlas-Liberty, 228
Automobile Workers, *see* United
Auto Workers Union, 145

Baker, Jacob, 266
Beal, Fred E., 144
Beck, David, 193
Bell Transportation System, 228
Bendix strike, 166
Bennett, Harry, 116, 117, 118
Benson, Gov. Elmer A., 275
Berry, George L., 16, 148

285

INDEX

Bethlehem Steel Corp., 73, 80, 83, 85, 88, 108, 110, 111, 112
Bittner, Van A., 46, 47, 86
Bituminous Coal Commission, 40, 41
Black Legion, 93, 94
Bland Committee, 41
Blue Card Union, 62
Book and Magazine Guild, 258
Bookkeepers, Stenographers and Accountants Union, 257
Boot and Shoe Workers Union, 229
Borah, Senator William E., 61
Boysen, George E., 99
Bridges, Harry, 47, 48, 147, 148, 150, 152, 153, 189–94, 197, 198, 231, 239, 240, 260, 261, 272
Brockton Brotherhood, 229
Brooklyn *Daily Eagle*, 250
Brooklyn-Manhattan Transit Company, 227
Brophy, John, 27, 36, 38, 48, 49, 148, 191, 193, 197, 223, 230, 242, 253, 271
Brotherhood of Railway Conductors and Trainmen, 111
Broun, Heywood, 150, 247, 248, 251, 252, 253, 254, 256
Browder, Earl, 139
Bruère, Robert, 208
Buck, Robert M., 252, 253
Buick strike, 166, 167
Building Trades Industrial League, 145
Bukharin, Nicolai, 139
Byne, Moe, 201
Byrnes Act, 107

Cadillac strike, 166, 167
Cambria, *see* Bethlehem Steel Corp.
Cameron, William J., 118
Campbell, Douglas, 109
Campbell, Lawrence W., 108, 112
Canadian fur workers, 144
Cannery, Agricultural, Packing and Allied Workers, United, *see* United
Carey, James P., 219
Carnegie-Illinois Steel Corp., 66, 77

Carpenters, United Brotherhood of, *see* United
Caruso, Angelo, 116
Catholic Church, 99, 222
Catholic Trade Unions, Association of, *see* Association
Catholic Worker, The, 222
Chevrolet strike, 166, 168
Chiang Kai-shek, 138
Chicago *Tribune*, 249
Chinese Revolution, 138
Chrysler, Walter P., 169
Chrysler Motor Company, 121, 238
Chrysler strike, 169, 174
Citizens' National Committee, 112
Clark, Capt. William A., 85, 110, 112
Cleveland *News*, 246, 250
Cleveland Newspaper Guild, 246, 247
Cleveland *Plain Dealer*, 246
Cleveland *Press*, 246
Coefield, John, 22
Coeur d'Alene, 61, 63
Collective Security, 143, 177, 194, 201, 202, 222, 268, 276
Collins, William, 158, 159
Commercial Telegraphers' Union, 240
Committee for Industrial Organization, 12; early history, 26–31; and charter unions, 46–9, 56, 60, 61, 65; and steel workers, 70, 71; and vigilantism, 97–101; and factionalism, 126–34, 141–50; and automobile workers, 156–60, 166; and maritime workers, 187–99; and new unions, 206–67; future, 268-281
C.I.O. News, 47
Commonwealth Federation, 275
Communist, The, 147
Communist International, 129, 136, 137, 138, 139, 141n., 145–7, 276
Communist Manifesto, 123
Communist Party (*see also* Stalinists), 69, 87, 90, 129–32, 135, 142–50, 152, 154, 160, 170, 171, 177, 189, 192, 201, 205, 219, 222,

INDEX

Communist Party *(Continued)* 223, 225, 233, 240–3, 257, 260, 275, 276
Conemaugh and Blacklick Railroad, 81, 111, 112
Congress of American Industry, 106
Consolidated Edison Company, 219, 221, 222
Consolidated Oil Company, 64
Consumers Power Company, 223, 224
Continuous Discharge Book, 194, 197
Cooks and Stewards Union, 152, 195, 198
Coughlin, Father, 95, 99
Coxey, General, 123
Crawford Clothing Stores, 262
Crown Cork and Seal Company, 80
Curran, Joseph, 150, 197, 201, 203–205

Daily Worker, 123, 177, 178, 184, 185, 227
Dalrymple, S. H., 215
Damich, Bozo, 87
Darrow, Clarence, 61
Daughters of the American Revolution, 93
Davey, Gov. Martin L., 85, 113
Davis, James, 43
Davis-Kelley bill, 43, 44
De Caux, Len, 47, 253
De Leon, Daniel, 57, 124
Democratic Party, 56
Department Store Organizing Committee, 262
Dillon, Francis J., 22, 159, 160
Dubinsky, David, 19, 21, 24, 34, 57, 60, 61, 126, 149, 152, 234, 277
Dunne brothers, 130
Dyer, Dr. Gustavus, 112

Eagle-Picher Co., 62
Earle, Gov. George H., 71, 85, 108, 110, 274
Easley, Ralph M., 100
Eastman, Max, 144
Eddy, Jonathan, 251, 254

Edwards, George, 165
Electrical, Radio and Machine Workers, United, *see* United
Electrical Workers, *see* International Brotherhood of
Elser, Ralph (Youngstown sheriff), 113
Emerson Electrical Manufacturing Company, 219, 220
Evans, Sidney D., 108, 110

Fagan, Pat, 46
Fairless, Benjamin F., 78
Farmer-Labor Party, 130, 275
Farrington, Frank, 36
Federal Agricultural Workers, 242
Federal Employees, National Federation of, *see* National
Federal Workers of America, United, *see* United
Federated Press, 172
Federation of Architects, Engineers, Chemists and Technicians, 151, 264, 265
Federation of Flat Glass Workers, 151, 237
Federman, Max, 144, 232, 233
Fifth Avenue Coach Company, 227
Fink Book, *see* Continuous Discharge Book
Firestone Tire and Rubber Company, 215–7
Fischer, Ben, 133
Fisher Body strike, 166, 167, 176
Flat Glass Workers, Federation of, *see* Federation
Flaxer, Abram, 150, 267
Fleetwood strike, 167
Flint Alliance, 99, 167
Food Workers Industrial Union, 145
Ford, Edsel, 119
Ford, Henry, 115, 117–9
Ford Brotherhood, Inc., 119
Ford Motor Company, 99, 117–9, 169, 170, 185
Ford Service Men, 116, 117, 118
Foster, William Z., 67
Franco, General, 139, 140, 254

INDEX

Frankensteen, Richard, 118, 160, 163–4, 172, 179, 180–2, 184–5
Franklin, J. A., 22
Frey, John P., 10, 19, 20, 22–3, 30
Fremming, Harvey, 64
French Cable and Telegraph Company, 241
Friends of New Germany, 93
Friends of the Soviet Union, 139, 154
Fuller, Paul, 239
Fur Workers Union, International, see International

Gallagher, Daniel, 173
Garment Workers, United, see United
Garst, Delmond, 184
Gary, Judge Elbert H., 67
Gastonia strike, 207, 208
Gebert, B. K., 171, 179
General Electric Company, 17, 221
General Motors Corp., 76, 120–1, 164, 166–70, 175, 176, 178, 181, 238
Gimbel Bros., 262, 263
Girdler, Thomas, 79, 81, 82, 112, 114
Globe Wireless Corp., 241
Gold, Benjamin, 231–4
Golden, Clint, 79, 86
Gompers, Samuel, 5, 7, 30, 31, 35, 37, 124
Goodrich Company, B. F., 121, 216
Goodyear strike, 98, 214–6
Gorman, Francis J., 208, 210
Government Employees, American Federation of, see American
Grace, Eugene, 81, 82
Grange, David, 198
Green, John, 187
Green, William, 10–12, 16, 17, 22, 26, 30, 45, 68, 70, 125, 148, 157–159, 196, 236, 272, 274, 275, 278, 279
Guaranty Trust Company, 73
Guffey, Senator Joseph F., 71
Guffey-Snyder coal bill, 46
Guide Lamp Company strike, 167
Guild Reporter, 254

Gulf Oil Company, see Mellon interests

Haessler, Carl, 172
Hall, Edward, 160, 164, 165, 171, 184, 185
Hall, Lee, 87
Hapgood, Hutchins, 230
Hapgood, Norman, 230
Hapgood, Powers, 230, 231
Hapgood, William, 230
Harding, William G., 9
Hart, Schaffner & Marx, 49
Hatband Group, 211
Hatchet Gang, 80, 97
Hatters, Cap and Millinery Workers, United, see United
Hayes, Frank, 37
Haywood, Bill, 61, 62
Hearn, George H., 204
Hearn Department Stores, 262, 263
Hearst newspapers, 250
Henderson, Donald, 150, 242, 243, 244
Henson, Francis A., 132
Herrick, Mrs. Elinore, 198
Hillman, Sidney, 16–19, 21, 49–55, 61, 126, 149, 210–13, 262
Hillquit, Morris, 124, 129
Hitler, Adolph, 96, 138, 146, 280
Hoan, Mayor Daniel W., 133
Hogan, Austin, 227
Homestead strike, 66, 86
Hoover, Herbert, 9, 42, 43
Hopkins, Harry, 266
Hosiery Workers, United, see United
Howard, Charles P., 21, 23, 24, 27, 64, 278
Howard Clothing Company, 259
Howat, Alex, 36
Hudson, Roy, 201
Hutcheson, William L., 10, 11, 22, 26, 45

Independent Labor League of America, 130, 132
Industrial Union of Marine and Shipbuilding Workers, 151, 187

Industrial Workers of the World, 32, 61, 190
Inland Boatmen's Union, 198
Inland Steel Company, 80, 81, 88
Interborough Rapid Transit Company, 227
International Association of Machinists, 25, 225, 226
International Brotherhood of Electrical Workers, 17, 25, 219, 221
International Fur Workers Union, 14, 148–9, 151, 154, 231, 232, 234, 256
International Labor Defense, 143
International Ladies Garment Workers Union, 13, 14, 18, 27, 49, 52, 56–60, 131, 151–3, 210, 248, 272
International Longshoreman's and Warehouseman's Union, 261
International Longshoreman's Association, 188, 196, 198
International Maritime Union, 154, 195
International Mine, Mill and Smelter Workers Union, 19, 25, 27, 61, 62, 151
International Seaman's Union, 189, 195–9, 202
International Typographical Union, 245
International Woodworkers of America, 131, 239
Iron and Steel Institute, 75, 81
Iron, Steel and Tin Workers, *see* Amalgamated Association of

Jacksonville Agreement, 42, 43
Jefferson, Thomas, 123
Jewish Daily Bulletin, 250
Jewish Daily Forward, 57, 134
John Price Jones Corp., 109, 110, 119
John Q. Public League, 98
Johnson, Gen. Hugh, 18, 45, 70, 148
Johnson, Walter O. R., 113
Johnstown Citizens' Committee, 84, 85, 108–12, 113

Johnstown strike, *see* Little Steel strike
Jones, John Price, 109, 110
Jones and Laughlin, 79, 80

Kelley, Clyde, 43
King, Jerome, 202, 203, 204
Kiwanis Club, 100
Knights of Dearborn, 99
Knights of Labor, 4, 5, 37, 56
Know Nothing movements, 86, 92, 93, 214
Kuhn, Loeb and Company, 73
Ku Klux Klan, 86, 92, 93, 96, 98, 152, 214

Labor's Non-Partisan League, 56, 130, 273, 274, 275
La Follette, Robert M., 281
La Follette, Robert M. Jr., 106
La Follette Committee, 76, 101, 106, 115, 119, 121
La Guardia, Fiorello, 273
Lamont, Thomas, 47, 76, 77, 109
Lauck, W. Jett, 44, 175
Law and Order League, 114
Lawrence strike, 207
Lawrenson, Jack, 201, 203, 204
Layton, George, 111
Lee, Algernon, 134
Lenin, V. I., 48, 123, 136, 137, 141, 150
Leonard, Lewis, 71
Lester, J. G., 112
Lewis, Edgar, 79
Lewis, John L., 12, 14, 16, 17, 19, 20, 21, 23, 24, 26, 27, 29, 32–40, 41–8, 55, 56, 61, 64, 68, 70, 72, 74, 77, 78, 80, 82, 86, 90, 91, 100, 112, 126, 147, 148, 149, 159, 161, 168, 169, 171, 172, 175, 176, 183, 185, 190, 191, 197, 214, 223, 224, 230, 242, 243, 248, 253, 265, 266, 271, 273, 278, 279
Lewis, Thomas, 36, 37
Lewis, Tom, 43
Libby-Owens-Ford Glass Company, 238

Lion Clubs, 100
Little Steel strike, 47, 73, 81, 87, 89, 98, 99, 106, 107, 121
Long, Huey, 92, 97
Long Island *Daily Press*, 250
Longshoremen's and Warehousemen's Union, International, see International
Longshoremen's Association, International, see International
Los Angeles Industrial Union Conference, 153
Lovestone, Jay, 132, 184
Lovestoneites, 129–32, 177, 184
Ludlow Resolution, 90, 181
Luhman, Rev. Roland, 113
Lundeberg, Harry, 189–93, 195, 196, 202, 205

Machinists, International Association of, see International
Mackay Cable Corp., 241
Macy, R. H. & Co., 262, 263
Mahon, William B., 226
Mahoning Valley, see Little Steel strike
Mahoning Valley Citizens' Committee, 113
Marine and Shipbuilding Workers, Industrial Union of, see Industrial
Marine, Firemen, Oilers, Water-Tenders and Wipers Association, 195
Marine Workers Industrial League, 145
Marion strike, 208
Maritime Federation of the Pacific, 193–5
Maritime Union, International, see International
Maritime Union, National, see National
Mark, James, 87, 88
Marlin, Gen., 114
Martin, Francis C., 108, 110
Martin, Homer, 34, 132, 144, 149, 152, 160–4, 170–9, 181–4, 212, 223

Massillon Citizens' Committee, 113
Master Weavers Institute, 211
Matles, James, 224
Maverick, Maury, 274, 275
May's Department Store, 262
Mayes, Barney, 144, 193, 194
Mayo, John, 87
McBride, John, 31
McCabe, Glen W., 238, 239
McCormick, Col. R. R., 249
McDowell, William, 118
McMahon, Thomas, 207
Mechanics Educational Society, 158
Mellon interests, 64, 73, 237
Memorial Day Massacre, 114
Merchant Marine Act, 200
Mergenthaler Linotype Co., 218
Merrill, Lewis, 259, 260
Metal and Steel Workers Industrial Union, 145
Method, George, 176
Milwaukee *Wisconsin News*, 250
Mine, Mill and Smelter Workers Union, International, see International
Mine Workers, United, see United
Minneapolis Central Labor Union, 275
Mitch, William, 46
Modern Age Books, 258
Mohawk Valley Formula, 102, 106–108; text, 102–6; in action, 107–114
Molly Maguires, the, 93
Monthly Labor Review, 55
Mooney, Capt., 115
Mooney, Rena, 35
Mooney-Billings Defense Committee, 35
Morgan, House of, 72–4, 76–8
Mortimer, Wyndham, 160, 164, 171, 176, 179, 181, 184, 185
Moscow Trials, 131, 140, 143, 178
Mossman, W. T., 79, 80
Moyer, Charles, 61
Munger, William, 132
Murphy, Gov. Frank, 168–9, 180, 224, 274

INDEX

Murray, Philip, 46–7, 64, 71, 77–8, 82, 86, 90–1, 126, 152, 212, 271, 278
Mussolini, Benito, 96
Myers, Blackie, 201
Myers, Carl, 114

Nation, The, 98, 249, 258
National Association of Manufacturers, 97, 102, 106, 107
National Association of Newspaper Publishers, 249
National Civic Federation, 99–100, 152
National Committee for the Organizing of Iron and Steel Workers, 67
National Federation of Federal Employees, 265
N.I.R.A., 15, 43, 44, 56
National Labor Relations Board, 63, 82, 88, 102, 106, 110, 112, 117, 198, 213, 216, 220, 224, 237, 272
National Maritime Union, 150, 198–201, 203, 205, 256, 273
National Miners Union, 145
National Negro Congress, 143
N.R.A., 15–18, 24, 36, 45, 53–6, 58, 59, 62, 63, 68, 158, 187, 208, 214, 217, 245, 247, 257, 261, 265
National Shoe and Leather Workers Union, 229
National Steel Corp., *see* Weirton Steel Company
National Textile Workers Union, 145
Needle Trades Workers Industrial Union, 145
Nessin, Samuel, 239
Newark *Ledger*, 250
New Deal, 14, 16, 77, 269, 276
New Republic, 249, 258
Newspaper Guild, American, *see* American
New York City Department of Welfare, 267
New York City Omnibus Company, 227
New York City Projects Council, 260
New York *Daily News*, 250
New York *Herald Tribune*, 252
New York *Post*, 250
New York Shipyards, 187
New York *Times*, 152
New York *World-Telegram*, 250
Niagara-Hudson Power Corp., 74
Nicely, Rev. George W., 108
Norris, Rev. Frank J., 99

O'Brien, Judge, 186
October Revolution, 131, 135–7, 141
Office and Professional Workers of America, United, *see* United
Ohio National Guard, 114
Ohrbach's, 262
Oil Field, Gas Well and Refinery Workers, 27, 63
Oil Workers International Union, 151
Oneal, James, 134
O'Shea, Thomas, 226
Owens, George, 111

Parmelee System, 228
Partido Obrero Unificación Marxista, *see* P.O.U.M.
Passaic strike, 10, 207
Paterson strike, 207
Pegg, Louis A., 111
Pegler, Westbrook, 12
Pennsylvania State Federation of Labor, 19
People's Press, 225
Perkins, Frances, 82, 112
Petroleum Workers Organizing Committee, 64
Phelps-Dodge Company, 63
Philadelphia Storage Battery Company, 217, 219, 220
Phillips, Fred, 202–4
Pickands, Mather, 73, 74
Pinkerton National Detective Agency, 66, 120
Pittsburgh Plate Glass Company, 238
Plumb Plan, 36
Postal Telegraph Company, 241

P.O.U.M., 140
Printing Pressmen, 16
Pritchett, Harold, 239, 240
Quill, Michael J., 226–7
Radio Corporation of America, 220, 241
Radio Telegraphists' Association, American, *see* American
Railway Conductors and Trainmen, Brotherhood of, *see* Brotherhood
Rand, James B., Jr., 102
Randau, Carl, 251, 254
Random House (Modern Library), 258
Rank and File Pilot, 203, 204
Rathborne, Mervyn, 150, 197, 240, 241
Ray, Tom, 201
Remington-Rand strike, 102
Republic Steel Corp., 73, 79, 80, 82, 114–5
R.O.T.C., 93, 99
Retail Clerks International Protective Assn., 261–4
Retail and Wholesale Employees of America, United, *see* United
Reuther, Roy, 160, 165, 180
Reuther, Victor, 160, 165, 180
Reuther, Walter, 118, 160, 165, 166, 172, 176, 177, 180, 181
Richberg, Donald, 18, 70
Rickert, Thomas, 53
Rieve, Emil, 210
Robinson, Reid, 63
Rockefeller interests, *see* Standard Oil Company
Roosevelt, Eleanor, 208
Roosevelt, Franklin D., 14, 15, 55, 70, 82, 112, 208, 246, 254, 274, 276, 277
Rotary Clubs, 100
Rubber Workers, United, *see* United
Runciman, Walter, 75
Russian-American Industrial Corporation, 52
Russian Revolution, *see* October Revolution

Ryan, Joseph, 188, 196, 198
Safeway Stores, 260
Saginaw Valley, 223, 224
Sailors' Union of the Pacific, 190, 192, 195, 196, 199–200, 205
San Francisco Industrial Association, 260
Santo, John, 227
Schiefelbein, John, 184
Schlossberg, Joseph, 50
Schoellkopf, J. F., Jr., 74
Scripps-Howard newspapers, 250, 252
Seabrook Farms strike, 243
Seafarers' Federation, 195, 196
Seamen's Defense Council, 197
Seamen's Union, International, *see* International
Seattle *Post Intelligencer*, 250
Second International, 129
Sharecroppers Union of Alabama, 242
Shell Oil Co., 64
Sherman Anti-Trust Act, 44
Sherwood, John M., 63
Shields, Mayor Daniel, 108, 110
Shoe and Leather Workers Union, *see* National
Shoe Workers Industrial Union, 229
Shoe Workers Organizing Committee, 230
Shoe Workers Protective Association, 229
Shoe Workers Union, United, *see* United
Sinclair, Upton, 123
Sinclair agreement, 64
Smith, Ferdinand, 203
Smith, Rev. Gerald L. K., 97
Social Democratic Federation, 130, 134
Socialist Labor Party, 57
Socialist Party, 129–30, 132–4, 165, 187, 204, 230
Socialists, 31, 133–5, 140, 180, 183, 242, 260

INDEX

Socialist Workers Party, 130
Social Security Board, 266
Society of Designing Engineers, 265
Sokolsky, George, 97
Soulounias, Charles, 232
Southern Tenant Farmers Union, 242–3
Stachel, Jack, 147
Stahlmate Clubs, 98
Stalin, Joseph, 136–9, 141
Stalinists, in A. F. of L., 13–14; Lewis's attitude toward, 34; in steel union, 70, 87; in international labor movement, 135–41; in American labor movement, 142–53; in U.A.W., 161–5, 170–85; in maritime unions, 189–204; in new unions, 218–9, 222–5, 227–8, 231–6, 240–2, 249, 251, 256, 262-267; role in CIO, 271–81
Standard Oil Company, 64
Stanton, Rev. John H., 108, 112
State, County and Municipal Workers of America, 150, 266
Steel Labor Board, 70
Steel Workers Organizing Committee, 71, 72, 74–92, 107, 149
Stettinius, Edward R., Jr., 77
Steunenberg, Frank, 61
Stevens, Thaddeus, 93
Stonkus, Albert, 221–4
Street, Electric Railway and Motor Coach Employees, Amalgamated Association of, *see* Amalgamated
Student Americaneers, 98
Sunshine Radio System, 228
Sunshine Silver Mine, 62
Survey, 208
Switter (Massillon Chief of Police), 114
Swope, Gerard, 17
Symes, Lillian, 133

Talmadge, Eugene, 92, 98
Taylor, Myron, 47, 72, 74, 75, 77, 78
Teachers, American Federation of, *see* American

T.V.A., 266
Terminal System, Inc., 228
Textile Converters Association, 211
Textile Labor Relations Board, 208
Textile Workers of America, United, *see* United
Thermidor, 136–8, 140–1
Third Avenue Railway Company, 227
Third International, *see* Communist International
Thomas, Arthur, 204
Thomas, Elbert D., 106
Thomas, Norman, 132, 133, 144, 242
Thomas, Rolland J., 162, 172
Thomas, Roy, 113
Throop, Rev. Frank, 98
Thyssen, Fritz, 101
Tighe, Michael, 66–71, 78, 207
Todd-Robins Dry Dock Co., 188
Torres, Charles, 204
Townsend, Gov. M. Clifford, 88
Trade Union Unity League, 145, 146, 229, 240, 243, 257
Transport Workers Union, 150, 151, 225, 226
Travis, Robert C., 160, 164, 165, 223
Tri-State Metal, Mine and Smelter Union, 62
Trotsky, Leon, 130, 131, 136, 137, 141, 218
Trotskyites, 129–31, 177, 275
Tugwell, Rexford Guy, 242
Turner, Capt. Arden S., 98
Typographical Union, International, *see* International

Ullman, Carl, 113
United Automobile, Aircraft and Vehicle Workers, 157
United Automobile Worker, 132
United Automobile Workers, 118, 120, 132, 133, 144, 149, 152, 153, 156–9, 160, 166, 170, 173, 185, 186, 205, 213, 223, 256, 265, 273

INDEX

United Brotherhood of Carpenters, 17, 239
United Cannery, Agricultural, Packing and Allied Workers, 152, 241
United Electrical, Radio and Machine Workers, 149, 151, 217, 218
United Federal Workers of America, 266
United Garment Workers, 53
United Hatters, Cap and Millinery Workers, 19, 27
United Hosiery Workers, 207, 210, 211
United Mine Workers, 13, 17, 27, 31, 32, 36, 37, 45–7, 49, 77, 87, 91, 120, 151, 171, 219–22, 225, 230, 270, 278, 279
United Office and Professional Workers of America, 151, 257
United Progressive Furriers, 233
United Retail and Wholesale Employees of America, 261
United Rubber Workers, 120, 151, 213–15
United Shoe Workers Union, 153, 230
United States Maritime Commission, 191, 200, 201
United States Steel Corp., 45, 66, 72, 73, 75–8, 91, 188
United Textile Workers of America, 10, 27, 207, 210
Updyke, Calvin, 111
Utility Workers Organizing Committee, 223

Van Gelder, Philip, 187, 188
Vanguard Press, 258
Veterans of Foreign Wars, 93, 99, 100
Viking Press, 258
Vladeck, B. Charney, 135
Voice of the Federation, 144, 193, 194

Wagner Act, 89, 111
Waldman, Louis, 132, 134, 135
Walsh-Healy Act, 76
Watson coal stabilization bill, 43
Weinstein, Charles, 210
Weinstone, William, 171, 174, 179
Weir, Ernest T., 74, 83
Weirton Steel Co., 80
Welles, Walter, 181, 184, 185
Wersing, Martin A., 221–2, 223
West Coast Commercial Radio Men's Protective Association, 240
West Coast CIO, 49, 148, 190, 191
West Coast Firemen and Oilers, 144, 152, 195, 273
West Coast Longshoremen, 150
Western Federation of Miners, 61
West Side Conveyer, 172
Wetmore, Fred, 237
Wharton, Arthur O., 10, 11, 21
Whelan Drug Stores, 263
White, Lloyd, 246
Williams, Kempton, 223
Wilson, Woodrow, 40, 129
Wolchok, Samuel, 261, 262
Woll, Matthew, 99, 100, 148
Women's National Association for the Preservation of the White Race, 93
Woodworkers of America, International, *see* International
Woolworth Company, F. W., 262
Workers Alliance, 260
Workers Council for Social Justice, 99
Workers Party, 13
W.P.A., 254, 260, 264

Young, Owen D., 76
Young Nationalists, 98
Youngstown, Pa., *see* Little Steel strike
Youngstown Daily Vindicator, 113
Youngstown Sheet and Tube Company, 74, 80, 81, 88, 113

Zaritsky, Max, 21
Zimmerman, Charles S., 131, 210, 234
Zonorich, N. A., 236, 237

American Labor: From Conspiracy to Collective Bargaining
AN ARNO PRESS/NEW YORK TIMES COLLECTION

SERIES I

Abbott, Edith.
Women in Industry. 1913.

Aveling, Edward B. and Eleanor M. Aveling.
Working Class Movement in America. 1891.

Beard, Mary.
The American Labor Movement. 1939.

Blankenhorn, Heber.
The Strike for Union. 1924.

Blum, Solomon.
Labor Economics. 1925.

Brandeis, Louis D. and Josephine Goldmark.
Women in Industry. 1907. New introduction by Leon Stein and Philip Taft.

Brooks, John Graham.
American Syndicalism. 1913.

Butler, Elizabeth Beardsley.
Women and the Trades. 1909.

Byington, Margaret Frances.
Homestead: The Household of A Mill Town. 1910.

Carroll, Mollie Ray.
Labor and Politics. 1923.

Coleman, McAlister.
Men and Coal. 1943.

Coleman, J. Walter.
The Molly Maguire Riots: Industrial Conflict in the Pennsylvania Coal Region. 1936.

Commons, John R.
Industrial Goodwill. 1919.

Commons, John R.
Industrial Government. 1921.

Dacus, Joseph A.
Annals of the Great Strikes. 1877.

Dealtry, William.
The Laborer: A Remedy for his Wrongs. 1869.

Douglas, Paul H., Curtis N. Hitchcock and Willard E. Atkins, editors.
The Worker in Modern Economic Society. 1923.

Eastman, Crystal.
Work Accidents and the Law. 1910.

Ely, Richard T.
The Labor Movement in America. 1890. New Introduction by Leon Stein and Philip Taft.

Feldman, Herman.
Problems in Labor Relations. 1937.

Fitch, John Andrew.
The Steel Worker. 1910.

Furniss, Edgar S. and Laurence Guild.
Labor Problems. 1925.

Gladden, Washington.
Working People and Their Employers. 1885.

Gompers, Samuel.
Labor and the Common Welfare. 1919.

Hardman, J. B. S., editor.
American Labor Dynamics. 1928.

Higgins, George G.
Voluntarism in Organized Labor, 1930-40. 1944.

Hiller, Ernest T.
The Strike. 1928.

Hollander, Jacob S. and George E. Barnett.
Studies in American Trade Unionism. 1906. New Introduction by Leon Stein and Philip Taft.

Jelley, Symmes M.
The Voice of Labor. 1888.

Jones, Mary.
Autobiography of Mother Jones. 1925.

Kelley, Florence.
Some Ethical Gains Through Legislation. 1905.

LaFollette, Robert M., editor.
The Making of America: Labor. 1906.

Lane, Winthrop D.
Civil War in West Virginia. 1921.

Lauck, W. Jett and Edgar Sydenstricker.
Conditions of Labor in American Industries. 1917.

Leiserson, William M.
Adjusting Immigrant and Industry. 1924.

Lescohier, Don D.
Knights of St. Crispin. 1910.

Levinson, Edward.
I Break Strikes. The Technique of Pearl L. Bergoff. 1935.

Lloyd, Henry Demarest.
Men, The Workers. Compiled by Anne Whithington and Caroline Stallbohen. 1909. New Introduction by Leon Stein and Philip Taft.

Lorwin, Louis (Louis Levine).
The Women's Garment Workers. 1924.

Markham, Edwin, Ben B. Lindsay and George Creel.
Children in Bondage. 1914.

Marot, Helen.
American Labor Unions. 1914.

Mason, Alpheus T.
Organized Labor and the Law. 1925.

Newcomb, Simon.
A Plain Man's Talk on the Labor Question. 1886. New Introduction by Leon Stein and Philip Taft.

Price, George Moses.
The Modern Factory: Safety, Sanitation and Welfare. 1914.

Randall, John Herman Jr.
Problem of Group Responsibility to Society. 1922.

Rubinow, I. M.
Social Insurance. 1913.

Saposs, David, editor.
Readings in Trade Unionism. 1926.

Slichter, Sumner H.
Union Policies and Industrial Management. 1941.

Socialist Publishing Society.
The Accused and the Accusers. 1887.

Stein, Leon and Philip Taft, editors.
The Pullman Strike. 1894-1913. New Introduction by the editors.

Stein, Leon and Philip Taft, editors.
Religion, Reform, and Revolution: Labor Panaceas in the Nineteenth Century. 1969. New Introduction by the editors.

Stein, Leon and Philip Taft, editors.
Wages, Hours, and Strikes: Labor Panaceas in the Twentieth Century. 1969. New introduction by the editors.

Swinton, John.
A Momentous Question: The Respective Attitudes of Labor and Capital. 1895. New Introduction by Leon Stein and Philip Taft.

Tannenbaum, Frank.
The Labor Movement. 1921.

Tead, Ordway.
Instincts in Industry. 1918.

Vorse, Mary Heaton.
Labor's New Millions. 1938.

Witte, Edwin Emil.
The Government in Labor Disputes. 1932.

Wright, Carroll D.
The Working Girls of Boston. 1889.

Wyckoff, Veitrees J.
Wage Policies of Labor Organizations in a Period of Industrial Depression. 1926.

Yellen, Samuel.
American Labor Struggles. 1936.

SERIES II

Allen, Henry J.
The Party of the Third Part: The Story of the Kansas Industrial Relations Court. 1921. *Including* **The Kansas Court of Industrial Relations Law** (1920) by Samuel Gompers.

Baker, Ray Stannard.
The New Industrial Unrest. 1920.

Barnett, George E. & David A. McCabe.
Mediation, Investigation and Arbitration in Industrial Disputes. 1916.

Barns, William E., editor.
The Labor Problem. 1886.

Bing, Alexander M.
War-Time Strikes and Their Adjustment. 1921.

Brooks, Robert R. R.
When Labor Organizes. 1937.

Calkins, Clinch.
Spy Overhead: The Story of Industrial Espionage. 1937.

Cooke, Morris Llewellyn & Philip Murray.
Organized Labor and Production. 1940.

Creamer, Daniel & Charles W. Coulter.
Labor and the Shut-Down of the Amoskeag Textile Mills. 1939.

Glocker, Theodore W.
The Government of American Trade Unions. 1913.

Gompers, Samuel.
Labor and the Employer. 1920.

Grant, Luke.
The National Erectors' Association and the International Association of Bridge and Structural Ironworkers. 1915.

Haber, William.
Industrial Relations in the Building Industry. 1930.

Henry, Alice.
Women and the Labor Movement. 1923.

Herbst, Alma.
The Negro in the Slaughtering and Meat-Packing Industry in Chicago. 1932.

[Hicks, Obediah.]
Life of Richard F. Trevellick. 1896.

Hillquit, Morris, Samuel Gompers & Max J. Hayes.
The Double Edge of Labor's Sword: Discussion and Testimony on Socialism and Trade-Unionism Before the Commission on Industrial Relations. 1914. New Introduction by Leon Stein and Philip Taft.

Jensen, Vernon H.
Lumber and Labor. 1945.

Kampelman, Max M.
The Communist Party vs. the C.I.O. 1957.

Kingsbury, Susan M., editor.
Labor Laws and Their Enforcement. By Charles E. Persons, Mabel Parton, Mabelle Moses & Three "Fellows." 1911.

McCabe, David A.
The Standard Rate in American Trade Unions. 1912.

Mangold, George Benjamin.
Labor Argument in the American Protective Tariff Discussion. 1908.

Millis, Harry A., editor.
How Collective Bargaining Works. 1942.

Montgomery, Royal E.
Industrial Relations in the Chicago Building Trades. 1927.

Oneal, James.
The Workers in American History. 3rd edition, 1912.

Palmer, Gladys L.
Union Tactics and Economic Change: A Case Study of Three Philadelphia Textile Unions. 1932.

Penny, Virginia.
How Women Can Make Money: Married or Single, In all Branches of the Arts and Sciences, Professions, Trades, Agricultural and Mechanical Pursuits. 1870. New Introduction by Leon Stein and Philip Taft.

Penny, Virginia.
Think and Act: A Series of Articles Pertaining to Men and Women, Work and Wages. 1869.

Pickering, John.
The Working Man's Political Economy. 1847.

Ryan, John A.
A Living Wage. 1906.

Savage, Marion Dutton.
Industrial Unionism in America. 1922.

Simkhovitch, Mary Kingsbury.
The City Worker's World in America. 1917.

Spero, Sterling Denhard.
The Labor Movement in a Government Industry: A Study of Employee Organization in the Postal Service. 1927.

Stein, Leon and Philip Taft, editors.
Labor Politics: Collected Pamphlets. 2 vols. 1836-1932. New Introduction by the editors.

Stein, Leon and Philip Taft, editors.
The Management of Workers: Selected Arguments. 1917-1956. New Introduction by the editors.

Stein, Leon and Philip Taft, editors.
Massacre at Ludlow: Four Reports. 1914-1915. New Introduction by the editors.

Stein, Leon and Philip Taft, editors.
Workers Speak: Self-Portraits. 1902-1906. New Introduction by the editors.

Stolberg, Benjamin.
The Story of the CIO. 1938.

Taylor, Paul S.
The Sailors' Union of the Pacific. 1923.

U.S. Commission on Industrial Relations.
Efficiency Systems and Labor. 1916. New Introduction by Leon Stein and Philip Taft.

Walker, Charles Rumford.
American City: A Rank-and-File History. 1937.

Walling, William English.
American Labor and American Democracy. 1926.

Williams, Whiting.
What's on the Worker's Mind: By One Who Put on Overalls to Find Out. 1920.

Wolman, Leo.
The Boycott in American Trade Unions. 1916.

Ziskind, David.
One Thousand Strikes of Government Employees. 1940.

Soc
HD
8055
C75
S7
1971